UNIVERSAL RELIGIONS IN WORLD HISTORY

THE SPREAD OF BUDDHISM, CHRISTIANITY, AND ISLAM TO 1500

UNIVERSAL RELIGIONS IN WORLD HISTORY

THE SPREAD OF BUDDHISM, CHRISTIANITY, AND ISLAM TO 1500

DONALD JOHNSON

Professor Emeritus, New York University

JEAN ELLIOTT JOHNSON

Friends Seminary

Boston   Burr Ridge, IL   Dubuque, IA   Madison, WI   New York
San Francisco   St. Louis   Bangkok   Bogotá   Caracas   Kuala Lumpur
Lisbon   London   Madrid   Mexico City   Milan   Montreal   New Delhi
Santiago   Seoul   Singapore   Sydney   Taipei   Toronto

Higher Education

UNIVERSAL RELIGIONS IN WORLD HISTORY: THE SPREAD OF BUDDHISM, CHRISTIANITY, AND ISLAM TO 1500

Published by McGraw-Hill, a business unit of The McGraw-Hill Companies, Inc., 1221 Avenue of the Americas, New York, NY, 10020. Copyright © 2007 by The McGraw-Hill Companies, Inc. All rights reserved. No part of this publication may be reproduced or distributed in any form or by any means, or stored in a database or retrieval system, without the prior written consent of The McGraw-Hill Companies, Inc., including, but not limited to, in any network or other electronic storage or transmission, or broadcast for distance learning.

Some ancillaries, including electronic and print components, may not be available to customers outside the United States.

This book is printed on acid-free paper.

1 2 3 4 5 6 7 8 9 0 DOC/DOC 0 9 8 7 6

ISBN: 978-0-07-295428-9
MHID: 0-07-295428-0

Vice President and Editor-in-Chief: *Emily Barrosse*
Publisher: *Lyn Uhl*
Senior Sponsoring Editor: *Jon-David Hague*
Editorial Coordinator: *Allison Rona*
Editorial Assistant: *Liliana Almendarez*
Marketing Manager: *Katherine Bates*
Managing Editor: *Jean Dal Porto*
Project Manager: *Meghan Durko*
Art Director: *Jeanne Schreiber*
Art Editor: *Ayelet Arbel*
Cover Designer: *Srdjan Savanovic*
Interior Designer: *Karen LaFond*
Photo Research Coordinator: *Natalia Peschiera*
Senior Production Supervisor: *Janean A. Utley*
Composition: *10/13 Palatino by Techbooks*
Printing: *45 # New Era Matte, Quebecor World*

Library of Congress Cataloging-in-Publication Data

Johnson, Donald, 1931–
    Universal religions in world history: The Spread of Buddhism, Christianity, and Islam to 1500/Donald Johnson, Jean Elliott Johnson.
        p. cm.—(Explorations in world history)
    Includes index.
    ISBN-13: 978-0-07-295428-9 (soft cover: alk. paper)
    ISBN-10: 0-07-295428-0 (soft cover: alk. paper)
    1. Religions—History—Textbooks. 2. Church history—Textbooks. 3. Islam—History—Textbooks. 4. Buddhism—History—Textbooks. I. Johnson, Jean, 1934-II. Title. III. Series.
    BL80.3.J64 2007
    2009.9—dc22

2005053126

The Internet addresses listed in the text were accurate at the time of publication. The inclusion of a Web site does not indicate an endorsement by the authors or McGraw-Hill, and McGraw-Hill does not guarantee the accuracy of the information presented at these sites.

www.mhhe.com

❦ CONTENTS ❦

A NOTE FROM THE
SERIES EDITORS

World history has come of age. No longer regarded as a task simply for amateurs or philosophers, it has become an integral part of the historical profession, and one of its most exciting and innovative fields of study. At the level of scholarship, a growing tide of books, articles, and conferences continues to enlarge our understanding of the many and intersecting journeys of humankind framed in global terms. At the level of teaching, more and more secondary schools as well as colleges and universities now offer, and sometimes require, World History of their students. One of the prominent features of the World History movement has been the unusually close association of its scholarly and its teaching wings. Teachers at all levels have participated with university-based scholars in the development of this new field.

The McGraw-Hill series—Explorations in World History—operates at this intersection of scholarship and teaching. It seeks to convey the results of recent research in world history in a form wholly accessible to beginning students. It also provides a pedagogical alternative to or supplement for the large and inclusive core textbooks which are features of so many World History courses. Each volume in the series focuses briefly on a particular theme, set in a global and comparative context. And each of them is "open ended," raising questions and drawing students into the larger issues which animate world history.

Don and Jean Johnson have been long-time practitioners of the craft of world history, with a special focus on Asia and on religious topics. In this volume they explore what is surely the most enduring legacy of the premodern era, its great religious traditions. Focusing on Buddhism, Christianity, and Islam, they trace the origins and spread of these "world" or "universal" religions, inviting students to consider similarities and differences in the meanings they ascribe to human life. Furthermore, the book highlights repeatedly the relationship between religious and cultural life and the political and social context in which it is embedded.

Finally, the authors call attention sharply to the issue of cross-cultural encounter, certainly a major theme in any telling of world history. What happened to these religions as they spread far beyond their points of origin? How were they received and understood by distant peoples, and in what ways were they transformed as they entered new cultural environments? In these ways, *Universal Religions in World History: The Spread of Buddhism, Christianity, and Islam to 1500* provides a distinct lens through which to engage our students in the history of the premodern world.

Robert Strayer
Kevin Reilly

ACKNOWLEDGMENTS

The writing of most books requires the support and advice of many people. This one owes much to several scholars and readers. We were honored when Robert Strayer and Kevin Reilly, the series editors, invited us to write this manuscript. Both provided constant support and encouragement throughout the writing process. Each of them carefully read the drafts and offered concrete suggestions for improving the work, and both responded immediately to our questions and concerns.

We are also indebted to many scholars whose insights and interpretations we relied heavily on throughout our research and writings. These scholars represent the specific religious areas as well as the field of world history. Jerry Bentley, Richard Bulliet, Bart Ehrman, John Kieschnick, Ira M. Lapidus, Nehemia Levtzion, Xinru Liu, Wayne Meeks, Elaine Pagels, Morris Rossabi, Tansen Sen, Donald Swearer, and John Voll, as well as the anonymous readers who reviewed the manuscript, are but a few of the many specialists we drew upon for the best available scholarship.

Finally, we express our genuine gratitude to the editors at McGraw-Hill. Lyn Uhl oversaw the preliminary steps in the development of the manuscript and provided the initial encouragement for the project. Jon David Hague later assumed editorship of the volume, and his rapid responses to our revisions enabled the manuscript to move swiftly through the editorial process. Finally, we owe special thanks to Allison Rona for her careful attention to all details of publication and for her warm and supportive presence during the final stages of the process.

UNIVERSAL RELIGIONS IN WORLD HISTORY

THE SPREAD OF BUDDHISM, CHRISTIANITY, AND ISLAM TO 1500

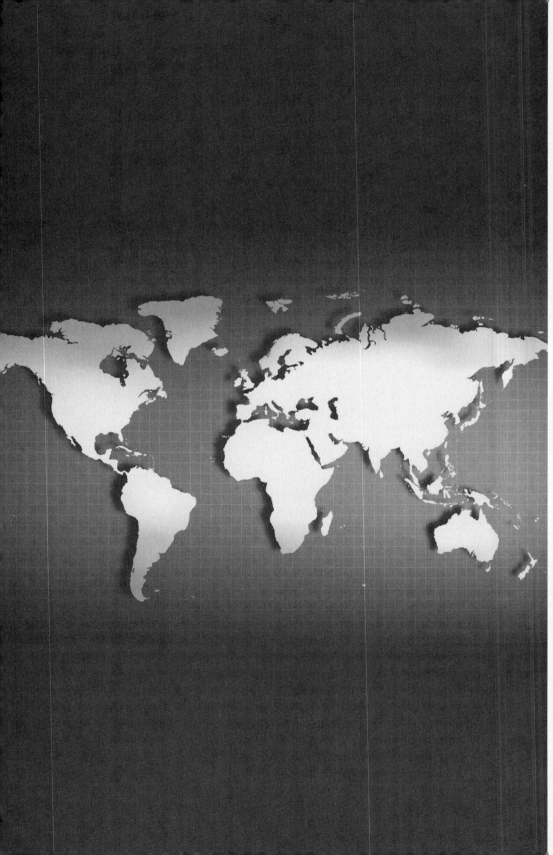

THE ORIGINS OF BUDDHISM, CHRISTIANITY, AND ISLAM

> **GETTING STARTED ON CHAPTER ONE:**   Why do we refer to Buddhism, Christianity, and Islam as "universal religions"? In what historic circumstances did each of these religions begin? How did each of them reflect the religious traditions that preceded them? What made it possible for the teachings of the Buddha, Jesus, and Muhammad to be accepted by peoples outside their own cultural groups? "All religions are basically similar." After reading the chapter, how would you respond to this statement?

INTRODUCTION

What is it about human beings that moves them to think, feel, and reach beyond the everyday struggles for food, shelter, survival, and safety? Very early they realized they could not survive as isolated individuals and had to learn to cooperate by helping others and accepting help. Once they became aware of suffering and loss and knew that one day they would die, humans began to question why they were born, what would happen after they died, and what values should guide the way they lived. Throughout the world and over the vast expanse of human experience, people have tried to imagine how life came about, how the world was created, and how it works, and they have made efforts to symbolize their insights and pass them on to future generations.

Humans have included in their insights an important place for a sense of the sacred: some transcendent reality, truth, or moral principle that explains the way the world works, gives comfort and can be relied on for help. They often worshiped forces in nature such as the sun, sky, thunder, trees, and snakes, as well as a variety of tribal gods that they

3

hoped would take special care of them. They called on war gods and goddesses to lead them to victory and on gods of fire and light to illuminate their days and bring security and prosperity to their lives. They knelt before images of divinity, prostrated in prayer, sat in quiet contemplation of the infinite, engaged in philosophical arguments about the nature of the divine, and stood in awe and wonder at the magnitude and glory of the universe. As they tried to make sense of it all, they sought collective meanings that they could share.

Early peoples in China, India, the Mediterranean basin, and west Asia offered sacrifices to please the divine forces and convince them to keep the world going. These sacrifices grew in complexity, and over time specialists developed who claimed to know the right way to speak to the divine powers and the proper way to perform the sacrifices. The communities believed the gods and goddesses would have to answer prayers as long as the rituals were performed correctly, and they looked to special men and women to help them grasp sacred realities: priests and priestesses, shamans, brahmins, monks and nuns, ministers, gurus, diviners, mullahs, hojas, ascetics, griots, and a host of others who offered ways to make meaning out of life's joys and suffering as well as ways to manage, if not control, events.

As cities developed and business, manufacturing, and trade supplemented herding and agriculture, nature gods personifying sky, storm, thunder, and fire, or agricultural deities representing the earth and seasonal cycles began to lose their potency. Besides, there were so many gods and goddesses, each promising, but not always delivering, special protection and prosperity for its own special group. How could these tribal gods satisfy the competing demands, especially in matters of warfare, when groups were constantly at each other's throats? Prayers often went unanswered, and sacrifices became empty rituals, making priests rich rather than appeasing and influencing the divine. In more complex, interdependent, insecure urban environments, constantly threatened by war, some people questioned the possibility of any kind of universal order and longed for effective ways to deal with the changeable and arbitrary nature of their lives.

Moreover, in small communities humans, bonded from birth to family, clan, and community, felt concern for the needs of their less fortunate members, and kinship ties and common blood moved them to compassion and charity. However, in larger urbanized societies, where a select few were growing rich by living off the labor of a vast number of poor peasants and laborers, the fellow feeling born of blood ties was often absent. Who would take care of the widows and orphans in these societies, the sick and disabled, the young and the elderly? Urban dwellers clearly understood the seeming capriciousness of life and knew firsthand that even if they observed all societal rules, things could still often turn out badly. Why did good people suffer and why was there so much evil in the world? How could justice and mercy be balanced and what should be the proper goals of life? People are still asking these questions today.

As human communities confront these ultimate mysteries and struggle to develop a coherent view of the world, they most often look to some form of religion as the wellspring of meanings. Of course, as the Buddhists know so well, no one bathes in the same river twice. History flows, even when it meanders and sometimes turns back in the opposite direction. The collective meanings that religions endeavor to supply are constantly changing as new historic circumstances demand adjustments, calibrations, and sometimes reformations in these faiths.

Meanings and the symbols that embody religious worldviews are as basic to survival as bread. In the words of Herbert Gutman, a noted historian, "It is not so much what happened in history as the meanings we make of what happened."[1] To make sense of what we experience, we pass it through our cultural filter and its symbols. Among the factors that shape how we interpret experience and give meaning to events, perhaps none has been more significant than religion.

Religious insights and the faiths that embody the collective meanings and transmit them to future generations are crucial factors in human history. These insights and faiths guide both everyday actions and illuminate cosmic concerns. Religious values help people know what to eat and when, which holidays to celebrate, how to mark events in our lives such as births, becoming an adult, marriage, and death. Religion helps humans find solace in suffering and, perhaps most important, how to face and find meaning in death. Religious faith and its teachings have inspired much art, literature, and music and provide a guide for what to hold sacred and how to live a moral and aesthetically sensitive life.

Religion also serves many social functions, such as fostering communal identity, cementing group cooperation, and both legitimizing and challenging dominant elites in the society. Religion also encourages the relationship and interaction of all strata of society. Merchants and political leaders often look to religion for legitimization for their burning ambitions. Through history the majority of people have been and still are poor, and they sometimes mobilize around their faith to battle for reform. More often, the poor settle for some form of eternal justice: When the Day of Judgment comes, "the meek shall inherit the earth," but until then, they often have to be satisfied with "a haven in a heartless world."

According to the eminent anthropologist Clifford Geertz, religion establishes in humans, "powerful, pervasive, and long-lasting moods and motivations . . ."[2] by "formulating conceptions of a general order of existence."[3] Religion protects us from the impending chaos that threatens our collective and individual lives on at least three levels: our ability to understand the universe and how it works, our ability to endure suffering, and our ability to face evil. It gives direction to people's lives and infuses them with a sense of how to think and feel about what is happening.[4] Religions are not mere abstractions or lists of beliefs and practices. Nor are they merely things that individuals do and believe in one isolated compartment of their lives, unrelated to other dimensions of life, such as changes in technology, the production and exchange of goods, and war. The loyalty that each faith commands from its believers fosters intense and impassioned feelings and actions. Religious faith can inspire the most horrible violence and even genocide. That same faith can also move people to sacrifice their lives for others, go on peace marches, and participate in worldwide efforts to feed the hungry and heal the sick. Whatever direction the force of faith takes, students of history must take religion seriously; it is intertwined in all of human life and is an integral part of history.

UNIVERSAL RELIGIONS

One of the most significant aspects of the first millennium C.E. was the development of religions that were open to anyone and whose teachings were valid for all people. Scholars such as Edward Farmer and others[5] have identified these faiths as "universal" because they are not linked to blood, racial, ethnic, or national groups, and anyone can join them. In societies that worshiped local gods and goddesses and where only elites had access to the sacred knowledge, mass participation in religion was a revolutionary idea.

Universal religions have several characteristics beside the fact that they welcome all who believe. Each of these faiths was founded by a historic person who synthesized a variety of teachings current during his lifetime and created a new path. Worship is usually focused on a single, all-powerful divinity that transcends the world, but also seems to intervene in human experience. Universal religions promise believers the possibility of salvation, often in some form of life after death in a heaven. This reward generally results from devotion and obedience to the divine power and observance of the rules of the faith. Heaven offers a form of postponed justice. Things may not seem fair in this world, but even a peasant or destitute person can expect to be rewarded with heaven for living a good life or having faith.

Universal religions provide saints or other intermediaries to help believers reach or realize salvation, so believers do not have to strive totally on their own. Intermediaries such as a messiah or a bodhisattva also can provide a personal link between divinity and humanity. In addition, the message is in a language average people understand, and the insights are often given in stories and parables. These faiths incorporate existing practices and mix elite religious concepts with popular rituals, making the faith accessible to people far from where it originated.

Finally, universal religions address and deal with the everyday problems and insecurities that people are experiencing. They offer solace to those who feel their lives are hopeless or meaningless, and they answer questions about suffering and the presence of evil. They offer a common set of ethics for living a moral life and also promise forgiveness for sins and the possibility of ultimate salvation. They inform everyday life and give hope and comfort in a seemingly capricious and hostile world.

Certainly the beliefs and message of the founder are important to any religion, but so is the historical context surrounding its founding and spread. Faiths, like politics, economics, and technology, change over time and often stray far from their original formulations. What happens to a religion in a new cultural setting often depends on political forces, economic realities, even pure chance, as much as on the intrinsic attraction the faith has for potential believers. As diverse groups in different parts of the world encounter new beliefs and work to make them their own, they alter and adjust the message as they translate it into their own language, art, philosophy, and traditional values. Newly settled nomadic groups, men and women concerned with survival, political leaders seeking forms of legitimacy and strategies for unity, merchants looking for profit and peaceful zones of exchange, and common people desperately searching for explanations for suffering, inequality, and evil all found reasons for embracing one of these faiths, as well as ample ways to adjust that faith to their own needs and traditions.

Of all the numerous religious worldviews that had developed by the first millennium, only Buddhism, Christianity, and Islam meet the criteria established here for a universal religion. None of these faiths started out with a universal appeal, and their founders most likely would have been surprised at how their messages spread. Nevertheless, over time the followers of each faith calibrated the message so that it might appeal to anyone and everyone, no matter what their race, ethnic status, caste, or class.

An argument could be made to include Judaism and Hinduism as universal faiths because they also accepted converts, but neither of them has focused on conversion as a major goal. Hinduism is ambivalent about conversion. Groups that migrated into the Indian subcontinent adapted to Hinduism by becoming new castes, and brahmins journeyed outside of India spreading their insights. Interestingly, one of the most impressive Hindu temples in the world can be found in Cambodia and the Hindu worldview significantly influenced the development of both mainland and island Southeast Asia. Even so, most Hindus would say that one has to be born a Hindu. Judaism accepts converts as well, but being a Jew is most often considered a fact of birth as well as belief and practice. There is no doubt that Judaism and Hinduism have provided the ethos and historic roots for one or more of the universal religions examined here. It is sometimes said that Buddhism is Hinduism's vehicle for reaching a wider audience and that Christianity and Islam carried Judaism to the world.

This study focuses on how religions develop and spread to other areas, changing and adapting in the process. As you consider the history of these universal religions, you can ponder the attraction each had and how their original messages changed as they spread from their modest beginnings to distant lands. It is noteworthy that although their founders never traveled more than a few hundred miles from their homes in North India, Palestine, and Arabia, these religions now span the entire earth, The Buddha, Jesus, and Muhammad would likely be surprised that the ideas that they preached would one day attract two-thirds of the people in the world.

THE SETTING AND CONTEXT

Although the origins of Buddhism, Christianity, and Islam were separated by more than a thousand years, the contexts out of which they grew have some noteworthy similarities. Siddhartha Gotama, the founder of Buddhism, lived in the sixth century B.C.E, during a time when the tribal organization the Indo-Europeans had established in the Indian subcontinent centuries earlier was breaking down, and urbanization, accompanied by commercialism and cross-cultural contacts, was rapidly accelerating. Five centuries later in west Asia, during the time of Jesus of Nazareth, Hellenistic culture, and Roman military occupation, which threatened the tribal loyalties and survival of the Jews, was spreading across west Asia. Finally, in the seventh century

C.E., during the lifetime of Muhammad, the founder of Islam, the strong blood loyalty of the Arabian Bedouins was being undermined by the growth of trade and commercial contacts and the rise of towns in the Arabian Peninsula.

The migration of nomadic groups into settled areas and the subsequent slow movement from herding to settled farming, the development of towns and cities, and the emergence of larger political units that transcend tribal loyalties—a recurring cycle in world history—usually results in a search for new meanings. As people try to adjust to changing realities, gifted teachers emerge who offer creative responses that calibrate traditional worldviews into more timely and satisfactory cosmologies.

It is not surprising to find religious ferment when old values are threatened. As conditions change and established ways seem inadequate, people seek new meanings. This was true in North India in the early centuries of the first millennium B.C.E., in Palestine during the Hellenistic Age that followed Alexander of Macedonia's conquests, and also in Arabia during the early centuries of the Byzantine Empire. These eras of social turmoil all sparked an outburst of creative energy and reform. Out of these troubled times, new religious faiths that were innovative syntheses of the old and new were born.

THE INDIAN SUBCONTINENT

Indian civilization dates back at least 4,500 years when people built sophisticated cities in the Indus River valley. Archaeological evidence, including carefully constructed drains and waterways, suggest the Indus people were interested in ritual purity and probably worshiped a mother goddess or goddesses. Archaeologists have uncovered little evidence of warfare, and few weapons have been found. In addition, Indus seals depicting figures in the yogic "lotus" position suggest that the Indus people may have practiced meditation.

Sometime around 2000 B.C.E., a large number of nomadic tribal groups, collectively known as Indo-Europeans, began to move south and east into major urban centers from the Mediterranean to India. The Indo-Europeans who reached India around 1500 B.C.E., about the same time that the Achaeans arrived in Greece, were known as "Aryans."

The interaction of the nomadic Aryans with the urbanized people of the Indus civilization resulted in a common culture that was a blending of both ways of life. One of the major aspects of this synthesis was in the realm of religion and worldview. The Aryans brought a typical nomadic worldview that pictured the earth covered by a vast sky dome managed by a three-tiered collection of celestial, atmospheric, and terrestrial gods. Among the more important gods were Varuna, who governed the rhythms of the universe; Indra, the storm and war god; and Agni, the god of fire.

The Aryan religion centered on sacrifices that brahmins (priests) performed. Over the centuries these rituals grew more and more elaborate until they sometimes involved the slaughter of hundreds of cattle, sheep, and even horses. In addition, the brahmins followed strict rules of purity and avoided any kind of ritual pollution in performing the sacrifices. Every instrument used in the rituals had to be ritually purified, and only brahmins were allowed to touch them. Brahmin power steadily increased, and they claimed they could interpret the will of the gods. If they performed the rituals accurately, the gods seemed compelled to respond to their sacrifices, prayers, and supplications.

As the indigenous people and the Aryans mixed, their distinct worldviews gradually merged into one complete religious system. The Aryans' more masculine approach and the Indus people's inclination for the mother goddess fused, and these sky gods and earth goddesses blended into a synthesis, symbolized by paired father and mother divinities such as Ram-Sita, Shiva-Parbati, and Vishnu-Laxmi.

After 700 B.C.E., urbanization increased and ambitious tribal leaders sought to expand their power by conquering smaller tribes and creating multi tribal kingdoms. As the importance of tribal and blood loyalties decreased, men and women began to identify themselves not by tribes but as members of occupational groups, called *jatis* (which Europeans later called "castes"). Individual castes clustered together in specific parts of the cities and attempted to strengthen their unity by arranging marriages and sharing food with members of their own group. These castes, which often cut across geographic boundaries, provided a certain amount of security for their members as well as a new source of identity.

The brahmin emphasis on purity and pollution, which may well have been a legacy from the Indus culture, permeated the entire social structure, including the kinds of foods that one ate and shared with others. In caste rankings, those who dealt with impure things were considered impure and were slotted onto the lower rungs of the social ladder and often shunned. Those, like the brahmins, who dealt with pure things, stood at the top of the caste rankings, followed by warrior-rulers and administrators, known as *kshatriyas*. Every other group was ranked somewhere between the lowest outcastes and the highest kshatriyas and brahmins.

The brahmin/kshatriya alliance was crucial in the new kingdoms. Rulers looked to brahmin advisors to help them establish legitimacy. At the same time, many people, especially in the middle and lower castes, began to question the traditional brahmin dominance, to doubt the value of rituals and elaborate sacrifices, and to resist supporting them. As prayers went unanswered and the sacrifices no longer seemed to work, a desire for reform spread, especially in republics that bordered the larger kingdoms.

Besides antibrahmin sentiments and the significant shift from tribal loyalties to caste identification, the new urban culture was also upsetting the economic security of self-sufficient villages. Individual village artisans could not compete with craftsmen in far off cities who had established large caste/craft organizations and had access to cheaper raw materials and more efficient ways of producing goods. At the same time, village farmers, who were pressured to supply food to the growing cities, were often exploited and forced to pay taxes in the form of foodstuffs.

The increasing sense of inequality, dissatisfaction, and social flux left many unwilling to follow society's rules and questioning their inherited worldview. As a result, from approximately 900 to 600 B.C.E. in North India, large numbers of seekers after the truth wandered about the countryside searching for new meanings. When word of their insights filtered out to the larger community, others, disenchanted with their lives, sought out these wandering ascetics and often became their disciples.

The teachings of these ascetics are described in the Upanishads, one of Hinduism's most important texts. The Upanishads, composed between c. 700 and 200 B.C.E., introduced the concept of rebirth (*samsara*) and explained that one's rebirth depended on *karma*, the measure of how well one performed his or her *dharma*, actions that were appropriate to one's age, caste, and temperament. One's good and bad karma is calculated at each death and carried into one's future lives, determining the status into which each person is born. Good karma results in being born into a group with greater status and experiencing a better life; bad karma consigns one to less-fortunate future life. In addition, people who performed their appropriate dharma would be respected by their peers and experience some satisfaction in a life well lived.

Looking beyond the earlier Indo-European deities, the Upanishads introduced the concept of *Brahman* (Oneness, Ultimate Reality), giving a name to the growing sense of a cosmic unity. Brahman represents the invisible and indescribable force that animates the universe, the primal and unchanging energy infusing all things. "Being alone exists," the ascetics explained; everything in the created world, including the gods and goddesses, is but a manifestation of this Oneness. Each person and every thing emerges from and ultimately returns to Brahman.

The Upanishads taught that one could escape from karma and samsara by understanding that one's real Self is identical with Brahman: "You are That." Often called monism, this idea maintains that ultimately all aspects of the universe derive from one source and return to that source. Truly experiencing that unity leads to *moksha* (release, salvation): one breaks the bonds of karma and ends the cycle of rebirths. To experience moksha, the Upanishads taught each person had to recognize that all pairs of opposites, such as good/evil, right/wrong, rich/poor, etc., were not ultimate reality and humans had to find a discipline that would take them beyond dualism. The concept of "the oneness of all things" pervaded North Indian life for centuries, and nondualism was an integral part of the legacy that the Buddha would draw upon for his own message.

At the same time, the later Upanishads also taught forms of theism, the belief in a personal, all-powerful god. Whether through god or knowledge of Brahman, it was possible for the seeker to find release from samsara and to experience moksha. However, insights of the Upanishads had very little impact on average people.

By the sixth century, hundreds of teachers were popularizing and reinterpreting the insights from the Upanishads about samsara, karma, dharma, and moksha. Most of them were offering ways to break the bounds of birth and rebirth and the laws of karma, and many of them attracted large numbers of followers. The period became a testing ground for new ideas and new approaches within the vastly changed North Indian landscape. Given this context, it is not surprising that so many people questioned the older religious practices and sought new ways to make sense of their altered world.

In this milieu of reform the questioning groups of ascetics, almost entirely non-brahmins who most often came from small republics bordering larger kingdoms, began to teach new ways to moksha. Many of these ascetics taught that pursuing harsh lifestyles of renunciation of worldly pleasures could lead to moksha. Most refused to eat meat, some went without clothing, while others disdained sleeping in a shelter and lived instead under the open sky. Most of them rejected animal sacrifices, insisting sacrifices should be symbolic. One of these wandering teachers was Siddhartha Gotama, who would become the Buddha.

WEST ASIA

Whereas in North India several large kingdoms emerged that were capable of dominating much of the subcontinent, the small Hebrew kingdom in Palestine was constantly at the mercy of more powerful neighboring empires, such as Assyria, Chaldea, Selucia, and Rome, and its survival and identity was relentlessly at risk. Members of the Jewish community, struggling to survive as a distinct ethnic group, clung tenaciously to their separate identity as descendents of Abraham who, according to their tradition, had once served as slaves for the pharaohs in Egypt. They believed that with the intervention of their god YHWH, they had managed to escape from Egypt and eventually conquer Canaan and, by 1000 B.C.E., they had built a small kingdom under their leader David.

The Jews grew out of a long-standing tradition of monotheism that dates back to at least the Egyptian Pharaoh Ikhnaton (r. 1350–1254, B.C.E.), who tried to elevate Ra as the single god of his kingdom. In neighboring Persia, Zoroaster had also advanced a worldview based on a sharply divided universe of light and darkness with Ahura Mazda as the god of light. However, the Jews were probably the first west Asian group to formulate the idea that the God of their people also presided over the history and affairs of non-Jews.

Jews cherished the Torah, the first five books of the Old Testament, which recorded how God had given Moses the laws and had formed a covenant relationship with them as his chosen people. Implicit in this Covenant was the belief that if they keep the laws, YHWH would protect them and answer their prayers. Furthermore, Jews looked to the example of the prophets such as Elijah, Amos, Hosea, Jeremiah, and Isaiah as well as to the Psalms for guidance.

When the Assyrians overran Israel in the eighth century B.C.E., and the Chaldeans conquered Judah in 586 B.C.E. and sent the Jews into captivity, many feared that their lack of faith had contributed to these disasters. The Jews responded by adhering even more strictly to their traditional rituals and laws. After Persia conquered the whole area, Cyrus, the Persian emperor, permitted the Jews to return to Judea and rebuild their temple, and he allowed them to reestablish Mosaic Law and rituals. He appointed a governor who served as the nominal head of the community and worked closely with the high priest of the temple in Jerusalem on most local matters.

Jewish life revolved around the temple where priests fastidiously observed rules governing purity and pollution in their sacrifices as well as in their daily lives. These rituals and the importance of purity and pollution were not unlike brahmin sacrifices in northern India at about the same time. Although the brahmins addressed numerous gods and goddesses, whereas Jews believed in a single divine power, both groups paid close attention to the exact sounds, proper cleaning and storing of utensils, and the precise layout of the surroundings as they performed their rituals. Observant Jews could not take food with non-Jews, and they followed detailed rules for life-cycle events. Anyone who violated the purity rules was punished and sometimes even banished from the community. In addition, Jews were required to undergo circumcision rites that identified them as members of the community.

For three hundred years after Alexander's conquests, Hellenistic values spread rapidly from the Aegean to the borders of the Indian subcontinent. New employment opportunities that opened up in the cities in the wake of his conquests attracted numerous job seekers. Using Greek as a common language for commerce enhanced trade, facilitated the exchange of ideas, and helped create an appealing cosmopolitan culture. Hellenism was the general term that referred to Greek culture, language, philosophy, its pantheon of Greek gods and goddesses, and other Greek (Hellenic) elements. Rich merchants and landed aristocrats flaunted their wealth by building extravagant homes, dining on exotic food, traveling, and patronizing the arts. These aristocrats prospered in large part by exploiting the labor of slaves, farmers, and laborers.

The Roman Republic was heir to Greek civilization, and the Romans were absorbing many Hellenistic ideas into their own culture as they made the transition to an empire. Although the Romans tolerated a great deal of religious and cultural pluralism, they were beginning to insist that their subjects, including the Palestinian Jews, pay homage to the ruler as the symbol of the Roman state.

Many Jews living outside of Palestine found work in the cities of the Mediterranean basin where, instead of preserving their unique Jewish identity, they readily blended into the Hellenistic society. The allure of the cosmopolitan culture must have been hard for many to resist, even though their experience in exile might have steeled them against such temptations. It was becoming increasingly difficult to remain committed to traditional values such as justice, equality, and concern for the poor and downtrodden, or to continue to rely on the protection of the Covenant amidst the swirl of conflicting ideas.

It was even more difficult to turn away from the respect and status that wealth seemed to offer. Diaspora Jews were becoming far more urbane than their compatriots in Palestine and generally more heavily influenced by Hellenistic values. Even within Palestine, doubts about the efficacy of the rituals spread as similar doubts had spread in the Indian subcontinent. If that were not enough, when the Roman legions conquered west Asia and established the province of Judea, Jews had ample reason to fear that Rome would soon absorb and destroy Judaism once and for all. Roman leaders had difficulty appreciating Jewish concerns, and tension mounted, especially because of the oppressive taxes the Romans imposed.

Groups of Jews reacted in different ways to Roman rule and the threat of being destroyed or absorbed into the larger society. Those who had benefited most from the spread of Hellenism tended to embrace the urbane life of secular learning and sumptuous lifestyles. More orthodox Jews thought their cosmopolitan brothers were violating God's will and not keeping their side of the Covenant, not unlike their predecessors whose lack of faith had resulted in exile. Those who had been pushed aside by the cosmopolitan Hellenistic culture gravitated to the conservative Jewish sects and parties that promised a return to the simple agrarian justice of traditional Jewish life.

In the century before the birth of Jesus, many Jews increasingly longed for their independence and turned to the biblical promise of the coming of God's kingdom, which most assumed meant an earthly kingdom. Most were convinced this kingdom would come in the future, for some sooner rather than later, although no one was quite sure what would happen when that awaited time occurred. One thing was certain—when it did come, the enemies of the Jews would be destroyed and his chosen people would be saved. Many were looking for someone who might hasten this event and usher in the kingdom.

The Pharisees (Separated Ones) championed a reform movement that would recapture the imagined purity of an earlier time, and they focused on intensive study of the Torah. They were highly political and advocated a continuation and expansion of traditional legal systems and strict observance of purity and pollution in matters of personal health, food preparation, dining, and social relations.

The Sadducees, who controlled temple rituals, had their own version of traditional Jewish law. This group was mainly composed of conservative, wealthy landowners. Whereas the Pharisees believed there was life after death, the Sadducees argued that there was no scriptural basis for such beliefs.

The Zealots, a third group of Jewish reformers, were politically the most radical. They formed armed guerilla groups who battled not only the Romans but also their own king Herod because they thought he was too Hellenized and acted too much like a Roman ruler.

The Essences, a fourth major faction in Jewish society, resembled the Indian ascetics. Their members had dropped out of society and were living celibate lives, sharing their resources. The Essences rejected the interpretation of Judaism that the Pharisees and Sadducees preferred. They disdained rituals and laws and were thoroughly disgusted with the dominant Hellenistic lifestyle. They believed that the end of time was imminent and that the "Messiah," the "anointed one," would defeat the forces of evil and darkness and usher in a new kingdom where God would be king, and a new age of freedom and prosperity would emerge for all Jews.

At the same time, many Jews were hoping that an earthly messiah, a descendant of the line of David, would serve as the arm of God, end Roman occupation, and restore the Jewish people to their privileged place in history. It was into this context of Jewish prophecies, especially in the writings of the Prophet Isaiah and in the apocalyptic writings of the Essenes, that Jesus was born around 4 B.C.E. into a humble family of Nazareth.

THE ARABIAN PENINSULA

The Arabian Peninsula, further to the south, was divided between a relatively prosperous and urbanized southern area in Yemen, which had several flourishing kingdoms, and a less-populated north, peopled by pastoral nomads known as Bedouins. By the start of the Common Era, the southern states, famous for their production of frankincense and myrrh, were already engaged in a lively trade north to Syria and Anatolia and across the Indian Ocean. Bedouins had been living for millennia in the desert and steppe lands to the north. Most of them, like the Aryans and early Hebrews, survived by herding their flocks of sheep and goats, moving from oasis to oasis in search of water and grass for their animals. Mecca, Yahtrib (Medina), and Jewish agricultural settlements in the north punctuated the largely open desert where the Bedouins held sway.

Like other pastoral nomads, the extended family and clans and tribes related by blood formed the basis of Arabian society. Each tribe was led by a chief, chosen by the leading families and advised by a group of elders. Members of individual tribes felt intense loyalty to their own clans, and raiding other groups was a common means of obtaining needed resources when times were hard. Heated rivalries over grazing areas, access to water, or for honor were common. As a result, clans and tribes engaged in periodic warfare.

After the third century C.E., as Roman power waned and the Yemenite urbanized states in the south declined, Bedouins filled the power vacuum, overwhelming peasant farmers and urban craftsmen. Bedouin warriors easily conquered entire communities and even threatened Byzantine and Sasanid cities further north.

Although Bedouin survival and success were based on pastoral nomadism supplemented by raiding, cross-cultural contacts and exchanges overland and by sea were becoming increasingly important. New trade routes helped bring Bedouins into the commercial network. A major caravan route from southwestern Arabia all the way to Palestine and Syria made important stops in Mecca and Yahtrib. These new routes helped Petra and Palmyra, two northern states, rise to power. These states were greatly influenced by Hellenistic and Roman culture.

By 500 C.E., both land routes and maritime traffic across the Indian Ocean linked Arabia to the outside world, and Arabian traders were well positioned to transport goods from seaports to camel caravans that carried goods overland through Palestine to Constantinople or east to central and east Asia. Oases, where traders could rest and find water and food, dotted the caravan routes.

As these way stations grew into towns and cities, an increasing number of wealthy mercantile clans developed, and tribes that could best take advantage of the commercial opportunities rapidly grew in wealth and importance, resulting in a growing gap between rich and poorer tribes. Some clans became increasingly prosperous while others experienced social dislocation and a crisis of identity. Since Bedouins traditionally believed in equality and sharing all wealth, the new commercialism leading to stratified classes spawned increasing friction that threatened to undermine the social order.

New ideas were also challenging Bedouin society. As caravans wended their way through the Arabian Peninsula, people exchanged not only goods but opinions, innovations, inventions, and insights. Ideas came from the cosmopolitan Greek culture, the Roman Empire, and traders from the Indian subcontinent. New information fanned throughout Arabia from trading centers and towns, creating an atmosphere of inquiry and doubt about the old gods and goddesses and traditional ways of doing things.

The extraordinary place of poetry in Arabian society offered a fertile avenue for ideas and a response to changing conditions and values. Bedouins often say that poetry was "the archives of their history, the evidence of what they consider right and wrong, . . ."[6] Imrul-Kais (d. 540), a Bedouin tribal leader, was an important poet who attracted many others. His circle of poets helped create Arabic as a language, and Arabic-speaking Bedouins were soon identified as Arabs. Poets began to write beautiful verse and complex religious texts in Arabic.

The major religious practices in sixth-century Arabia focused on deities embodied in spirits associated with wells, trees, and forces of nature that were believed to protect a particular tribe. Most of these deities were more feared than loved, and worshipers propitiated them with gifts, prayers, and pilgrimages.

A variety of monotheistic groups also lived in the region. Communities of Jews and Christians, as well as other groups who rejected polytheism and preached about one true God, were scattered throughout Arabia, including a significant Jewish settlement in Yahtrib and a number of Christians in Mecca and some Arabian coastal trading towns. There Arabs learned about their neighbors' monotheistic tradition. Najran, a city south of Mecca, was home to a large Christian community, and in 530 Abyssinia, a Christian state, invaded and took over much of southern Arabia. Many Jews had adopted Arabic practices and began to give their children Arabic names. By 600, some Arabs had already converted to an Arabized form of Judaism. Moreover, Arab caravan traders regularly met Christians, Jews, and Zoroastrians on their journeys north.

Beyond the attraction of Christianity and Judaism, some groups were already expressing belief in a single God whom they identified as Al-Hal. Although they were not organized as a sect or community, these *hanifs,* as they were called, revered Abraham as the best example from ancient times of someone who believed in a single all-powerful divinity.

Mecca and Yahtrib were small but growing urban centers. Mecca was an important pilgrimage site because a shrine enclosing the Ka'ba, a sacred black stone that was probably a meteorite, was located there. Bedouins made a yearly pilgrimage to Mecca, praying at the Ka'ba and placing images of their gods and goddesses around it. Warfare was suspended during the pilgrimage, and pilgrims were expected to leave their weapons outside the city limits. Merchants and traders in and around Mecca managed a prosperous business feeding and lodging the pilgrims. Tribes such as the prosperous Quraysh benefited most from the urbanization and rise of commercialism.

The competition among tribes for a role in the newly developing commercial opportunities and the increasing prosperity that accompanied them contributed to increasing unrest in Arabia, not unlike what had happened in India in the sixth century B.C.E and in Palestine in the first century C.E. In addition, contact with the more sophisticated centers left some Bedouins unsettled about their lifestyle. Muslims later called this period the "time of ignorance" (*Jahilia*), but it was also a period of intellectual ferment and experimentation with new forms of faith. In 570, in Mecca, during this efflorescence of ideas and speculation, Muhammad was born.

THE SPIRITUAL WORLDS OF BUDDHISM, CHRISTIANITY, AND ISLAM

Each of the charismatic individuals who founded the three universal religions grew up in a specific cultural context and historical past that informed his message. By weaving together threads of their own traditions, borrowing from other teachers, and speaking a faith language accessible to those they sought to teach, they all created something new and exciting and, in the process, redirected the histories of large areas of the world.

THE BUDDHA

Siddhartha Gotama, the founder of the first of the universal religions, was definitely not an ascetic in his early life. He was a young prince living in a small kingdom near present-day Nepal. The Buddhist tradition claims that as a young man he lived a life of luxury in a pleasure palace, isolated from any hardships. When he realized the suffering that sickness, old age, and death bring, he is said to have fled from the palace, leaving behind his beautiful wife and his newborn son, and he sought solace with ascetics in the countryside. After intensive study and practicing extreme forms of asceticism, including starving himself, followed by temptations of sex and power, doubt and fear, Siddhartha suddenly experienced enlightenment and became a "Buddha," one who has "woken up."

According to Buddhist sources, the Buddha realized that existence is filled with suffering (*dukkha*). Desire, he taught, is the root cause of suffering: desiring what we do not have and desiring to keep what we do have. Most of all, people fear death and desperately cling to life. If individuals could stop all desires, he preached, suffering would end. This insight was the basis of what became known as the Four Noble Truths: Life is filled with suffering; suffering is caused by desire; one can end desire and therefore put an end to suffering; by following the Eightfold Path one will be able to end desires, lead a moral life, and at death find final release from birth and rebirth in nirvana.

To experience nirvana, which is very close to the Hindu concept of moksha, required a radical change in consciousness. There is no permanent self, the Buddha taught, only a collection of stimuli stored in the brain. People's minds organize sensory impressions into categories such as beautiful/ugly, sweet/bitter, good/bad, etc., and they mistake these mental images for reality. If they can change their understanding and consciousness, they will experience nirvana, the dissolution of the ego, and escape the endless rounds of birth and rebirth.

FIGURE 1-1   THE BUDDHA IN TEACHING POSE
The teaching Buddha in Sarnath, Gupta style.

Buddha's Eightfold Path suggests how leading a moral and ethical life can help one realize nirvana. The first two steps—Right Understanding and Right Resolve—include the sincere belief that the Four Noble Truths are correct and the intention to strive earnestly to end desire by following the Buddha's path and letting go of the idea of a self. Steps three through five—Right Speech, Right Action, and Right Livelihood—involve ethical commitments that include benevolence and not harming living things. Believers should practice right speech by not telling lies or spreading gossip; right conduct includes not killing, not stealing, and remaining chaste. Right Livelihood advises people to avoid jobs that harm others, such as butchers, hunters, soldiers, fishermen, jailers, slave traders, or liquor salesmen.

Steps six through eight outline one's spiritual development. Right Effort involves banishing envy, lust, and jealousy and guarding the mind against all unhealthy thoughts and images. Right Awareness means paying close attention to the sensations that enter one's body and mind, keeping calm, and being indifferent to pain and pleasure. Finally, in step eight, Right Concentration, one undertakes deep meditation that leads beyond all pairs of opposites. Freed from sensations, thoughts, and categories, one has finally realized nirvana.

Clearly the Buddha's teachings formed a synthesis of many of the ideas and values that were circulating among other ascetics. He took ideas such as karma, samsara, and moksha from the Upanishads and made them accessible to a wider audience, regardless of gender, caste, or tribe. He was able to combine mystical goals leading to nirvana with everyday ethical concerns such as diet, relationships, and personal values such as truth telling, honesty, compassion and nonviolence. His stress on right livelihood probably appealed to the growing numbers of merchants and traders, many of whom would become his most enthusiastic supporters.

The Buddha's teaching also addressed some of the disquiet people had about the role of brahmins in society. Many had growing concerns about the slaughter of so many animals and the enormous expense of the extravagant sacrifices brahmins were performing in an effort to influence the gods. Buddha denied the existence of gods and goddesses and argued that sacrifices were irrelevant. He also rejected the idea that certain people are born ritually purer than others. No one is born a brahmin, he stated. A person becomes a brahmin only by his actions. Right livelihood also undercut the idea of hereditary caste occupations because he insisted that no one should perform a job that was harmful to any living being, either human or animal.

Karuna, compassion, lay at the center of the Buddha's teachings. He advocated a "middle way" between extreme asceticism and brahminic sacrificial ritualism. Recognizing that no one can be perfect, he suggested that one should try to do as little harm as possible. These values of moderation appealed to large numbers of people who eschewed the extreme discipline and self-mortification that many ascetics of that time were practicing. Although the Buddha's teachings appear to have focused more on psychological insights than on deities and rituals usually associated with a religion, his audiences were familiar with many of the concepts he was using, such as release from karma, and his followers likely heard his words as an invitation to an exciting spiritual quest.

During the last 40 years of his life, the Buddha wandered across the Gangetic Plain preaching to kings, merchants, and common people, and he advised his closest disciples to go by twos and spread his message. Some who accepted the Buddha's Four Noble Truths and wished to follow his Eightfold Path became monks who renounced the world; others were lay followers who expected to continue to lead their normal lives in the world while supporting the monks.

The Buddha, like most successful reformers, offered many innovations for the new age, but as he did so, he worked within the traditions and worldview of the existing north Indian society. When he spoke of karma, samsara, and release, he was referring to familiar principles that he had adapted for his own new message. The Buddha also added a significant ethical dimension to these earlier concepts. Reformers and teachers in other areas, while accepting many of the historic values and belief from their societies, were also offering innovative solutions to the crises of their own times. One of them, about 500 years later, was Jesus of Nazareth.

JESUS

The first century B.C.E. in the Jewish community in Palestine was quite different from life in North India. Instead of release from rebirth, Jews were hoping for the coming of a messiah. Speculation over what sort of person he would actually be covered a wide spectrum of possibilities from a militant political leader to a spiritual redeemer. Whereas the Essenes anticipated that the messiah would bring about the end of time, the Zealots hoped he would lead a revolt against Roman rule and reestablish a powerful Jewish kingdom. In this atmosphere of great expectation, Jesus of Nazareth was one of many itinerant preachers, Jewish reformers, and candidates for messiahood that emerged in Judea.

Jesus is said to have lived from about 4 B.C.E. to about 30 C.E., and knowledge gained from recently discovered manuscripts known as the Dead Sea Scrolls places his period of teaching at the time of Roman emperor Claudius. Almost nothing is known about his personal life, although tradition claims his father was a carpenter. After his baptism by John the Baptist, another ascetic, he was inspired by the possibility of the imminent realization of the kingdom of God. He is said to have wandered over the countryside during the last three years of his life, preaching that the kingdom was already coming and using parables to illustrate his insights.

In addition to his message of the coming kingdom, Jesus' deep concern for poor and marginalized people living miserable lives in the Hellenized society also attracted followers. Adapting the Ten Commandments handed down by Moses, Jesus emphasized two commandments, which some Jews also emphasized: "Love the Lord your God with all your heart and all your mind," and "Love your neighbor as yourself." (Matthew 22:37–40) Like the Buddha before him, he stressed compassion and love of one's neighbor. He also advocated peace and nonviolence, symbolized by turning the other cheek. "You have heard it said you shall love your neighbor and hate your enemy," he said. "But I say to you, Love your enemies and pray for those who persecute you." (Matthew 5: 43–4)

Jesus was not only a spiritual and ethical teacher, but also a healer. During his brief ministry, his acts of healing and exorcism made up a major part of his mission. The Gospels, which summarize his life and teachings, speak often of Jesus' compassion and his responses to the suffering of afflicted persons. Many of those healed were social outcasts such as lepers, a bent over woman, and those with physical disabilities such as blindness. Many New Testament passages testify to the healing miracles Jesus performed, such as raising a man from the dead and restoring sight to the blind. Jesus healed by simply saying to a paralytic, "Get up, pick up your bed and go home." (Mark 2:11) In an age that sorely distrusted physicians and looked to miracle workers, Jesus' power to heal certainly attracted followers. When asked how he differed from John the Baptist, Jesus replied, "Go and tell John what you hear and see: the blind receive their sight, the lame walk, the lepers are cleansed, and the deaf hear, the dead are raised up" (Matt. 11:4–5, Luke 7:22)

Jesus tempered Jewish dedication to justice by telling his followers, "Judge not lest you be not judged." When a mob was about to stone a woman caught in adultery, he suggested that whoever was without sin should cast the first stone. He advocated a communal life where people shared what they had, and, instead of amassing treasures on earth, he advised them to prepare for the coming kingdom.

Jesus preached about God's love and forgiveness. One of his parables told of a shepherd who was extremely upset over the loss of one of his sheep. Another was about how joyous a poor widow was when she found a lost coin. He told about a prodigal son who had left home, gotten into trouble, and squandered his inheritance. When he returned home, his father rejoiced and celebrated his return. Jesus likened God to that father.

Many Jews, especially the Pharisees, probably saw Jesus as a significant threat to their own status and someone who would both anger the ruling Roman officials and upset the social structure of Jewish society. Certainly, his followers who were anticipating a political messiah wondered when Jesus would make a move against Roman rule. Instead, he spoke about a heavenly kingdom where people would dwell with God after they died. Even so, fearing Jesus would stir up unrest, the Romans, with support from some members of the Jewish community, crucified him in Jerusalem when he was only 33 years old.

FIGURE 1-2   JESUS TEACHING
The teaching Jesus from artwork.

It looked as though that was the end of Jesus' story, but three days after his crucifixion his followers believed that he had been resurrected and that he had appeared to some of them. At the celebration of Pentecost, which Jews traditionally commemorate 50 days after the seder (a common feast at the time of Passover), Jesus' followers felt the Holy Spirit in their midst and the Christian community was born. The focus changed from Jesus the preacher to Jesus the risen one. Believers, called Christians, preached the "Good News" that Jesus Christ has conquered death. By believing in him, one could gain eternal life.

MUHAMMAD

Muhammad was born into the powerful Quraysh tribe, but his parents died when he was very young, and a granduncle raised the orphaned boy. Muhammad supported himself in a variety of jobs until Khadija, a widow 20 years his senior who had substantial business interests, hired him to work in her caravan business. Khadija was said to have been so impressed with Muhammad's integrity and sensitivity that she married him, even though he was many years her junior. Their marriage gave Muhammad financial and emotional security. Khadija was a constant source of support for her young husband, and she is revered as his first convert.

As Muhammad accompanied his caravans north into parts of the Sasanid and Byzantine empires, he came in contact with traders from other cultures including Jews, Christians, and other monotheistic groups in the area. No doubt Muhammad also talked with Waraqa, his wife's cousin, who had converted to Christianity. These contacts may have made him uneasy with the rituals directed toward numerous local gods and especially to three major goddesses.

Even as a young man, Muhammad was said to have inclined toward spirituality. It was his custom to spend time each year meditating, fasting, and praying in a cave on Mount Hira. Khadija encouraged his religious quest.

During a period of fasting and prayer in 610, when he was 40 years old, Muhammad had a mystical experience in which the angel Gabriel brought him divine revelations. At first he was deeply troubled with these revelations and hesitated sharing them with others. But Khadija took the revelations seriously and believed he had received a divine revelation, and soon others began to believe as well. Over the next 22 years, Muhammad continued to receive revelations that he shared with his followers.

The most important of these revelations was an uncompromising monotheism: "There is no God but God (Allah)." The Quran states:

> Say, He is God the One and Only,
> God the Eternal, the Absolute:
> He begetteth not nor is He begotten,
> and there is none like unto Him (Sura 112: 1–4)

Allah is both transcendent and personal, "as near as the vein in one's neck."[7] Followers were to submit totally to Allah. Islam means submission, and anyone who submits to Allah is a Muslim. These revelations established Muhammad as the messenger of God. He insisted he was not a god nor was he to be worshipped.

Muhammad's revelations also included the belief in a final judgment and heaven and hell. He stated that on Judgment Day, each person would face Allah and have to account for his or her individual choices and actions. Those who had submitted to Allah would go to heaven, whereas nonbelievers would be condemned to a fiery hell.

Muhammad did not intend to create a new religion, but rather to correct and complete the message of his predecessors. The Quran makes numerous references to events and persons in the Old and New Testaments. God had sent prophets to the Jews and had sent Jesus for the Christians. Finally there were revelations in Arabic for Arabs.

In some ways Muhammad was trying to revive existing Bedouin values, especially the commitment to equality. Those who surrendered to Allah promised they would support and protect one another and never attack other Muslims. But the number of converts remained small, and for 10 years Muhammad and his followers struggled against the leaders of Meccan society who resented his emphasis on strict monotheism, which clearly threatened the profitable pilgrimage trade in Mecca. They also feared that his criticism of money lending, unequal contracts, and harsh treatment of orphans and widows might undermine the leaders' privileged status. Some Meccans refused to trade with Muslims and threatened them, so in 622 Muhammad and his followers secretly left Mecca and went to Yahtrib. This migration, known as the *hegira*, established the Muslim community. The hegira was a major turning point in Islamic history, and 622 became Year One of the Islamic calendar.

Impressed with Muhammad's integrity, and preferring to accept the leadership of an outsider rather than give power to any one of the groups in the city, the various factions in Yahtrib allowed Muhammad to take charge. Unlike the Buddha or Jesus, who focused on preaching and stayed away from politics, Muhammad became not only a religious prophet but an important political and military leader as well.

Muhammad thought he would work closely with the Jewish community in Yathrib composed of diaspora Jews and Arabs who had converted to Judaism. After all, they were worshiping the same God. However, leaders of the prominent Jewish tribes refused to accept Muhammad as a genuine prophet, and some saw his authority in Yahtrib (which became known as Medina, the "city of the Prophet") as a threat to their position. Having little opportunity to support themselves as traders, the Muslims started raiding caravans, some belonging to members of Muhammad's tribe, the Quraysh. These raids violated tribal law that forbade attacking members of one's own tribe, and they forced the Muslims to defend themselves against the vastly larger Quraysh forces. The success of Muhammad's followers convinced more people to surrender to Allah.

In 628, after a decisive victory against the Meccan army, Muhammad decided to return to Mecca. Instead of attacking the city, however, he directed his followers to put away their weapons and participate in the annual peaceful pilgrimage, the *hajj*. This daring move resulted in a treaty between the Muslims and the Quraysh leadership. When the Quraysh violated the treaty, Muhammad led a large army to Mecca and the city surrendered without a fight. By the time he died in 632, one tribal leader after another had pledged his loyalty to him; most of the Arabian Peninsula was united under Arab Muslim control, and warfare among the tribes in Arabia had decreased significantly. Just before he died, Muhammad preached to his followers:

> Know ye that every Muslim is a brother unto every other Muslim, and that ye are now one brotherhood. It is not legitimate for any one of you, therefore, to appropriate unto himself anything that belongs to his brother unless it is willingly given him by that brother.[8]

CONCLUSION

The founding and early spread of Buddhism, Christianity, and Islam suggest both general similarities and many particular differences. The founders of all three faiths offered their followers specific answers to the concerns that many faced. In all three settings, people were struggling with crises of meanings and the Buddha, Jesus, and Muhammad all responded to these crises by first diagnosing the problems and then prescribing solutions. Each talked in the symbolic language of his own historic tradition and taught within an inherited worldview that shaped his message. Buddhism was created within a thoroughly Indian world that saw life as an endless round of births and rebirths that were determined by one's personal karma. The Buddha was one of many teachers offering a way out of this cycle. Further to the west, Jesus and Muhammad, both "children of Abraham," accepted the basic Jewish worldview of the supremacy of a single God in heaven who is revealed to human beings by prophets, and they offered ways to reach heaven after they died.

Like large rivers reaching the deltas, the universal religions began to spread outside their places of origin to new groups of people with different cultural traditions. As each faith moved to new settings, its followers tried to cling to the basic teachings and ethical values of its founder while adapting the message so it made sense in the new surroundings.

In the process of spreading their faiths to new cultural groups, the leaders and missionaries for the universal religions faced two formidable problems. First, they had to make concerted efforts to form a coherent consensus on what their particular faith believed, what rituals were required, and how they would maintain their institutions and community. Each faith also had to find ways to deal with those who deviated from the core beliefs and those charismatic reformers who threatened to undermine the faith or even launch new religions of their own making. This dimension of the history of the universal religions may be called their inner history.

Studying the inner history of Buddhism, Christianity, and Islam involves analyzing how each religion was institutionalized and how that institution, whether *Sangha*, Church, or *Ummah*, changed over time. The inner dynamics include analyzing how each faith strove to remain true to its core message as it became increasingly involved with commercial and political power. Frequently, the institutional form of the faith deviated far from the founder's teachings. Cycles of worldliness usually stimulated reform movements within each of the faiths. The inner dynamics also address how the institutional religions managed dissent and conflicting interpretations of the core beliefs.

The universal religions faced a second daunting problem: how much adaptation to new settings they should tolerate. This issue may be identified as the conflict between universalism—the beliefs and practices all members of a given faith must affirm—and localism—adaptations to the historic and cultural traditions in the areas to which it spread. As missionaries carried their religions to new areas, they constantly questioned how much of the established doctrine and ritual practice they should insist on and how flexible they could be in infusing the faith with new practices and local beliefs.

As these faiths spread, each had to adapt its message for people who spoke other languages, had lived different histories, and shared unique cultural worldviews. Much was lost in translation and much new was added. Those who wanted to share their faith adapted its core message to new cultural contexts by appropriating similar local beliefs and practices. They also looked for symbols, rituals, and ideas familiar to potential converts that could be identified with the message of the faith they wanted to spread. Those who were successful succeeded in balancing their beliefs and practices with aspects of the local culture and were able to forge a new synthesis that included both the central message of their faith and liberal portions of familiar local beliefs and practices. Pouring new wine into old bottles, they related new insights to what prospective converts already knew.

Spreading the new religions was like walking on a tightrope. If the carriers of the faith accepted too many of the local cultural traditions, the new faith's influence and meaning would be superficial at best. However, if they insisted on too much orthodoxy, few potential converts would understand or care to listen to the message. Both the challenge of remaining true to the faith and the necessity of adapting to changing circumstances are important themes in the history of the spread of Buddhism, Christianity, and Islam.

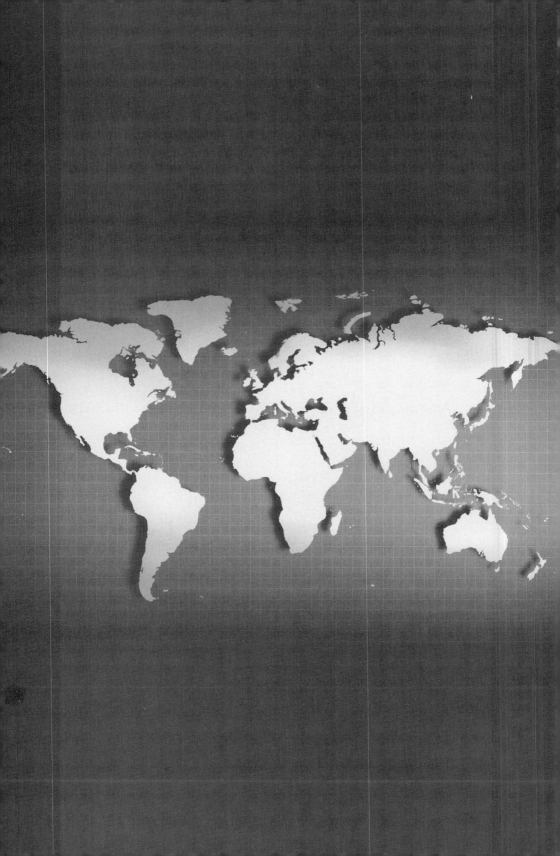

CHAPTER TWO

THE EXPANDING WORLD OF BUDDHISM: BUDDHIST ENCOUNTERS FROM SOUTH TO EAST ASIA

GETTING STARTED ON CHAPTER TWO: How did the Buddha's followers try to organize a community and define a common doctrine following the death of their teacher? What was the appeal of Buddhism for women, merchants, rulers, lower castes, and other groups? Why was Buddhism able to spread so widely beyond its Indian home base? And why did it decline in the Indian subcontinent? How did Buddhism change as it took root in new cultural settings? What differences, conflicts, and controversies divided the world of Buddhism as the religion spread? What relationship did Buddhism develop with political authorities? How did the support or opposition of kings and emperors affect its evolution?

The Buddha gained enlightenment and preached his message of compassion and release in the enormously pluralistic religious environment of sixth-century North India. He was only one of many ascetics wandering the countryside, offering new insights, and seeking followers. This charismatic teacher provided a prescription to ease life's suffering and lead those who followed his path to nirvana. In his message, called the *Dhamma,* he taught that suffering results from a desire for permanence in a world of constant flux. The way to end suffering, he explained, is to stop desiring. Be content with what you have, cultivate compassion, and try to do as little harm as possible. Give up the idea of a permanent self and seek to experience oneness with the totality of the universe, an experience that will result in nirvana and release from the cycles of rebirth.

BUDDHISM'S EARLY GROWTH

Early Buddhists probably included men and women of all social strata and cut across castes as well. The new faith had great appeal to the increasing number of merchants in the cities in the Gangetic Plain. It also resonated with princes and kings who hoped that the Buddha's message might foster unity within their states by offering their subjects a common set of beliefs and ethical practices.

As the number of followers increased, it became apparent that the Buddha and his closest disciples would have to provide housing and food for them. As a result, the Buddha organized his followers into the Sangha, a society that included all who wanted to follow his path, whether monks or members of the lay community. Soon, however, the Sangha included only men who were ordained as monks. Monks took the vows of celibacy, truth telling, and nonstealing, and they gave up their possessions and dedicated their lives to preaching, healing, and helping others. The monks' example of simplicity, meditation, and service set an example for the lay community. The Buddha, the Dhamma, and the Sangha—known as the "Three Jewels of Buddhism"—form the core of Buddhist faith. Members of the lay community were encouraged to build good karma by supporting the monks.

Initially, the Buddha resisted including women in the Sangha and only men joined. His adopted mother and close companion asked the Buddha twice if he would let women join, and both times he refused. When Ananda, one of his most trusted disciples, spoke up for the women, the Buddha reluctantly agreed that they could join the order on the condition that they followed eight additional rules that underscored their inferior status.

His resistance to including women may have been caused in part by his fear that their presence would distract the monks and snare them in the web of worldly concerns, the very state they were working to transcend. Early Buddhist texts presented women as both compassionate caregivers who minister to people in need and also as sexual temptresses whose allure stands in the way of a devotee letting go of the world.

In spite of the initial resistance to including women, large numbers aspired to become nuns. Many were drawn to the Buddha's message and wanted to devote their lives to following his discipline and to living with others who had made the same commitment. Their community provided a home and security for women who had no family to protect them, although a good many of the early nuns came from wealthy families where finances were not an issue. Becoming a nun offered a socially acceptable alternative to marriage and childbearing and a way to escape from an unhappy marriage. Some women also wanted a chance to develop their intellect, a path that was denied to most women.

Technically, the Sangha was the entire Buddhist community and included monks, nuns, laymen, and laywomen. However, the Sangha is often used to refer only to celibate monks and nuns who lived in communal groups according to a strictly enforced discipline with written codes of conduct that governed all aspects of behavior. They were expected to work on their own spiritual development to achieve the status of an *arhat* (a saint or fully enlightened being), one who has completed the Eightfold Path and attained enlightenment.

The following story of the "still beautiful" Isidasi, who wants to work off her bad karma, illustrates why some women might have wanted some respectable alternative to marriage. She explains to the Buddha why she became a nun:

> In the great city of Ujjani my father was a merchant of high repute.
> I was his only daughter, deeply loved and pampered. A wealthy merchant sent noblemen from the city of Saketa to arrange a marriage, and my father gave me to be his son's wife. Day and night I humbled myself to honor my in-laws—my training made me bow my head down at their feet. When I saw my husband's sisters and brothers I cringed and crept away to free my seat for them. I kept fresh-cooked food and drink and spiced pickles ready to serve their demands.
>
> I woke early every morning to scrub my hands and feet before I crossed the threshold to beg my husband's blessing. Like a slave girl, I took combs and scented oils and my mirror to groom him. I cooked his rice gruel, I washed his bowl, I waited on this husband like a mother doting on her son. Though I was diligent and humble, meticulous and virtuous in serving him, my husband despised me. He begged his parents, "Give me your leave. I must go away. I will not stay in this house with Isidasi!"

To placate their son, his parents took Isidasi back to her father's house and her parents arranged another marriage for her, but it only lasted a month. Then they got an ascetic to marry her but he only stayed two weeks. Isidasi wanted to kill herself, but decided instead to become a nun.

> My father argued, "My child, you may follow the Buddha's way by giving food and drink to holy men and Brahmin priests." I pleaded in tears, begging his blessing, "I must destroy the evil I have done!" My father blessed me then, "Attain enlightenment and the Buddha's way that leads to liberation!" . . .[9]

From the outset the Buddha accepted lay believers: individuals who remained in the world to keep society functioning. Lay people were expected to observe the first three steps on the road to becoming arhats, which included donating financial and material support for the monks and nuns. Because monks and nuns had no reliable source of income, the Buddha instructed them to spend time each day seeking food and other necessities from the lay community. Lay people earned "merit" for their services to the monks and nuns, and merit built up good karma. The symbiotic relationship between the monks and nuns and the lay community that supported them set a pattern that would also be followed by Christianity.

There were many reasons why the Buddha's message attracted so many followers. For one thing, joining his movement did not require a drastic change in worldview for many. The Buddha taught in Pali, the language of the people, rather than in Sanskrit that brahmins used. He wanted all people to understand his teaching and be able to apply it to their own lives. He accepted most of the older concepts common to Indian religions such as dharma (performing the action appropriate for one's age, caste, and gender), karma (the consequences of one's actions), and rebirth. Most Indians were familiar with these ideas and already accepted them. However, the Buddha's criticism of the caste system and of the brahmins, who were at the top of this hierarchical structure, had a huge appeal for the lower castes.

The Buddhist goal of nirvana was also very similar to the Hindu concept of moksha (release from rebirth). He offered an innovative combination of mystical union with the ultimate, the philosophic system developed earlier in the Upanishads, and a new ethical system that stressed human equality. The Buddha recast these familiar ideas into a more contemporary message that included several ethical and moral concerns as well and made that message accessible to anyone who would listen.

The Buddha offered a "middle way" between the Brahminic religion that focused on animal sacrifices and observance of strict rules of purity and pollution and the purely individual quest for moksha espoused in the Upanishads. He also offered a middle way between a hedonistic life of personal gratification and the austere reform movements that required total renunciation of the world, absolute adherence to nonviolence, and strict dietary restrictions that severely limited one's choice of food.

The Buddha also spoke to the general uncertainty caused by the disruption of traditional social norms and the increasing social mobility. In the charged atmosphere that accompanied the rapid rise of the cities along the Gangetic Plain, an entrepreneurial spirit prevailed as merchants struggled to achieve a higher place in the social system. Merchants were attracted to the Buddha's rejection of the strict hierarchy, which relegated them to relatively low status. They also profited from his appeal to nonviolence, for traders need large areas of stability to carry on commercial activities.

At the same time, the growing desire for more possessions and the enjoyment of physical pleasures were not bringing the satisfaction or peace of mind people hoped for. Their desires never seemed to be satisfied. The more they had, the more they wanted. The Buddha warned that acquisitiveness could only cause more anxiety and suffering and would never result in human happiness. This was a radical idea for any period in history, but his messages obviously struck a chord with many people in sixth-century India.

Moreover, many popular religious practices, including some that were centuries old, began to creep into Buddhism. One example was the worship of sacred serpents called *nagas,* a long-standing tradition in India (and one that continues to this day). In a popular story about the Buddha's enlightenment, a giant naga sheltered him from a violent storm. Before images of the Buddha were made, much attention was focused on the Bodhi tree under which the Buddha gained enlightenment. Tree worship had already had a very long history in India, and the Buddha's enlightenment gave the sacred tree new symbolic meanings. Perhaps most important, meditation, by which the Buddha realized enlightenment, had probably been practiced in the subcontinent since the Indus civilization some 2,000 years earlier. Buddhism prospered by infusing new meanings into these and other age-old beliefs and practices.

THE FORMATION OF THE CANON

The Buddha did not designate a successor before he died. He told his followers, "The Dhamma will be your leader," and instructed Ananda to "be a lamp unto yourself. Pursue your own salvation with diligence." With such seemingly vague instructions, his followers soon began debating what his parables and metaphors really meant and in what form they should pass his message on to others. The Buddha, like the founders of Christianity and Islam, was a charismatic preacher with a burning message of salvation, not a systematic philosopher whose statements fit into a logical system.

Many of the texts collected in the first centuries after the Buddha's death were his disciples' recollections about issues, and the meanings were often ambiguous. Moreover, the Buddha is said to have told his disciples to spread his message in the local languages, and followers tried to translate his teachings into languages used outside the Buddha's north Indian setting. With so many followers translating the message and the many individual interpretations that got inserted into the texts, discrepancies about the core meanings of the Buddha's teachings were unavoidable.

Buddhists wanted to establish a common basis for their faith so that those who carried the message to different areas could share a common set of teachings. To achieve this goal, the Sangha attempted to compile a Buddhist Canon in Pali. A series of all-Buddhist councils were convened to carry out the major work of completing the Canon.

At the First Council, held in 483 B.C.E. just a few months after the Buddha's death, and the Second Council, held a hundred years later, the Buddha's disciples recited his sermons that they had memorized, and scribes wrote them down. (It is hard for us to imagine, in an age of e-mail, what prodigious feats of memory these monks had perfected to remember these texts. Memorizing a single source might take a lifetime.) The Third Council, held in 225, revised the collected texts, added two scholarly commentaries, and produced the "Three Baskets" or "Tripitaka": the Basket of Discipline, the Basket of Discourses, and the Basket of Scholasticism.

EARLY SCHISMS   Serious disagreements on several contentious points arose during the Second Council as the growing Buddhist community strove to create a common set of texts and formulate a common core of beliefs and practices. One was over the role of the arhat. One group, the Theravadans (Followers of the Teaching of the Elders), insisted that the Buddha was a human being who had taught that each person, individually, had to go through the same stages the Buddha had experienced in order to become completely detached from the world and experience nirvana. The group known as the Mahasanghika (Great Assembly) ridiculing this notion, claiming the Buddha was not human but an all powerful, almost godlike presence whose appearance on earth was an apparition. They argued that as a divine being, the Buddha could help take away karma and assist people in their quest for nirvana.

The Mahsanghikas also wanted to relax some of the rules in the Sangha and accused the Theravadas of being too concerned with their own personal salvation. Instead, they stressed the idea of the bodhisattva. Bodhisattvas were saints who could renounce the world but chose instead to work for the salvation of others. They focused on the Buddhist teachings about mental discipline and stressed the concept of emptiness: freeing oneself from all categories whatsoever. The councils were unable to resolve this split and disagreements continued.

THE ROLE OF ASHOKA IN SPREADING BUDDHISM   Emperor Ashoka, who ruled the Mauryan Empire in India from 270 to 232 B.C.E., tried to help heal this split, and he also played an important role in the initial spread of Buddhism outside the subcontinent. In his early career, Ashoka acted like anything but a Buddhist. He intrigued to gain power and probably ordered the assassination of all his brothers so he could become king. However, after his bloody campaign against the state of Kalinga that resulted in thousands of deaths, he was filled with remorse at what he realized was a needless slaughter of innocent people. His change of heart probably contributed to his conversion to Buddhism.

Being careful not to impose Buddhism on his subjects, Ashoka transformed the Buddhist concept of Dhamma into a set of social and ethical principles that supporters of any religious persuasion could follow. He then had these principles carved on numerous pillars, which were placed from Afghanistan to southern India to mark the boundaries of his empire. One edict states that he spread his message to Sri Lanka and neighboring Greek kingdoms. Another edict defines dhamma as

> . . . non-slaughter of animals for sacrificial purposes. Non-violence toward human beings, proper attention to kinsmen, proper attention to Brahmins and ascetics, welfare of mother and father, welfare of the aged and many other kinds of moral behavior . . . (Rock Edict IV)

Ashoka also made use of Buddhist relics. Tradition claims that the Buddha's bones and teeth that had remained after he was cremated had been divided into eight equal portions and placed inside eight stupas, solid semicircular burial mounds, in eight regions of the empire. Emperor Ashoka is reported to have ordered that these relics be retrieved, divided, and re-enshrined in 84,000 stupas that he ordered built all over his kingdom.[10] In a nod to the importance of naga worship, it was said that Ashoka did not disturb the relics that were buried in the stupa the nagas guarded because the nagas were taking such good care of them.

Although this legend is much exaggerated, Emperor Ashoka did commission the building of stupas, such as those at Sanchi, and excavations near Nepal record that he gave relics for the stupas built there. In addition, many stupas constructed in the third century B.C.E. as repositories of Buddhist relics have been excavated, and more edict pillars have been discovered.

Ashoka convened the Third Buddhist Council at his capital in Pataliputra, which was the largest city in the world at that time. He encouraged Buddhist missionaries to carry the faith to Sri Lanka and mainland

FIGURE 2-1   STUPA AT SANCHI, INDIA
One of the earliest stupas of Buddhist India.

Southeast Asia. Some Buddhists probably also traveled as far west as Egypt, North Africa, and Greece.

Emperor Ashoka's use of Buddhism and especially Buddhist relics illustrates the symbiotic relationship between religion and politics. Heads of state need more than sheer force to establish their legitimacy and authority. To govern effectively, their subjects must believe that their leaders have the right to rule and their laws should be obeyed. Religion helps give them this legitimacy. A common set of beliefs that has moral and ethical appeal and promises some form of deferred justice, especially general ones that everyone can accept, such as the dhamma rules Ashoka promoted, can help bring stability. These values also appeal to military rulers who seek additional forms of legitimacy. Paradoxically, often the support of political leaders, especially kings and emperors, helps a foreign set of beliefs gain acceptance in a new area. The Persian kings had already been instrumental in the spread of Zoroastrianism. Now Emperor Ashoka's support was proving significant in the spread of Buddhism.

In about 247 B.C.E., Ashoka's son converted the king of the Sinhala dynasty in Sri Lanka to Buddhism. A monastery was built in Anuradhapura, its capital, and one of Ashoka's daughters is said to have taken a sprig of the Bodhi tree from Bodhgaya where the Buddha attained enlightenment and planted it in Sri Lanka. (Sri Lankans claim that tree is still living.) By the second century, many among the Sinhalese nobility and commoners had embraced Buddhism. Sri Lankan Buddhists built universities, temples, and stupas, and commissioned statues of the Buddha. Sri Lanka has been a Buddhist society ever since—the longest continuous Buddhist state.

BUDDHISM SPLITS INTO SCHOOLS

Despite Ashoka's efforts to keep the entire Buddhist community united, subschools split off from both the Theravadans and Mahasanghikas. By the first century C.E., these groups had coalesced into two major divisions within Buddhism: the Theravada and Mahayana traditions, something like Catholics and Protestants in Christianity or the Sunni and Shia in Islam.

The main issue dividing the Theravadans from the Mahayanists was a Buddhist's vocation. Should a good Buddhist focus on his own salvation and strive to become an arhat or postpone that goal and stay involved in the world as a bodhisattva to help others? Theravada Buddhists believed individuals should seek to become an arhat on their own, without help, so some referred to this school as Hinayana, or Lesser "*hina*" Vehicle "*yana*" Buddhism.

Mahayana Buddhists knew it was difficult for individuals to seek their own salvation without assistance. For them, the Buddha was a transcendent being, a savior who came to earth to take away bad karma and help individuals realize nirvana. They urged people to try to become bodhisattvas and work for the salvation of all beings. The Buddha and bodhisattvas were vehicles for salvation, so this group was called Mahayana Buddhists, Great "*maha*" Vehicle Buddhism. Theravadans believe realizing nirvana is possible only through one's individual efforts, but the Buddha and bodhisattvas offer Mahayanists help in overcoming or removing karma. For Theravadans, nirvana means permanently leaving the world, whereas Mahayanists believe experiencing nirvana means becoming conscious of one's identity with totality.

The following example illustrates the difference between an arhat and a bodhisattva: Two men, lost in the desert and slowly dying from thirst and hunger, approach a high wall. On the other side of the wall they can faintly hear singing birds and a gurgling waterfall. One man climbs over the wall and slides down into the paradise on the other side. He has chosen to be an arhat and experience nirvana on his own. The other man thinks how wonderful it would be to climb over the wall, but he hesitates and then goes to help other lost travelers find their way to the lush oasis. He has decided on the path of the bodhisattva. In theory, anyone who dedicates him- or herself selflessly to help others may become a bodhisattva.

Theravadans and Mahayanists also disagreed over the concept of Buddhahood. Theravadans maintain that the Buddha was a human being, a great teacher, and a model for anyone to follow. Mahayana Buddhists argued that humans do not have souls and that all is emptiness and nothing endures. It is possible for anyone to pierce through the illusion of phenomenal reality and see into the deeper truth and attain enlightenment. The Buddha's death was also an illusion, and his spiritual self remains available to assist his devotees. Mahayana Buddhists gradually turned the Buddha into a god and added a three-tiered system made up of a transcendent Buddha, a transcendent bodhisattva, and an earthly historic Buddha. Eventually Mahayana Buddhists systematized all the Buddhas and bodhisattvas into 33 sets of three trinities each.

The differences between these two major divisions of Buddhism are historically significant, but Buddhists have never gone to war with one another over interpretations of doctrine nor condemned and executed any Buddhists for following "wrong" ideas. To this day, the various sects and schools go to each other's temples and worship together in peace.

By the first century B.C.E., artists and craftsmen were not only building stupas to represent the Buddhist faith, but also excavating elaborate

FIGURE 2-2   CAVE SANCTUARY AT AJANTA, INDIA
There are some 5,000 cave santuaries in Western India. The most impressive Buddhist caves are in Ajanta. Cave sanctuary construction traveled from India to China, Korea, and Japan.

cave sanctuaries that served as homes for monks during the rainy season and as magnificent worship centers. The Theravada school did not initially make images of the Buddha, but the Mahayana followers sculpted images of the Buddha and bodhisattvas according to prescribed rules. In some of the cave sanctuaries such as at Ajanta, the stupa and the Buddha are the objects of worship. The stupa and these unique cave sanctuaries were widely copied in other areas where Buddhism spread.

BUDDHISM IN THE KUSHAN EMPIRE

Following Ashoka's death in 232 B.C.E., waves of invaders from Greece, Iran, and Afghanistan migrated into North India, weakening the Mauryan Empire. The Kushanas, the most successful of these newcomers, left the fringes of China when the Han Chinese discouraged them from trading there. Sometime around the first century C.E., the Kushanas established an empire that included northern India and present-day Afghanistan. Their court, situated on a major crossroad of trade and exchange, attracted artists, poets, musicians, monks, and merchants from across the hemisphere.

Under King Kanishka, who ruled for more than 20 years around 100 C.E., the Kushanas became devout supporters of Mahayana Buddhism. After he converted to Buddhism, the king actively promoted the faith in Central Asia. Traders and monks from his court took miniature stupas with them as they sought to spread Buddhism along the major trade routes to China.

Buddhists and Christians mixed in this area during the first century as Mahayana Buddhism took its essential form. This contact may explain why Buddhists and Christians share some similar stories and legends. For example, the parable of the prodigal son, the story of a wayward son who is welcomed home by his father, the parable of the mustard seed, and the story of walking on water are found in both faiths, but are used to illustrate different meanings. Because Mahayana Buddhists had made the Buddha a god, they also shared the concept of the earthly incarnation of a transcendent god who was a savior to humankind. It may be that the Christian concept of the Christ influenced Mahayana Buddhism or that the bodhisattva ideal from Mahayana Buddhism influenced early Christianity, or perhaps influences went in both directions.

BUDDHISM IN SOUTHEAST ASIA

In the first century C.E., Theravadan missionaries carried their school of Buddhism not only to Sri Lanka, as Ashoka had directed, but eastward to Southeast Asia. Brahmins and Buddhists often accompanied Indian merchants who were part of the highly developed Indian Ocean maritime trade between India and China. They went initially to Funan, the first center of power in mainland Southeast Asia, and then to smaller states along the Malay Peninsula and to Srivijaya (c. 300–1200), a kingdom that included parts of Sumatra and Java. These merchants and religious leaders did not try to colonize Southeast Asia or build military kingdoms there. Instead, the traders were seeking lucrative commercial opportunities. Meanwhile, brahmins and Buddhist missionaries spread their faiths to the courts of Funan and Srivijaya.

Brahmins spread information about Hinduism, including *bhakti,* a devotional form that was developing in South India. They taught that by intense devotion a ruler could realize a close relationship with divinity, often identified as Shiva or Vishnu, two major Hindu gods. If, through intense asceticism, a leader experienced oneness with Shiva or Vishnu, he could become a *cakravartan,* one who can maintain order in the cosmos, or even a *devaraja,* a divine king. The brahmins told local tribal chiefs about ceremonies South Indian leaders performed that established their ritual authority and gave them control over villages clustered around their royal centers. They stressed that the Indian rulers found that manipulating religious symbolism was a more effective way to enhance their legitimacy than military force.

The brahmins and Buddhists knew that the key to spreading their faith was finding ways to adapt Indian concepts to local beliefs and practices. The idea of a ruler using rituals and possessing divine authority touched familiar cords in many would-be leaders who were competing with one another to attract subjects to their ports and courts. In that setting, a leader's legitimacy did not depend on his lineage or military might, but on his status as a "big man," a charismatic figure whom people believed possessed supernatural powers. Followers were attracted to him because they hoped somehow to share his spiritual substance.

These local rulers were not primarily military leaders, nor could they claim that they controlled specific territory or a large bureaucracy. Instead, they gained their legitimacy by controlling the distribution of wealth that trade created, and by personal qualities that seemed to ensure prosperity in their realm. An aspiring ruler's authority also derived from his subjects' desire to be identified with the splendor of his court.

Would-be "big men" must have enthusiastically welcomed ideas and rituals from India, which they regarded as a highly prestigious civilization. Even more to the point, they believed that these new ideas could enhance their own ritual authority. When they heard stories of Emperor Ashoka's semidivine status as a Cakravartan and that he had supervised the building of 84,000 stupas, these ambitious leaders probably wanted to copy the example of this powerful monarch who was said to have governed so justly and righteously.

As time went on, Indian merchants and religious visitors shared legends about Ashoka that told of his initial violence and how, after the carnage of Kalinga, he had gained enlightenment and converted to Buddhism. Many of the Southeast Asian rulers had to fight for power, but once established, they wanted to be admired for their moral qualities. Ashoka provided a model for their own lives: By imitating him they could make amends for their early cruelty and excesses and also rule with righteousness and justice, supporting the monastic orders, ensuring political and religious harmony, and guaranteeing peace and prosperity in their kingdoms.[11]

Besides Ashoka's example, the acceptance of other Indian concepts that resonated with existing beliefs also helped Buddhism spread among the ruling elites in Southeast Asia. Reverence for nagas was a common belief there as in India. Nagas were thought to live in palaces at the bottom of rivers, lakes, and seas and were widely believed to be sources of fertility, prosperity, and earthly health. As guardians of the life energy and the oceans' wealth, they had the power to attract and control rain.

The myth of the founding of Funan illustrates how leaders adapted Indian beliefs and practices and appropriated naga symbolism. The story relates how Kaundinya, an Indian brahmin, came to Southeast Asia and, on landing, threw his spear into the ground, marking the spot where the future capital of Funan would be built. He then married Soma, a local princess and daughter of the naga king. According to Southeast Asian tradition, this couple was the origin of the ruling house of Funan and neighboring Champa, and their union guaranteed the prosperity of the land that their descendents would rule. Reverence for the naga is also reflected in the many Southeast Asian images of the naga king spreading his hood to shelter the Buddha.

Reverence for mountains, believed to be sacred in both the Indian subcontinent and Southeast Asia, provided another way to make Indian ideas appealing. In Southeast Asia, people believed mountains were the abode of ancestral spirits that were responsible for prosperity and the source of powerful spiritual forces. The word "Funan" may be associated with both mountain and a national guardian spirit. Mountains were also important symbols in pre-Buddhist Java. The Javanese believed supernatural power hovered around mountain peaks, and they built numerous sanctuaries on high places. Leaders in Sailendra, which controlled central Java in the eighth and ninth centuries, called themselves "mountain kings." The prevalence of volcanoes in island Southeast

Asia—there were 20 active volcanoes on Java alone—suggests another reason why people considered mountains a source of great power.

The shape of the Buddhist stupa resembles a mountain. Burial mounds can be found throughout Asia, and the stupa may have developed from these mounds. Although originally associated with the Buddha's death and liberation from rebirth, the stupa came to symbolize not only a reliquary and memorial but also the cosmic mountain, the navel of the universe, the generative womb, and an ascending pathway leading to nirvana. It also represented the creation of the universe, and its axis symbolized the world pillar, or *axis mundi*. In Southeast Asia, the stupa also represents the symbiotic relationship between sacred cosmology and kingship.[12]

Borobudur offers a vivid visual expression of the synthesis of holy mountain and giant stupa because it can both represent and symbolically merge royal authority, sacred mountains, and Buddhism. This impressive monument was probably built between 760 and 830 under the supervisions of the Sailendra Dynasty. It seems to have represented indigenous royal power identified with sacred mountains and may have been built as a tribute to the power and authority of the Sailendra kings. It can also represent an ascending pathway leading pilgrims to liberation. This monument illustrates how Southeast Asian rulers used Buddhism to lend "luster, authority, and a sense of legitimacy" to their rule.[13] Their patronage proved to be the crucial factor in Buddhism's strong roots in Southeast Asia.

FIGURE 2-3   BOROBUDUR: THE MONUMENTAL BUDDHIST STUPA ON
JAVA, INDONESIA

The mountain also symbolizes the universe in both Mahayana and Hindu cosmology. Mahayana Buddhism identifies the universe as three realms with Mt. Sumeru at the center, and in Hindu cosmology, the cosmos is a round, flat continent, ringed by concentric chains of mountains and oceans from whose center Mt. Meru, the cosmic mountain and abode of the gods, reaches into the heavens. If a local chief could construct a temple that resembled both the local sacred mountain and the Indian sacred cosmos and could ritually identify himself with the locus of divine power that resided in the sacred mountain-temple-palace, he could not only significantly increase his authority, but also increase it with familiar and accepted symbols of ritual power. No wonder Southeast Asian rulers ordered the construction of walls (to represent the chains of mountains) and moats (to represent the oceans) around a central holy temple mountain. These cosmic temple/court complexes served as earthly imitations of the Hindu/Buddhist concept of the universe and underscored the ruler's divine status.

Temple/court complexes are the foundation of what political scientists call "theater states." Here the grandeur of the buildings symbolizes a leader's magical powers, and the elaborate performances and festivals dazzle individuals and draw them to the court as if by a magnet. Leaders in theater states in Southeast Asia often relied on these strategies rather than on military force to win allies and to attract settlers to their realms.

The distinguished scholar James Scott argues that would-be Southeast Asian rulers always lacked substantial populations that could provide the services they required, so they were constantly searching for ways to attract more people. If the activities at the court were not impressive enough, leaders would sometimes go to war to capture slaves, but the lure of impressive rituals was a more appealing method for ensuring an adequate number of submissive subjects.[14] From the second to the tenth centuries, various Southeast Asian rulers experimented with both Hindu and Buddhist ideals of kingship, and often the two forms blurred together.

THE KHMER KINGDOM

At the end of the eighth century, a prince from the Sailendra court brought both Hinduism and Buddhism to the area around the Mekong River, the third-largest river in Asia, where peasant farmers practiced recessive agriculture, planting rice in the receding flooding waters. Following a successful military campaign, he established the Khmer kingdom (802–1431) near the Great Lake (Tonle Sap), and brahmins installed him as a god-king. He named his capital "Mountain of the Great King of the Gods" and modeled his palace after the Hindu/Buddhist idea of the cosmos. Subsequent kings wanted to make their own cosmic cities, and they supervised the construction of even larger palace/temple complexes. Even though the kings looked to Hinduism and Buddhism to legitimate their rule as *devarajas* (God Kings), the vast majority of people continued to worship various local spirits and their ancestors' spirits.

Suryavarman II, who ruled from 1113 to at least 1145, was one of the greatest Khmer kings and the force behind the building of Angkor Wat, his cosmic temple-mountain. The walls of this awe-inspiring complex are covered with exquisite reliefs, including numerous depictions of lovely nature spirits and the Churning of the Ocean episode from Lord Vishnu's turtle incarnation. The buildings are positioned to mark where the sun rises on the solstices and equinoxes. After his death, the king's divine essence was believed to reside in the temple.

Jayavarman VII (r. 1181–1218) was the country's greatest builder. He adopted a form of Mahayana Buddhism as the state religion, but most of his subjects continued to practice aspects of their earlier spirit worship. He commissioned Angkor Thom, a two-mile-square city. Giant smiling faces that look out in four directions from the towers of the Bayon, his temple-mountain complex, may represent Avalokiteshvara, the Buddhist Boddhisatva of Compassion, or perhaps they symbolize the ruler's power radiating in all directions over the land, or both. These magnificent palaces and temples attracted a large number of people who

FIGURE 2-4   BODHISATTVA FACES FROM THE BAYON, ANGKOR CITIES, CAMBODIA

These lovely faces of Bodhisattvas adorn the towers of the Bayon in northern Cambodia.

farmed and fished in the Tonle Sap as its waters receded and who provided the enormous supply of labor needed to construct these temple complexes.

Pagon, near the Irrawaddy River in Burma, was another theater state that shared the same worldview. As the well-known anthropologist Clifford Geertz writes, the power of these rituals and architecture "lies in the fact that it pictures the ultimate structure of existence in such a way that the events of everyday life seem repeatedly to confirm it."[15]

Beginning in the thirteenth century, Southeast Asian Buddhism changed significantly. As a result of Mongol incursions into the area and the increasingly powerful Thai military threats, the Khmer and Burmese kingdoms declined dramatically. By the fifteenth century, the Thais controlled what had been the Khmer state and much of Burma as well, and everyday life became increasingly insecure. Mahayana Buddhism had mainly been the religion of kings and courts. With the decline of royal power and the accompanying insecurity, a popular form of Theravada Buddhism attracted widespread popular support, transforming the culture of the region.

As the majority of people converted to Theravada Buddhism, they began to emphasize karma, the cosmic tabulation of one's appropriate or inappropriate actions, and building up personal merit, the aspects of the faith that met their everyday concerns. A popular Theravada text states: "Each of us comes into the world rich or poor, man or woman, healthy or deformed depending on the amount of good karma that comes with us."[16] The most important way that people can change their karma is by building merit, which means doing good deeds such as performing rituals, praying, fasting, acting morally, and giving alms to Buddhist monks.

Indigenous popular pre-Buddhist beliefs that monk reformers of the thirteenth and fourteenth centuries helped infuse into Theravadan Buddhism increased the appeal of the faith. Most farmers and artisans believed that the world was alive with ghosts and spirits that they tried to propitiate with rituals that the shamans performed. They also believed that the movement of heavenly bodies shaped daily life, so they practiced astrology as well. Many thought that personal deities could affect karma and improve one's daily life, so worshiping numerous gods and goddesses also became part of popular Buddhist practice. Additionally, they tended to believe that images of the Buddha or Bodhisattvas exude a potent power, which a worshiper can tap. Most Southeast Asian Buddhists hoped that these local beliefs and practices would aid them in accumulating merit and good karma.

Southeast Asians also transformed the concept of nirvana, the core idea of classical Buddhism. The Buddha had taught that nirvana was a

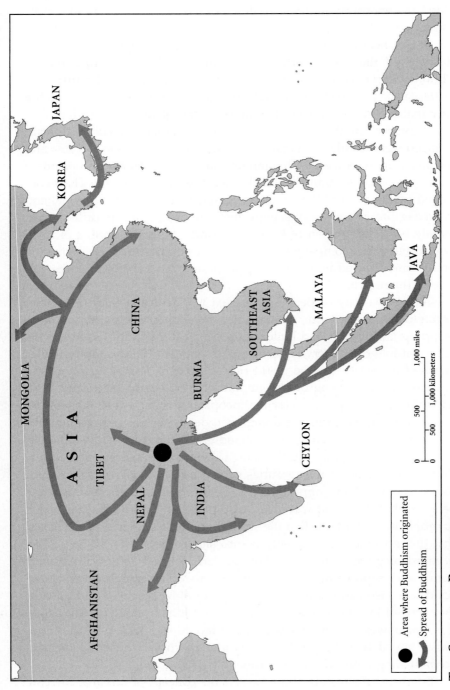

THE SPREAD OF BUDDHISM

This map shows the journey of Buddhism from its beginnings.

Area where Buddhism originated

Spread of Buddhism

distant goal that took many lifetimes to achieve, but popular Buddhism accepted faster routes. One popular shortcut was the belief that sponsoring the building of a shrine, temple, or monastery would cause a person to be reborn when Sri Ariya Maitreya, the future Buddha, returned (5,000 years after the historical Buddha). Once in the presence of Maitreya, a person would be assured enlightenment.

Buddhism found a welcome reception in Southeast Asia, in large part by integrating local beliefs and practices. Local chieftains had initially adopted the new faith to enhance their legitimacy. Kings sponsored the construction of elaborate temple and court complexes that replicated the Hindu/Buddhist cosmos to underscore their legitimacy and enticed farmers and workers to become subjects and live near the impressive cosmic courts. After the eleventh century, Southeast Asians transformed Buddhism into a popular faith by surrounding the quest for merit, good karma, and nirvana with a comforting panoply of traditional beliefs in gods, spirits, and ghosts.

MAHAYANA BUDDHISTS CARRY THE FAITH TO CHINA

By the first century C.E., Mahayana Buddhism had developed the characteristics identified with a universal religion, including a focus on a divine being and the promise of salvation for all believers and intermediaries that help individuals achieve salvation. By this time, many Mahayana Buddhists had begun to think of the Buddha as a personal savior and then as a transcendent god. Mahayana Buddhism also had absorbed some Indian deities and transformed them into Buddhas or bodhisattvas.

By the end of the first century, Buddhist monks were buying and selling religious items, such as sacred images of Buddhas and bodhisattvas, incense, cloth, and other items used in worship, and actively carrying Buddhism along the Silk Roads. Historical records report that in 68 C.E., two Indian Buddhist monks, Kasyapa and Dharmaraksha, arrived at the court of the Han dynasty (220 B.C.E.–220 C.E.). Other sources suggest a Parthian monk brought Buddhism to the Han capital around 148 C.E. Indian traders also traveled to China by sea, and Buddhist missionaries, consciously trying to carry the faith farther east, journeyed on to Korea and the Japanese archipelago.

It is not surprising that when Buddhism first reached China during the last part of the Han Dynasty, it made little immediate impact. At the time of their initial contact, Buddhist and Confucian values appeared quite incompatible. The Indian worldview based on spiritual discipline and renunciation of worldly pleasures was very different from the Chinese concern for harmony in social relationships and disdain for metaphysics. Those who dropped out of society to seek enlightenment could not fulfill their filial responsibilities, a central value in Chinese culture, because renouncing the world and becoming a monk would leave one's parents without support.

Blending sophisticated Buddhist philosophy with the Chinese emphasis on practicality and concrete thinking must have seemed daunting, if not impossible, to the early Buddhists. Indian texts are exceedingly metaphoric and its philosophic writing is very abstract, whereas the Chinese literary tradition is filled with concrete metaphors largely drawn from nature. The Indian tradition had a complex and developed psychological analysis, whereas the Chinese tradition had little interest in analyzing personality. The Indian sense of time deals in eons aimed at understanding the infinite; the Chinese tradition deals in lineages and focuses on the finite. The Indian tradition sought otherworldly goals, whereas Confucianism focused on how to build a harmonious society.[17] Chinese Daoism had mystical dimensions, but its emphasis was also directed toward building a better society.

The first Buddhist missionaries in China encouraged translations of their texts into local languages, but early attempts were difficult. Indian Sanskrit and Pali and Chinese are distinctly different. Indian languages have an alphabet and an elaborate grammar; Chinese is uninflected (does not change word endings to indicate gender, tense, etc.), ideographic (uses symbols to express things and ideas), and has no systematized grammar, unlike alphabetical languages normally have. Few Indian Buddhists knew Chinese, and their Chinese colleagues were not familiar with Indian languages and had difficulty identifying Chinese words or concepts that carried the same meaning as the Indian terms. In spite of these problems, between 60 and 317 C.E., about a thousand Indian texts were translated into Chinese.

Initially many Daoist terms were used to express Buddhist ideas. The central Buddhist concept of Dhamma, which means the teaching of the Buddha, was translated as "the Dao" (the way) in Chinese. Sometimes "Dao" was also used for *"Bodhi"* (enlightenment). The Buddhist word arhat was translated as *"Chen-jen,"* a Daoist term for immortals. Nirvana became *"wu-wei,"* the Daoist idea of nonaction.

The Chinese Buddhists also readily appropriated Confucian concepts. The Indian concept *sila* (morality) was translated as *"hsiao-hsun"* a Confucian term for "filial submission," significantly altering the Indian meaning. *Chung,* loyal devotion to authority, a value long known in Daoism and Confucianism, was identified with Buddhism's stress on karuna, compassion for all beings.[18]

Most significantly, the bodhisattva ideal helped bridge the gulf between Confucian filial piety and Buddhist renunciation, because bodhisattvas wanted to help all living beings along their path to nirvana, including one's parents and other family members.

Not only was it difficult to express important Buddhist concepts in Chinese, deep cultural divides also made it difficult for the Chinese to understanding familiar Indian Buddhist metaphors. The sexual analogies Indians commonly used to symbolize spiritual ideas were anathema for the more puritanical Chinese elite. Common images such as kissing and embracing a bodhisattva were totally eliminated in official Chinese translations. Mentions of breast, love, or sexual union were turned into terms such as bird or breeze. Because the Indian and Chinese social structures were different, many Indian Buddhist concepts were also changed. "Husband supports his wife" was translated as "The husband controls his wife." "The wife comforts her husband" became "The wife reveres her husband" when rendered in Chinese.[19]

People living during the social and political unrest and instability during the Later Han and after the fall of the Han dynasty in 220 were more open to Buddhism. Confucian values of moral leadership seemed ineffective in the face of dynastic collapse and warfare. *Li* (proper actions) and *ren* (appropriate feelings) did not alleviate the hunger, sorrow, and insecurity people were facing. Buddhism taught people to change their attitudes about the problems they faced and learn to transcend the pain and suffering around them. In addition, Buddhist communities provided social services, including medical care and other charities that helped alleviate the suffering of the poor. Further, Daoism had long offered Chinese people a way to escape the sufferings of this world, and now Buddhists built on that tradition.

After the fall of the Han, centralized China disintegrated into disunity that lasted for three centuries. While China broke into some sixteen regional kingdoms, nomadic invaders gained control of several states along China's northern border. Many of the unlettered nomadic leaders sought out Chinese scholars to serve as administrators. At the same time, the Chinese-ruled kingdoms to the south invited nomads to serve in their military forces. Because the northern border was not well guarded, nomads as well as traders and missionaries easily entered China, and in the radically changed political and social climate, Buddhism took firm root in China.

Nomadic leaders of the small kingdoms in the north were very receptive to Buddhism. As foreigners and nomads, they could not claim legitimacy because they were related to any previous Chinese dynasties. But endorsing Buddhism, with its scholarly traditions and sophisticated ideas, lent luster and legitimacy to their rule. In addition, these non-Chinese rulers liked the fact that Buddhism was a foreign faith. They did not want to adapt Chinese ways completely, so endorsing Indian beliefs was more appealing than trying to adopt Chinese ones. As one northern nomadic king explained, "Buddha being a barbarian god is the very one we should worship."[20] Further, these aspiring leaders feared that the Confucian bureaucrats who worked for them were trying to subvert their authority by spreading Confucian values.

In 311 the Huns sacked Changan, one of the world's most glorious cities, causing many aristocrats to flee from the northern kingdoms, the heartland of Chinese civilization, to the sparsely settled Yangtze River valley. Many of them were conservative Confucians who had lost their estates and turned to neo-Daoism because its reverence for nature offered a refuge from the displacement that the political turmoil had caused. Well-educated scholars were drawn to Buddhist speculation and philosophy and to its cosmology. Moreover, spending one's days in quiet contemplation, scholarship, and meditation meshed well with the lifestyle of the Confucian gentleman scholar, another example of syncretism. They must have found Buddhist renunciation of power and wealth an attractive alternative to the political chaos they had experienced firsthand. Gradually, these Buddhist aristocrats began to attract the attention of would-be kings seeking scholars and administrators, significantly elevating Buddhism's status.

Buddhists often used magic and their superior knowledge to impress nomadic leaders and ingratiate themselves as indispensable functionaries in their courts. For example, after Loyang fell in 316, Fo-tu-teng, the founder of the northern Sangha, met the Hun leader. According to the Chinese tradition, instead of trying to impress him with Buddhist philosophy, Teng took out his begging bowl, filled it with water, burned incense, and said a spell. Out of the bowl sprang a blue lotus "with a color dazzling to the eyes." As a result, the ruler became a willing patron of Buddhism.[21] Many Chinese flocked to take refuge under this holy man who could protect them and mediate on their behalf with nomadic leaders. By 300, Buddhism was growing rapidly in several northern cities. In the early fourth century there were nearly 200 Buddhist institutions in China's two major urban centers, Changan and Loyang, and these cities supported some 3,700 Buddhist clergy.[22]

The support of Northern Wei leaders helped Buddhism spread through their kingdom, which lasted from 386 to 534. Northern Wei nomadic leaders were able to blend their shamanistic practices with the more sophisticated Buddhist system. These leaders claimed to be incarnations of the Buddha and they made Buddhism a political force at

Loyang, their capital city, and supported the construction of expensive temples, monasteries, and cave sanctuaries modeled after the Indian monuments at Ajanta. Emperor Wu of the Liang kingdom (502–49) also patronized Buddhism and actually took Buddhist vows and on occasion gave himself to a Buddhist temple, forcing his ministers to "ransom" him with huge gifts. He also required nobles, officials, and his own family to reject Daoism and embrace Buddhism.

A number of southern merchants from diverse ethnic groups including the Chinese also began to accept Buddhism. They modeled themselves after Vimalakirti, a rich and powerful merchant who had renounced the life of opulence to become a Buddhist teacher. Although this Chinese gentleman wrote a sutra (religious text), he could not completely renounce good food, comfortable housing, and other earthly pleasures. Vimalakirti was close to an ideal Confucian civil servant who enjoyed life's pleasures while still exemplifying and teaching proper etiquette. He seemingly was able to remove himself from the world while still enjoying its pleasures. In the Chinese setting where Buddhism mixed freely with Confucianism and Daoism, such contradictions did not seem to disturb new converts.

Buddhism did not immediately appeal to average Chinese in the north, which had been the site of impressive cities and the home of renowned philosophers, writers, and heroes. Many of these aristocrats had lost power and influence and were saddened to see their homeland overrun by "barbarians." Seeking some deeper meaning for the upheavals that had left them feeling like exiles in their own land, they began to study the new philosophy in earnest. Buddhism also appealed to those who were wary of the exclusiveness and narrowness of Confucian culture. Other marginalized groups, including women, landless peasants, and wandering craftsmen, were also attracted to Buddhism.

The Chinese adapted Buddhism to fit with their traditional cultural values, giving Chinese Buddhism its distinctive characteristics. As in Southeast Asia, converts did not have to forsake their belief in ghosts, spirits, numerous supernatural figures, and other aspects of their traditional beliefs. Regional heroes, mythical characters, and local deities were accepted as bodhisattvas. Devotees could still worship those familiar figures while adding another dimension to their power. Local fertility rites, life-cycle celebrations, and seasonal festivals were gradually absorbed into Buddhist practices as well. Moreover, Buddhism's ethical message of compassion, kindness, honesty, and abstention from lavish materialism supported and extended the Confucian tradition while embedding these values in a more complex philosophical system.

Chinese Buddhists, like their Southeast Asian neighbors, began to infuse the concept of merit into Buddhism. Giving one son to the monastery built merit for the entire family and would help one's parents achieve salvation. Becoming a monk to earn merit became a way of caring for parents. Merit accrued by personal donations formed the basis of the relationship between monasteries and the lay public. Rich merchants and aristocrats who hoped to build merit gave money to build stupas, monasteries, and temples. The wealthy could justify their prosperity by giving large gifts to Buddhist institutions or paying for the construction of new buildings. Political leaders could find justification for their decidedly non-Buddhist military exploits by donating land to Buddhist institutions and removing monasteries from the tax rolls.

Old records indicate that in the sixth century, eunuchs, government officials, "foreigners," generals, aristocrats, emperors, and two prosperous butchers all gave homes to be converted into monasteries.[23] Reportedly, one of the butchers decided to give his home as a monastery when a pig he was about to slaughter pleaded for mercy in a human voice.[24] In another case, when a widow's deceased husband appeared and accused her of marrying again before the proper mourning period for him was over, the terrified woman donated her house as a monastery. Clearly, donors seeking merit acted for a wide range of motives. Whatever the reasons, the result was the construction of a panoply of architectural gems, including monasteries, temples, tombs, and even bridges that have enriched the Chinese tradition. Building merit by performing acts of kindness and compassion became important within the Confucian ethical system, and it assured one of being reborn in a better state in the next life.

SCHOOLS OF BUDDHISM

Mahayana Buddhism was by far the most successful form of Buddhism in China, where several separate schools of Mahayana Buddhism developed, each with a distinctly Chinese flavor. These schools were usually associated with a founder and his favorite *sutra* sacred text. To fit into the Chinese ethos, with its enormous emphasis on family and ancestral roots, these schools created lineages beginning with their initial founder or, if he was unknown, with the first generation of devotees. Each of these schools enjoyed a long tradition in China, and most built elaborate monasteries, temples, and retreats, many in lovely settings on mountaintops. The two major Mahayana schools were Pure Land, and Ch'an (later Zen in Japan).

PURE LAND BUDDHISM   Pure Land Buddhism, which originated in India, found wide acceptance in China during the difficult days of the later Han period, and it gradually became the most popular form of Buddhism in all East Asia. Pure Land Buddhists put their trust in the compassion of Amitabha (the Sanskrit spelling, Amitofo in Chinese; Amida in Japanese), who is regarded as a much earlier mythological figure than the historical Buddha. He assured his devotees that if they had total faith in him and surrendered to him with absolute devotion, after they died they would go to the Pure Land, an ideal Buddhist paradise. This school takes its definition from the Pure Land Sutra that stresses faith and devotion as the keys to personal salvation. In some forms of Amitabha worship, devotees had only to say his name once in a lifetime to reach the Pure Land.

The Pure Land is described as rich and fertile and filled with gods and men, but with no expressions of evil, such as ghosts or demons. Flowers, trees, and abundant lotuses decorated with beautiful jewels abound. Rivers run freely and their perfumed waters make sweet music as they flow. Dwellers in the Pure Land hear nothing but the Buddha's dharma and teachings of compassion, tolerance, and peace. (Mahayanists use the Sanskrit term dharma, not the Pali term dhamma.) Technically the Pure Land was supposed to be an intermediate stopping-off place on the way to nirvana. However, the Pure Land proved so attractive that for many, reaching it after death became an end in itself. Pure Land Buddhism's paradise is not unlike the Christian and Islamic concepts of heaven.

Members of the Pure Land School practice reciting Amitabha's name to control their thoughts. Usually, the worshiper undertakes a large number of recitations while contemplating an image of Amitabha. Devotees also try to visualize Amitabha and his Pure Land. The goal of this meditation is to merge completely with the vision of Amitabha, which ensures rebirth in the Pure Land.

Amitabha is assisted by the Kwan-yin, the Bodhisattva of Compassion, who "hears the cries of the world." Kwan-yin is arguably the most popular bodhisattva in Asian Buddhism. (In Vietnam, she is known as Quan'Am; in Japan as Kannon; and in Bali as Kanin.) According to legend, she was about to enter heaven but, after pausing on the threshold as the cries of the world reached her ears, she turned back to minister to the sufferings of the world. Kwan-yin is the embodiment of compassionate loving kindness. Avalokitesvara, the original Indian Bodhisattva of Compassion, was male. However, by the twelfth or thirteenth century, as the image traveled to east Asia, it became female. Kwan-yin resonates with the Christian Mary, the Tibetan goddess Tara, and several compassionate Hindu goddesses.

CH'AN BUDDHISM   The Ch'an School was strongly influenced by the Hindu concept of meditation called yoga that became very popular in China, especially among educated people. The legendary founder and first patriarch of the lineage of Ch'an Buddhism was a monk named Bodhidharma who sailed from India to China in the sixth century C.E. Harking back to early Buddhists who believed the phenomenal world was transitory, Bodhidharma preached that all appearances were illusions. He stressed the importance of meditation and promised that when devotees get in touch with their true mind, they can experience pure wisdom. Bodhidharma said:

> To search for enlightenment or nirvana beyond this mind is impossible. The reality of your own self-nature, the absence of cause and effect, is what is meant by mind. Your mind is Nirvana. You might think you can find a Buddha or enlightenment somewhere beyond the mind, but such a place does not exist.[25]

Ch'an Buddhists focus mainly on meditation and direct experience, although they do not disdain the scriptures. Through meditation and other exercises, a believer may suddenly transcend all the pairs of opposites and sense the oneness of all things and for an instant experience true bliss.

Ch'an and Pure Land Buddhism are often called short cuts to salvation. Both emphasize personal practices and stress that eventually everyone will reach nirvana. Aristocrats and merchants were attracted to Ch'an because it stressed meditation and private self-cultivation. Pure Land attracted far more followers from all walks of life, and its supporters built huge temples where people could come to make offerings to Buddhist and bodhisattva images.

Instead of these schools competing as they might have done in the dualistic West, Ch'an and Pure Land Buddhism found ways to reconcile their approaches. The faithful practiced both meditation and called on the name of Amitabha or Kwan-yin for grace, combining both self-reliance and dependence on an outside power. By the sixteenth century, Pure Land practices were deeply imbedded in Ch'an Buddhism. Even today, "Homage to Amitabha Buddha" is regularly chanted in Ch'an monasteries.

In spite of the focus on the Pure Land and other interpretations of the faith, nirvana remained the ultimate goal. A story from the Lotus Sutra, which became perhaps the most important Buddhist text in China, illustrates the effort people made to help others experience nirvana. There was once a rich man whose house caught on fire while his three children were playing inside, oblivious of the danger. The father, desperately trying to save his children, called frantically to them to leave the burning building, promising that three magnificent chariots awaited them outside. The children, responding to this promise, left their games and raced outside, just ahead of the flames.

Life, the Buddhists taught, is like that burning house, and people play with its toys like careless children, unaware of their impending doom. Buddhists wanted to free people from their ignorance (playing in the burning house) and bring them to the safety of the Buddha's teaching. The three chariots represented the Three Jewels of Buddhism that await believers to save them from the fires of desire.

BUDDHISM HELPS THE SUI UNITE CHINA

The turning point for Buddhism in China came in 581 with the founding of the Sui Dynasty that unified China after more than 300 years of decentralized power. Emperor Wendi, the first Sui emperor (r. 581–604), sought to establish his dynasty's legitimacy by supporting Confucianism and exempting filial sons from taxation and corvee and by establishing schools and a national college for the study of the Confucian classics.

Wendi's wife was a devout Buddhist, and he also patronized Buddhism and used it to help unify his empire and enhance his authority. He was given the title "the Bodhisattva Son of Heaven" and claimed to be a true believer and a patron of the Buddhist community. He ordered the construction of Buddhist monasteries at the foot of China's five sacred mountains and ordered damaged temples and stupas repaired.

Emperor Wendi copied Emperor Ashoka's earlier example by sending monks to supervise the construction of stupas that delineated the boundaries of his kingdom. He had Buddhist relics enshrined in 111 stupas, all on the same day. Constructing these stupas and distributing relics were apparently important factors in the dynasty's initial success.

However, Wendi did not embrace Ashoka's commitment to nonviolence. The Sui Dynasty was one of the most violent in Chinese history, and the emperor used Buddhism to legitimate his military exploits. He commissioned Buddhist temples at the sites of his famous battles and issued the following edict in 581:

> . . . We regard the weapons of war as having become like the offerings of incense and flowers presented to the Buddha, and the fields of this world as having become forever identical with the Buddhaland.[26]

Chinese leaders, like Roman emperors after Constantine used Christianity, often turned to Buddhism to gain support for their rule.

The Sui Dynasty ruled only briefly and was replaced by the Tang Dynasty, ushering in one of China's most illustrious periods. During the early Tang, (618–906) Changan, the Tang capital, became the main center of Buddhist learning in East Asia, and monasteries and temples were built throughout the country.

PILGRIMS AND OTHER SCHOLARS

Some Chinese Buddhist scholars and pilgrims wanted to return to the source of the faith to retrieve the original teachings and obtain relics for worship. Perhaps the most famous Chinese pilgrim was Xuanzang, who went to India during the Tang Dynasty. Concerned over disparities among the Buddhists texts he had, Xuanzang decided, much against the emperor's wishes, to try and get original texts from India and to visit sites associated with the Buddha's life.

In 629, even though the emperor forbade him to leave, Xuanzang sneaked out of Changan and headed for India. For the next 17 years, he and companions who joined him along the way covered some 32,000 miles, enduring untold hardships. In addition to many Buddhist sites, Xuanzang visited Nalanda, the world's oldest residential university that employed 2,000 teachers and enrolled 10,000 students from all over the Buddhist world. Xuanzang also visited kings and debated scholars throughout his journey.

On Xuanzang's return to China, bearing precious relics, images, and many Buddhist texts, the emperor greeted him warmly and commissioned him to translate the scriptures. His adventures were later popularized in a classic novel, *Journey to the West,* which tells how a magical monkey, pig, and horse helped the monk make this journey.

The increased exchanges of people, goods, ideas, and values between India and China went far beyond religion, and they resulted in a number of unintended consequences for both countries. Chinese pilgrims brought back medical, scientific, and artistic knowledge from India as well. Faxian, one of the first Chinese pilgrims to arrive in India, was much impressed with the quality of public health there, especially the treatment of the poor, and the high quality of Buddhist medicine was a major asset in its spread.

Records indicate that some two hundred Indian scholars, including astronomers, mathematicians, and medical practitioners, traveled to China during the T'ang and Song periods. They made significant contributions to Chinese knowledge in such areas as more accurate calendars, trigonometry, and the use of zero and place numbers. Several of the scientists held important Chinese government positions in the

Chinese government, including the presidency of the Board of Astronomy. Chinese temple and bridge building was greatly influenced by Indian models. Even the common Chinese title of "Mandarin" may have derived from the Sanskrit "Mantri," meaning advisor.[27]

IMAGES, RELICS, AND PRINTING

Initially there were no images made of the Buddha. His enlightenment was symbolized by an empty chair under the Bodhi tree or a riderless horse and his message was symbolized by a wheel. About 300 years after the Buddha's death, images of him began to appear in northwestern India. All representations are expected to have certain common attributes and hand gestures (*mudras*). Among the 32 prescribed attributes are his elongated ears, indicating that when he was a prince he wore heavy, expensive earrings, a third eye symbolizing insight, three folds in his neck, and a top knot symbolizing his enlightenment. The Buddha was also to be shown in one of five postures: meditating, sitting, standing, walking, or lying down. In spite of these prescriptions, Chinese images of the Buddha were adapted to represent more familiar Chinese faces and body types. A favorite bodhisattva is the so-called Laughing Buddha, whose countenance is distinctly Chinese.

The stupa, which became the primary Buddhist symbol throughout Buddhist Asia,[28] developed into a pagoda as it traveled to China. The sacred umbrella that sheltered it was elongated and enlarged into a tower. The pagoda moved from China to Korea and Japan, where it was further adapted to local settings and often housed relics and texts.

Numerous cave temples that replicated cave sanctuaries in India were built along the Silk Roads and in north China. The world's largest Buddha image, sculpted in the third century C.E. in a cave at Bamiyan in present-day Afghanistan, was 150 feet tall. (Sadly, it was destroyed by the Taliban in the 1990s.)

The Northern Wei Dynasty imported Indian craftsmen to create cave sanctuaries, many of which were filled with images of Buddhas and bodhisattvas. The Longmen cave sanctuaries in Henan Province, 60 percent of which were dedicated during the Tang, contain 2,345 caves and niches with some 2,800 inscriptions, 40 pagodas, and more than 100,000 Buddhist images. The art represents a vivid portrayal of the Buddhists' view of the political, economic, and cultural conditions in Tang China. Another important site is the Mogao Caves in Dunhang, which has 95 carvings from the Sui period and 213 from the Tang. The Leshan Buddha, which was carved between 713 and 803, is the world's largest sculpture of its kind.

FIGURE 2-5   CHINESE BUDDHIST CAVE SANCTUARY AT YUNGANG, CHINA
The Chinese Cave sanctuaries owe their inspiration to the Indian caves at Ajanta. Likely,
Indian craftsmen worked on these caves.

Although the Chinese conducted lavish burial rites for family members, there was no comparable worship of relics in China prior to the
introduction of Buddhism. In 399, Fa Xian reported seeing a shrine con-
taining the Buddha's skull,[29] and gradually Chinese Buddhists collected
a repository of relics from the bodies of their own saints and some mum-
mified monks, a practice introduced in China in the third century. Relic
worship became so important that various monasteries fought over
them, and thefts of relics were common. Grave robbers engaged in the
sale of body parts also found a ready market in Chinese monasteries.
Asian political leaders who have used stupas and relics to symbolize and
legitimate their power extend from Ashoka in the third century B.C.E.
to the shrine of Chairman Mao, whose embalmed body lies in Beijing,
where thousands can view it each day.

Chinese Buddhists, especially Pure Land Buddhists, also worship
images of a whole array of bodhisattvas and Buddhas. Although these
representations were never as important as relics, devotees believe
images have spiritual power in their own right and are able to cure illness, grant offspring, take away pain and suffering, and be good friends.
Images are also known to cry, bleed, perspire, demand favors, and complain. Most of the supplications to these images, especially of Kwan-yin,

are for immediate, personal results: the birth of a baby, better treatment by a husband, or more food or money to sustain a family. Chan Buddhists, however, were opposed to image worship. Although they allowed the use of images for meditation, they did not believe that images contained the actual presence of the Buddha or bodhisattvas.

The most important ritual associated with images was a ceremony to "open the eyes" that brings the image to life and readies it for worship. Priests or authorized Buddhists ritually dot the eyes of the image, infusing the living presence of the Buddha or bodhisattva into it. After the fifth century, specially appointed "Masters of the Ceremony of Opening the Vision" officially conducted the consecrations of images.

The care of relics and the construction of images was an elaborate process involving all strata of society. Usually the community honored patrons who paid for making the images, and donors believed they received merit for their generosity. Chinese sculptors used so much iron creating Buddhist statues that dynasties in short supply of this important metal periodically tried to ban the process.

Chinese Buddhist monasteries and temples were modeled after Chinese imperial palaces and bore little resemblance to temples in India or other Buddhist countries. Chinese Buddhists built many of their monasteries on sacred mountains that were believed to be the homes of bodhisattvas, and over the centuries they became pilgrimage sites and centers of art and philosophy. Many of them replaced or supplemented Daoist shrines on the same sites. Wealthy Buddhist monasteries were able to hire leading artists and sculptors to design temples and pagodas and create images.

The tremendous urge to copy original Buddhist texts profoundly stimulated the Chinese printing industry. One of the earliest Mahayana texts, The Perfection of Wisdom, stated that "where this perfection of wisdom has been written down in a book, and has been put up and worshipped . . . there men and ghosts can do no harm, except as punishment for past deeds.[30] Paper, invented in China, had been in use from the second century C.E., and the Tang Dynasty printed books with wood blocks. The Diamond Sutra, the oldest extant printed text, was printed in China in 868. By the tenth century, printing books was widely practiced.

WHY DID BUDDHISM DECLINE IN CHINA?

Both the Sui and early Tang rulers were strong patrons of Buddhism, and the faith reached its height during the seventh to tenth centuries. As long as the Tang government prospered, the emperors could tolerate the ever-growing wealth and privileges of the Buddhist monasteries and temples. However, when the Later Tang was undermined by political revolts and an economic crisis, the government began to reconsider its attitude toward Buddhism.

By then, the number of Buddhist monasteries had increased dramatically and they served many important functions in Chinese society. People went there for help. Farmers in need of money or seeds for planting borrowed from monasteries. Travelers lodged there, and children went there to learn to read. Monastery hospitals offered the best health care available.

At the same time, in large part because of donations made to earn merit, Buddhist monasteries and temples had grown exceedingly wealthy and acquired large estates, animals, and even slaves, as well as precious gems, gold, and other valuable items. The Buddha was often pictured sitting on a carpet of diamonds or surrounded by gems and jeweled nets, and many statues of him were gold plated and studded with jewels. By the Later Tang, monasteries, which were exempt from taxation, supported around 260,000 monks, nuns, and administrators, more than 100,000 temple serfs, and hundreds of thousands of paid lay workers. Buddhism's enormous wealth was both an affront to the government and a tempting source of quick tax revenues to shore up the impoverished state treasury.

The obvious contradiction between the Buddha's very clear teaching that believers should overcome their desires for luxuries and pleasure and the growing wealth of Buddhist monasteries fueled anti-Buddhist sentiments among the populace. Buddhist monks knew that the Buddha had turned his back on his family's wealth and position and, when tempted by Mara, had replied: "Money and treasure bind hard and fast and pollute the mind."[31] It seemed paradoxical that the Buddha had emphasized spiritual matters but some of his ardent followers were amassing fortunes.

Instead of giving up worldly pursuits and pleasures and seeking truth, many monks enthusiastically embraced the material world. They supervised farmland cultivation, used slave labor to run mills and oil presses, and even launched businesses and indulged in pawn brokering and money lending, often neglecting their spiritual calling. An obviously disillusioned fifth-century monk asked his fellow Buddhists, "Why is it that their ideals are noble and far-reaching and their activities still are base and common? [They] become merchants and engage in barter, wrangling with the masses for profit."[32] Emperor Gaozu in the early seventh century noted that although Buddhists "give priority to purity, distancing oneself from filth, and cutting off greed and desire," they practice "inexhaustible greed" and are intent on "amassing ever greater quantities of goods."[33]

In 845, Wuzong, a Tang emperor, stipulated that monks who prac-tice magic, kept women, or violated Buddhist discipline would be stripped of their religious status and the government would confiscate their land and wealth. Four years later, the emperor took a census of all Buddhist property and then issued an edict that ordered the destruction of all but a few temples, the confiscation and melting down of images, the secularization of most monks and nuns, and state appropriation of Buddhist land and serfs. Within three years, about 250,000 monks and nuns had been forced to return to secular life, and 4,600 monasteries and 40,000 chapels were either destroyed or converted to secular purposes.

Chinese intellectuals and artists were urging a return to more authentically "Chinese" cultural forms, fueled by the heightened resent-ment against what leaders now labeled a foreign religion and foreigners in general. Perhaps challenges from threatening Mongol armies helped create the backlash against foreign ideas. Moreover, the growing hostil-ities between Daoists and Buddhists may have prompted the emperor, an ardent Daoist, to suppress Buddhism.

A more convincing argument, however, is that Buddhist institutions were actually operating as a parallel government, posing a genuine polit-ical and economic threat to the Tang leaders. Devoting a large sector of the economy to providing bronze and iron to cast Buddhist images seemed an enormous waste of resources. The edict noted the immense economic power of the Buddhists and forbade the use of gold, silver, copper, iron, and gems in the construction of Buddhist images and required that clay or wood be used instead.

The persecution that resulted was the harshest in China's history, and for many years historians in both China and the West concluded that these systematic attacks marked the end of Buddhism as a signifi-cant force in China. However, recent scholarship now clearly indicates that Buddhism continued to flourish in China for several hundred years after the Tang.

During the Song Dynasty (906–1279), Chinese Buddhism developed into a uniquely independent system. Song sources state that in 1021 there were 397,615 monks and 61,140 nuns, the most ever in Chinese history. Buddhists during the Song period also wrote important religious histo-ries, and the Chan and other schools produced sophisticated theoretical texts.[34] Pure Land Buddhism continued to prosper as a popular faith and merged with other local Chinese religions that relied on temple offerings given to gain material results, such as good fortune, sons, attractive spouses, and good harvests.

Even though many of the formal Buddhist institutions were destroyed, Buddhist influences continued to have a deep and long-lasting influence in Chinese society. It has become a permanent part of Chinese culture, offering both earthly ethics and mystical worlds beyond the senses. It would enjoy revivals during the Mongol Yuan (1279–1368) and Ming (1368–1644) dynasties. When modern political leaders such as Liu Shao–ch'i can write, "I can compose an essay that holds up the ideal Communist Party member as one who, 'grieves before all the rest of the world grieves and is happy only after all the rest of the world is happy,'"[35] we can readily discern the long lasting influence of Buddhism in China.

THE NEO-CONFUCIAN SYNTHESIS

Significant aspects of Buddhism lived on in China in the new philosophy of Neo-Confucianism. Many Song leaders, literary figures, and intellectuals wanted to return to earlier Chinese ideas, particularly the Confucian political ideal, and the Song revived and reformed the civil service exams based on Confucian texts. However, rather than totally rejecting Buddhism, the Chinese blended many Buddhist ideas with Confucianism and Daoist concepts into a new synthesis known as Neo-Confucianism. Neo-Confucianists hoped to re-create the ideal Confucian society that they believed had existed in ancient times, but in the process they incorporated popular Buddhists and Daoists ideas as well.

According to the major Neo-Confucian philosophers such as Chu Hsi (1130–1200), the universe is divided into *chi*, spirit, and *li*, matter. The universal spirit, or chi, infuses all matter and gives it life. In this way, the Chinese incorporated Buddhist teachings into one abstract principle known as chi.

Neo-Confucianism advocated self-cultivation in order to become a sage or "superior person." Confucius and Mencius had taught that humans were born with a tendency toward goodness, and that sincere effort, a proper education, and lifelong hard work at self-cultivation would bring that goodness to the fore. Theoretically, anyone could reach the elevated status of the superior person, but few women were allowed to study the texts. Neo-Confucianism's stress on self-cultivation owed much to the Ch'an emphasis on meditation and self-development.

Neo-Confucianism was a uniquely Chinese synthesis, and from the Ming Dynasty (1368–1644) until 1905, Neo-Confucianism dominated Chinese intellectual life. It was China's way of absorbing Buddhism's major concepts while seeming to reject a "foreign" faith. Many temples contained images of Lao Tzu, Confucius, and the Buddha side-by-side, symbolizing the coexistence of these ideologies.

BUDDHISM TRAVELS TO THE FRONTIERS OF EURASIA

BUDDHISM SPREADS TO KOREA

Korea's first contacts with China came in the fourth century C.E. when Korean aristocrats wanted to adapt the Chinese writing system that they identified with Confucianism. At the same time, Buddhist missionaries began taking their faith to Korea and trying to adapt their teachings to local shamanistic customs, such as reverence for nature spirits and mountains.

When Korean monks visited the Sui capital at Changan in the sixth century, they were impressed with the way Emperor Wendi used Buddhism to encourage Chinese unity and to justify his military conquests. They carried these insights back to their homeland, which at the time was divided into three major kingdoms.

Monks in the southern kingdom of Silla compiled Five Precepts that reflected Korean values, as well values from Buddhism and Confucianism. The Silla king hoped to be able to incorporate some of the new ideas to emphasize national defense and national unity as well as to elevate his own status.

> Serve the king with loyalty,
> serve your parents with filial piety,
> be faithful to friends,
> do not retreat in battle, and
> do not kill indiscriminately.[36]

Buddhism spread rapidly in the Korean Peninsula where Silla leaders used it to help provide the basis for a broad consensus that would enhance their efforts to unite the country. Its ideology could also enhance their legitimacy, especially if the rulers could be identified with the Buddha and with China's sophisticated worldview and high civilization. Aristocrats readily identified with the Buddhist idea of karma and rebirth, because it seemed to strengthen the idea that their exalted position in society was the result of their good actions in past lives. Poorer members of society were comforted by the idea that everyone could cultivate his or her Buddha nature and that all stood as equals in the Buddha's sight, and each person could seek nirvana.

When Pure Land Buddhism reached Korea in the ninth century, it attracted a wide following because it did not require a lot of abstract knowledge: one had only to invoke the name of the Buddha and surrender to his power. Pure Land provided a way to escape one's karma and promised rebirth in paradise for all those who were suffering. According to one of Korea's most famous Buddhist philosophers, "The deeper meaning of Pure Land is that it has always been for everyone, not just for Bodhisattvas."[37] The idea that good deeds performed for the sake of the dead would bring merit also attracted many people who already practiced rituals celebrating their ancestors. Buddhist monasteries, following the Chinese example, served the poor and offered assistance to the sick and needy.

In 668, Silla conquered the other two Korean kingdoms and united the country, an event that marked the independent development of the Korean people, and Buddhism became the central cultural force knitting the people of the peninsula together. Having everyone following the way of the Buddha paralleled the whole nation following a single king. From its inception, Korean Buddhists tried to avoid schisms and advocated a unified approach. During the Unified Silla period, its leaders worked diligently to promote patriotic feeling and unity. Various rituals they performed were intended to protect the land from foreign invasion. Buddhist monks were willing to take up arms and fight bravely to safeguard the country, and their faith helped give them courage to face death.

The voluntary conversion of Koreans to Buddhism was greatly enhanced by the syncretism between the new ideas imported from China and traditional local customs. Korean popular religion centered on female shamans who were believed to be able to help individuals contact ancestors and other spirits and perform rituals to appease them. Buddhism gradually incorporated shaman rituals into its own practices. Moreover, like the Southeast Asian reverence for the naga, Koreans shared a widely held and long-standing belief that the Dragon of the East Sea (Sea of Japan) guarded the Korean Peninsula. People believed that this sacred Dragon could move between the spirit and human worlds, protecting the country. As Buddhism spread, the Dragon myth merged with both the ruler's power and with Buddhist symbolism.

King Munmu, the Silla leader responsible for repulsing the Tang threat and unifying the three kingdoms, ruled United Silla until 681. Just before he died, Munmu directed his followers to cremate his body and bury his ashes in a tomb in the East Sea. He hoped to be united with the spirit of the Dragon of the East Sea and in that way continue to protect the country even after his death, particularly from threats such as Japanese pirates.

Sokkuram, a cave grotto constructed in 751, illustrates the close connection between the king and Buddhism and how Korean Buddhism combined both Buddhist and local beliefs. Sokkuram, which is actually a freestanding temple that had been covered with dirt, resembles other

Buddhist cave sanctuaries. Around its interior walls are reliefs of Buddhist pilgrims who came to Korea from a variety of countries. In the center is a beautiful seated image of the Buddha looking out to the sea. Worshippers can imagine that the Buddha is not only blessing Munmu's grave and protecting the kingdom, but warding off enemies as well. Gradually, Buddhist ideas merged with Korean shamanism and national aspirations to form another unique form of Buddhism.

After the Silla Dynasty weakened in the tenth century, the Koryo Dynasty assumed control of the country. At its inception, Koryo was a thoroughly Buddhist state. One of its first rulers stated

> The success of the great enterprise of founding our dynasty is entirely owing to the protective power of the many Buddhas. We therefore must build temples . . . [to ensure the dynasty's well-being].[38]

Gradually, however, Confucianism gained ascendancy over Buddhism, which was relegated to helping people attain spiritual tranquility and salvation. By the end of the Koryo Dynasty (1232), the state support that had made Buddhism the official religion had vanished. Buddhism was declared "destructive of the mores and ruinous of the state."[39]

Rulers of the Chosen Dynasty, established in 1392, adopted Neo-Confucianism. This move led to greater restriction and oppression of Buddhism. Temples could not be built near towns, and many were destroyed. Monks lost much of their status and, for some years, were not permitted to enter the capital. Even though the common people continued to go to the temples, Buddhism clearly had lost its central place in Korean life.

BUDDHISM TRAVELS TO JAPAN

From the sixth to the eighth centuries, Korean Buddhist and Confucian scholars carried information about China to Japan. Japanese leaders must have been impressed by these Korean and Chinese visitors who came from more developed cultures and could read and write. They brought stirring Buddhist scriptures, scholarly philosophical arguments, and awe-inspiring works of art that revealed advanced and highly developed cultures.

Initially, members of the Japanese aristocracy, hoping to build Japan into a complex society, welcomed Buddhism. However, average peasant farmers found Buddhism alien to many of their beliefs, and they were not very receptive to a philosophy that seemed to deny the world. On the other hand, many readily responded to the idea of reverence for ancestors and performing rituals to honor one's parents—practices already well established in Chinese Buddhism.

Because of the beauty of the countryside and the ever-present possibility of earthquakes or typhoons, the Japanese people believed that
nature was imbued with divine energy called *kami*. Anything that was
awe-inspiring—such as an old tree or a steep mountain or the rumbling
earth—possessed kami, and the Japanese directed life-affirming prayers,
filled with love and gratitude rather than fear and supplication, to the
kami. This appreciation for the power and beauty of nature and reverence for kami was known as Shinto. The people went to Shinto shrines,
usually in beautiful settings, where they ritually washed and gave
thanks to the kami.

The Japanese especially venerated the powers of fertility. Women
priestesses played a major role in religion because they seemed to have
magical powers and could contact kami. Crime was associated with pollution, as were such things as wounds, blood, and death. Purity was
associated with goodness, and worshipers ritually washed before saying
prayers. The entrance to a Shinto shrine was a gate called a *torii*. Step-
ping through the torii meant passing from mundane to sacred space.

Prince Shotoku, a member of the Yamato clan, who became crown
prince in 593 and ruled until 622, wanted to unite the various clans in
Japan and raise the cultural level of Japanese society. He initiated contact with the Sui Dynasty and sent scholars to learn about China. He
admired the Chinese governmental system and attempted to introduce
it in Japan. Contact with China, and especially the introduction of Pure
Land Buddhism during his reign, helped him achieve his goals. Along
with support of Confucian principles, Prince Shotoku wanted the constitution, written in 604, to support Buddhist ideals of peace and salvation for all beings and to urge people to adopt Buddhism.

At first only the aristocracy supported Buddhism, but by the Nara
period (710–784) the government strongly supported Buddhism and
commissioned the construction of numerous Buddhist temples and
gigantic Buddha images. Pure Land Buddhism attracted members of the
aristocracy and it gradually spread across Japan, taking root among average people. In 741, Prince Shomu, who ruled from 724 to 749, proclaimed
that every district should have a state-subsidized Buddhist temple. The
consecration of the Great Buddha statue in the Todaiji temple in Nara
that Prince Shomu commissioned was an international event. A brahmin
priest came from India to conduct the ceremony, and musicians from all
over East Asia played music for the celebrations.

As had happened in China, Buddhist institutions grew so powerful
that the fledgling Nara government felt threatened. As a result, the
Japanese leaders decided to build a new capital, first at Nagaoka and then,
in 794, at Heian (Kyoto), where it remained for almost four centuries.

During the Heian period (794–1186) the Japanese stopped sending diplomats and students to China and concentrated instead on their own development. In the process, both Buddhism and Confucianism were thoroughly blended into Japanese institutions and values that included the importance of the military. Religious leaders worked out a synthesis, and average Japanese saw no contradiction in following ideas from both faiths. Men and women maintained their long-standing respect for nature and reverence for kami, and used Shinto rituals when they married, but they also conducted Buddhist rituals for their ancestors and were usually buried by a Buddhist priest.

By the end of the twelfth century, Pure Land was the most widely practiced form of Japanese Buddhism. The most important Japanese Pure Land sect was the Jodo school. Its founder, Honen (1133–1212), believed that ordinary people have difficulty reaching the state of Enlightenment through their own efforts. For them to reach the Pure Land, they should repeatedly say "Namo Amida Butsu" ("I rely upon the Enlightened One who is Infinite Light and Eternal Life"). For the first time in Japan, the Buddha's message was within everyone's reach.

The power of the central government was severely limited during the Heian period, even though the members of the court in Kyoto lived in splendor. As centralism failed, a feudal society with power in the hands of an aristocratic warrior class was slowly developing. Led by a general known as a shogun, by 1192 land-owning military leaders had taken over the central government. They continued to support the emperor in Kyoto as the symbolic and religious leader of the country, but his functions were purely ceremonial.

The shogun was the actual leader of the highly decentralized country. Under him were the land-holding lords. The most powerful lords were called *damiyo*. Beneath the shogun and damiyo were lesser lords. Supporting them were their warriors, called samurai, who pledged absolute loyalty to their lords. There was a strict hierarchy within the nobility that rested on the majority peasant population. The peasants worked the land and raised the food that supported the nobility.

The Chinese-style bureaucracy recruited by examinations never took root in Japan. Chinese society had placed the warrior at the very bottom of society, maintaining that good men should not become soldiers. Japan rejected the Chinese disdain for the military. The shogun, damiyo, and samurai were securely at the top of the Japanese social structure. Below them in status were the peasants and then the artisans. In a society without major urbanization and trade, merchants were next to last. Samurai who had no lord to serve were the outcasts of the Japanese society.

During this era, several important sects of Buddhism were founded that embraced the rise of militarism. Two of the most important of these were the True Pure Land sect of the Jodo School, founded by Shinran in 1224, and the Nicheran Sect, founded in 1223. These and other similar sects, unlike most historic Buddhist movements, were particularly intolerant and often hostile to other sects and championed the use of force. Some of these newer sects even maintained their own armies and engaged in open warfare and increasingly supported Japanese nationalism and used Buddhism in much the same way as the Chinese emperor Sui Wendi had done centuries earlier. Gradually, in the 13th century these various sects of the Jodo school of Buddhism grew to dominate the religious landscape. In the process Japanese Buddhism increasingly took on both a highly nationalistic and martial face.

The Zen sect, which was also introduced from China, arrived in Japan soon after the beginning of the thirteenth century. Zen's complicated theories were popular, particularly among the members of the military class. Zen Buddhism's central concept is that human life is full of suffering due to illness, death, and the loss of loved ones. By getting rid of desires and attachments through discipline, meditation, and other mental exercises, one can achieve a state of *satori* (mental

FIGURE 2-6   THE GREAT BUDDHA AT KAMAKURA, JAPAN
The Kamakura Daibatsu is one of the largest Buddha statues in the world.

tranquility) and escape suffering and the cycle of reincarnation. If followers of Zen could become totally indifferent to whatever they faced, they would be able to move through life without fearing anything, including death.

Zen adapted the Japanese special reverence for nature and the highly developed sense of aesthetics that was at the core of the Japanese worldview. Beautiful Zen gardens that were usually small and placed near temples made minimal use of objects and a maximum appeal to the imagination. Zen garden masters even built dry gardens with sand suggesting water and a few rocks to suggest mountains. Perhaps the most compelling of these Zen gardens can be found at the Ryoanji Temple in Kyoto.

Although Buddhist teaching abhors war, Buddhist influence infused the Japanese attitude toward warfare. Few if any other cultures have elevated warfare to such a high aesthetic art. Like the knights in Europe who adapted Christian ideas to the Code of Chivalry, the samurai borrowed heavily from Buddhism, especially the Zen school, in its code of conduct called Bushido, the Way of the Warrior. Bushido also adapted Confucian and Shinto ideals and merged them all into a uniquely Japanese ethic.

Fearlessness in the face of death, an important part of the Bushido, is a central Buddhist concept. Like the cherry blossom that fades, the warrior is cut down in the prime of his life. The warrior must strive "to combine action and art like the flower that wilts and the flower that lasts forever." A warrior should welcome death before allowing harm or dishonor to come to his lord or to himself, and he should not fear death as long as he dies with honor.

Self-control was another aspect of Bushido, and self-control through meditation is also an important aspect of Buddhism. The warrior should never complain, even when he is in extreme pain: "When the stomach is empty, it is a disgrace to feel hungry."[40]

Gradually, Japan synthesized Buddhism, Confucianism, Shinto, and other indigenous beliefs and practices into a uniquely Japanese religion. Japanese Buddhists came to believe that kami could improve their karma and help them move up the chain of consciousness. Accordingly, devotees built special shrines (*Jinguji*) on the grounds of Shinto temples. Buddhist philosophers accepted kami as manifestations of the Buddha essence. Many Japanese believed that the kami were responsible for protecting their homeland from the Mongol attacks of the thirteenth century.

Gradually, the emperor became a living kami. Belief in the emperor's sacredness was greatly strengthened when two major typhoons destroyed the fleets of Mongol that were set to invade Japan in 1274 and 1281.

CONCLUSION

Throughout their 2,500-year history, Buddhists have resisted the move toward doctrinaire orthodoxy. Buddhism began with its founder's philosophic diagnosis of the world and his prescription for transcending suffering. Over the first centuries as it grew into the first universal religion, the faith evolved into an institutional faith based largely in the Sangha, but closely related to the lay communities that supported the monks and nuns.

For a thousand years, Buddhism flourished alongside Hinduism in India where it had originated, but gradually Indians absorbed much of the Buddha's message into Hinduism, and around 800, Buddhism as a separate religion began to decline in India. With the collapse of the Pala Dynasty in the twelfth century, Buddhism suffered another major defeat, and this time it did not recover. When Muslim armies destroyed Nalanda University in 1202, Buddhism all but disappeared from the land of its birth, although Buddhist values and insights continued to exert significant influence in the Indian tradition.

As missionaries, traders, and others carried the message to lands outside India, Buddhist missionaries were quite willing to translate the scriptures and adapt their faith to local customs and indigenous culture. Both Theravada and Mahayana Buddhism were significantly transformed as they took root in new areas. The original ideal of realizing nirvana by one's own efforts gradually gave way to performing good deeds that built up merit and helped one's family achieve salvation.

Local deities and heroes entered the Buddhist pantheon as bodhisattvas, and traditional rituals and popular beliefs—from reverence for nagas, mountains, and ancestors to Shaman and Shinto practices—were incorporated into everyday Buddhist rituals and beliefs. Buddhism grew into a popular faith that offered common people solace in the face of suffering, fine medicine, charity during difficult times, and the sense of belonging to something universal. Perhaps most important, by offering the possibility of life in paradise after death through faith alone, and with the healing grace of Kwan-yin, East Asian Buddhism was able to appeal to a vast number of people.

Ironically, Buddhism's success contributed to its demise in several areas. As the faith spread and prospered, it grew richer and more powerful, and it had to face the challenges worldly success brings. Rich merchants and kings made valuable donations, and many monasteries in China, Korea, and Japan became rich and lost sight of their essential values of simplicity, compassion, and spirituality. As Buddhist institutions grew rich enough to rival governments, they faced a backlash from political leaders and disillusioned lay people, leading to a general decline of the faith in east Asia.

John Fairbank, one of the foremost scholars of Chinese history, convincingly argues that the whole period from the mid-fourth century to the end of the eighth century might be called the Buddhist Age, not just in Chinese history but also in Asian history and world history. However, by the Song Dynasty in China (906–1279) Buddhism began to merge into Neo-Confucianism while continuing as a strong presence in China. In Korea, Buddhism had lost its vitality by the fourteenth century when Neo-Confucianism became the state philosophy there. In Japan, by the thirteenth century, nationalism was pushing Buddhism to the periphery as it merged with Shintoism and Neo-Confucianism in a unique Japanese approach to religion. In Southeast Asia, Buddhism continued to adapt the faith to suit new historical realities. Buddhism still flourishes in mainland Southeast Asia and has been successfully challenged by Islam only in present day Malaysia and Indonesia.

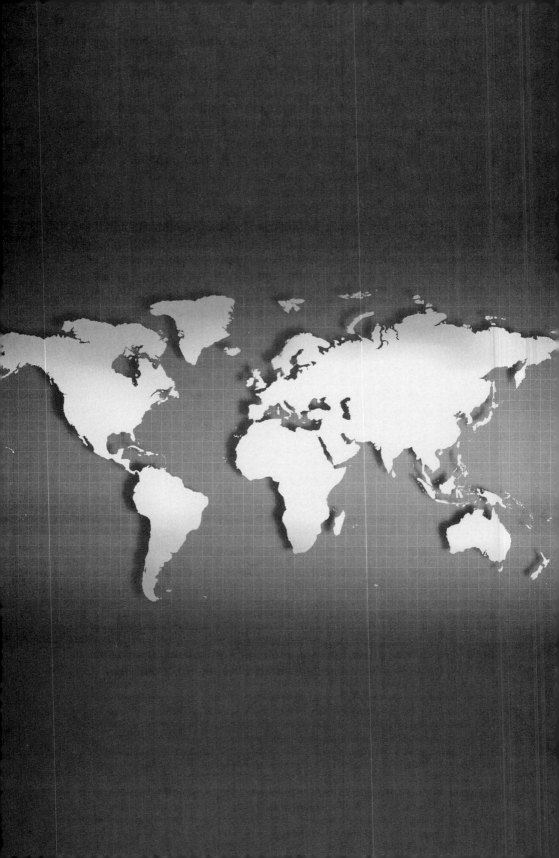

CHAPTER THREE

FROM MANGER TO METROPOLIS: THE EARLY SPREAD OF CHRISTIANITY

GETTING STARTED ON CHAPTER THREE: What was St. Paul's role in the early development of Christianity? Why did Christianity spread largely in urban areas? How did it appeal to large numbers of women, merchants, craftsmen, slaves, and other social groups? How did early Christianity serve to integrate various social groups into a single community? What kind of divisions and controversies tore at the unity of the early Christian community? What gave rise to the division between Roman and Eastern Orthodox churches as well as to the various Protestant movements that developed later? How did Christians adapt their teachings and practices to the various cultural areas to which the religion spread? Why was Christianity more successful in Europe than in lands to the East? How might you define the changing relationship of the church and various political authorities?

In contrast to Buddhism, which only gradually spread outside South Asia as a universal religion, Christianity met the criteria from its beginning. Within a generation after Jesus' death, missionaries had carried the Christian message beyond the land of its birth and had spent their lives sharing the "Good News" that Jesus had risen from the dead and conquered death. Christianity spread out of Palestine in all directions like spokes of a wheel. Believers sought prospective converts in Egypt, Syria, Ethiopia, Iraq, and Iran. Christian apostles carried the faith into the Hellenistic world of the Mediterranean basin and would later spread it in the Byzantium Empire and among the Germanic groups who settled in Europe.

PAUL'S EFFORTS TO PROMOTE CHRISTIANITY

The early missionaries focused their energies on city dwellers and tried to make the faith appealing to very diverse groups of people. In the process they adapted Jesus' agrarian metaphors of flocks of sheep and goats, plants, mountains, and water to urban symbols more relevant to city dwellers. Among the early Christians, no one shaped the message or helped spread it throughout the Mediterranean basin more effectively than Paul, often called the thirteenth apostle.

Paul was born in Tarsus, an active seaport town with a 2,000-year history, located on the northern Mediterranean shore of Asia Minor. A devout Jew, Paul initially persecuted Christians. However, after his dramatic mystical experience of the Holy Spirit, Paul embraced Christianity and soon became the faith's most articulate spokesman and effective missionary.

Paul's major contribution to early Christianity was his eagerness to take the news of Jesus' resurrection to gentile communities. Although a close reading of Paul suggests that he deeply respected Jewish law (Romans 9:4, Gal 5:14, 1 Cor 14:34, Phil 3:6), he especially wanted to reach out to non-Jews. In the letters of encouragement he wrote to the fledgling Christian churches, he explained that he saw no problem in adjusting the message to fit the cultural values of potential convents. "I must be all things to all people," he wrote (I Corinthians 9:16–23).

Jews such as Paul who had been influenced by Greek culture were flexible about Jewish rituals and personal habits, but many Jewish Christians were not enthusiastic about converting gentiles. Paul insisted that Jesus had brought a new and higher law that superseded traditional Jewish law and that faith in Jesus Christ was the sole criteria for salvation (Galatians, 3, 4). Paul encouraged Jews and gentiles to eat together, a practice Jewish law prohibited. Moreover, he did not insist that non-Jewish converts undergo circumcision, an important Jewish ritual. Paul feared that requiring gentile converts to follow Jewish law, including circumcision, would not only undermine his efforts to spread the Good News but would violate his understanding of the "New Covenant" established by Jesus.

Paul's contention that Jesus' message transcended Jewish law angered many of the more orthodox members of the Jewish Christian community in Jerusalem. James, probably Jesus' brother and the leader of this group, insisted that all Christians must adhere strictly to traditional Jewish law, including purity and pollution rituals and other personal habits, and they insisted that circumcision be a prerequisite for any male who wanted to become a Christian. Further, they stipulated that Jewish and gentile Christians must eat their meals separately.

In the mid first century, Christian leaders met in Jerusalem to resolve these divisive issues. The council decided that Paul should continue to work with non-Jews while James and his group would focus their efforts on Jews. Further, Paul and his colleagues did not have to insist that new converts observe Jewish law. This decision was critical in the spread of Christianity. If Paul's efforts had been curtailed, the Christian community would likely have become just another Jewish sect and would probably have been absorbed into Judaism. Instead, Paul and his fellow missionaries were able to spread the fledgling faith in non-Jewish urban centers.

Paul traveled to cities throughout the Mediterranean basin and may even have reached the Iberian Peninsula. Up until his execution in Rome in 64, Paul believed that Jesus' return was imminent. However, as the years passed and it became increasingly clear that Jesus was not returning soon, Paul and other new converts concentrated on building earthly institutions known as churches that would bear witness to the Good News until the "Second Coming" occurred. Paul's missionary efforts were greatly facilitated when the Romans destroyed the Jerusalem temple in 70 C.E., scattering the Jewish-Christian wing of the early Church. By 100, at least 70 small Christian communities could be found between West Asia and Iberia.

For the most part the early Christians met in homes, often in secret, and began to develop basic rituals. In 112 Pliny wrote to Emperor Trajan about what Christians were doing:

> They met regularly before dawn on a certain day, when they sang an anthem to Christ as to a god, and bound themselves by a solemn oath not to commit any wicked deeds, nor to practice fraud, theft and adultery, not to break their word, nor to deny a deposit when called upon to honor it. After this it was their custom to separate, and then to meet again to partake of food, but food of an ordinary and innocent kind."[41]

Early Christians commonly greeted one another with the "Holy Kiss," that Jesus and his disciples had used.[42] The usual order of worship included confessing one's sins and reconciling with one's neighbors. Then, following the Jewish tradition of sacrifice, the worshipers offered thanks over a cup of wine and a loaf, a ritual, which would come to symbolize the blood and body of Christ.

Services, which were held on Sunday, the day associated with Jesus' resurrection from the dead, often stressed moral exorcism through penance. A believer might appear in sackcloth and ashes to demonstrate his or her disgrace and beg the congregation for mercy and forgiveness. Church members also gave alms for the remission of their sins. The funds collected were used to support the religious community and its leaders. By the second century, the three official church positions were bishop, presbyter, and deacon. A diocese comprising several churches elected a bishop, the Greek word for overseer, and called their urban offices "sees."

The symbolic and political center of each bishop's authority was his cathedral (from the Latin word for "chair"). An archbishop had authority over several dioceses, and the archbishops in the five most important cities—Rome, Alexandria, Jerusalem, Antioch, and Constantinople— were called metropolitans. In the fourth century they were given the higher rank of patriarchs (fathers of the church). A clear line of authority ran from the patriarchs to archbishops, bishops, parish priests—who were in charge of individual churches—and finally to the laity, the community of believers.

THE ENVIRONMENT INTO WHICH CHRISTIANITY SPREAD

The pluralistic nature of the cultural environment into which Christianity spread had a profound effect on its development. The first Christians mixed and mingled with members of many diverse religious groups, including followers of Osiris/Isis, Cybele, various Greco-Roman gods, and especially Mithraism, probably the most popular religion of that time in the Mediterranean basin. Aspects of the Christian message that were similar to elements of these faiths made it easier for people to move from one faith to another. Meanwhile, Christians adapted some of the older religious practices and appropriated older sacred sites, making Christianity seem familiar and appealing to potential converts.

ZOROASTRIAN LEGACIES: THE COSMIC STRUGGLE BETWEEN GOOD AND EVIL

It is difficult to overestimate the influence of Zoroastrianism and its dualistic worldview. In the sixth century B.C.E., its Persian founder, Zarathustra, had stated that the world was starkly divided between the forces of light, presided over by Ahura Mazda, and the forces of darkness, associated with Ahriman. A cosmic struggle between Light (Good) and Darkness (Evil) was taking place, and each person had to choose which side to support. When the final triumph of the Good occurred, those who had sided with Ahura Mazda would be rewarded with heaven; those who had followed Ahriman would suffer in hell. Dualism, a final judgment, heaven and hell, and personal choice soon became part of Judaism and these concepts were important in Christianity as well. (The metaphor of light and dark remains central to contemporary Christian doctrine and reappears in many sermons, homilies, and hymns.)

Intriguing echoes from Elysian Mysteries in Greece, the Isis/Osiris myths of Egypt, and the Adonis and Cybele traditions of western Asia are all evident in early Christianity. Images of Mary nursing the baby Jesus looked very much like Isis nursing Horus. The myth of the death and rebirth of heroes or gods, exemplified in the Isis/Osiris myth, must have resonated with the death and resurrection of Jesus. The mystery religions associated with the agricultural cycle of death and rebirth also helped make Christianity's message of death and resurrection seem familiar. Moreover, stories of virgins being impregnated by gods and giving birth to special gods or heroes can be found in Hindu and Buddhist mythology and also became associated with Romulus, Egyptian pharaohs, Plato, Alexander, and Augustus.

FIGURE 3-1   ISIS NURSING HORUS AND MARY NURSING JESUS
Note the similarity of the two mothers and babies. The Egyptian Isis and Horus predate Jesus by many centuries.

THE MILIEU OF MITHRAISM

By the first centuries C.E., Mithraism, which had developed from Zoroastrianism, was thriving in cities throughout the Roman Empire. Mithraism retained Zoroastrianism's basic dualistic worldview, with Mithra struggling against the forces of evil. Mithraism's most important festival, which celebrated the rebirth of light, was held at the time of the winter solstice. Sunday was the important day of worship for followers of Mithra, and they also used baptism to wash away their sins.

As Christianity spread, Christians appropriated aspects of Mithraism but gave them new meanings. Although it is doubtful that Jesus was born in December, one reason early Christians celebrated the birth of Jesus in that month may well have been to appeal to devotees of Mithra who celebrated their major holiday around the time of the winter solstice. Christians, like followers of Mithraism, also made Sunday, associated with Jesus' resurrection, their day of worship, and they practiced baptism, confession, and forgiveness of sins.

Similarities abound between Mithraism's ritual sacrifice of a bull followed by ritual cleansing in the bull's blood and the Jewish practice of cleansing in the blood running from temple sacrifices. Devotees of Mithra believed that they would achieve everlasting life by eating the bull's flesh and drinking its blood. The Epistle to the Hebrews suggests how early Christians transformed this ritual into Christ's sacrifice.

> For if the blood of bulls and of goats, and the ashes of a heifer sprinkling the unclean, sanctifieth to the purifying of the flesh, how much more shall the blood of Christ, who through the eternal Spirit offered himself without spot to God, purge your conscience from dead works to serve the living God? (Hebrews Ch 9:13, 14)

Mithraism and Christianity also shared a belief in faith over works as the route to salvation and both believed that a savior/mediator between humans and God was a necessary aid to salvation. Both taught that believers could approach the savior by prayer and ascetic practices. Many scholars have argued that Paul's teaching about the End of Days and a single path to salvation were closer to the cosmology of Zoroaster and Mithraism than to the Jewish tradition. Many early converts probably did not see their shift to Christianity as a radical departure from many of the rituals and beliefs that already punctuated their daily lives.

THE PERSISTENT GHOST OF GNOSTICISM

Gnostics were a mystical group that had freely borrowed from early forms of mysticism, Zoroastrianism, and several Hindu and Buddhist concepts. Like Zoroastrians, Gnostics believed in the radical dualism between such opposites as light and darkness, good and evil, spirit and matter, and knowledge and ignorance. Human nature also has two natures: a perishable physical component and a "Divine Spark," a fragment of the Divine Spirit.

Gnostics believed they lived in a fallen world and the only way to escape was to discover the true meaning of existence and their inner Divine Spark. To do that they were to resist physical pleasures that tempted them to indulge their base passions. Gnostics taught that ignorance was the cause of sin: One must probe beneath the surface meaning of words and discover the hidden, esoteric message. In remarkable similarity to Hinduism, Gnostics believed that through knowledge (Gnosis) of the transcendent Divine Spirit and their inner Divine Spark, individuals can liberate themselves and allow their Spark to be reunited with the Divine Spirit. Believers could gain true knowledge though self-illumination, or a transcendent savior could teach them.

HELLENISM'S LONG SHADOW

Paul and his fellow missionaries' efforts almost always occurred within a Hellenistic milieu. Early Christians rejected the worship of Greek gods and goddesses and usually avoided civil events that involved sacrifices and prayers to them. However, Christian apologists were attracted to the learned works of the Greco-Roman philosophers such as Socrates, Plato, Aristotle, and especially the Stoics. That meant applying Greek modes of logic and analysis to Christian thought and borrowing from the current sophisticated philosophic systems.

Stoicism, one of several influential schools of thought that developed out of Hellenism during the first two centuries C.E., had a profound influence on early Christianity. Stoics stressed the inner consciousness of each individual. It counseled people to be calm in the midst of change, avoid excesses that might promote anxiety, and remain indifferent to the consequences of their actions. The Stoics taught that if one thinks the world is orderly, he or she could lead a virtuous life and serve as an example to others. Individuals could help build a better society by doing their duty. Stoicism had much in common with the principles expressed in the Indian Bhagavad Gita and Buddhism, both of which counseled individuals to be indifferent to the fruits of their actions.

WHY WERE EARLY CONVERTS ATTRACTED TO CHRISTIANITY?

Although the threads of earlier religions, Greek philosophy, and Hellenistic culture informed early Christian beliefs and practices, the essential message of the faith coupled with the moral and ethical examples of many early Christians were probably the major factors that attracted new converts. The Good News that Jesus had defeated death and risen from the dead, and the promise of eternal life in heaven for anyone who embraced Christianity, were extremely appealing. The Good News provided a cosmic concept of justice: You may suffer on earth, but on judgment day the "meek shall inherit the earth." Christianity's message of forgiveness of sins and compassion offered solace and hope for many struggling to find meaning in their lives.

Christian ethics were attractive to many. Jesus had preached more about helping the poor and dispossessed than any other topic, so it is understandable that early Christians carried on extensive charities, especially for those in need. According to one scholar, "Christian charity also attracted all those repelled by pagan brutality and inspired new virtues such as humility, while conspicuously caring for widows and building orphanages and the forerunners of hospitals."[43] Even the anti-Christian pagan emperor Julian (361–363) testified to the superior benevolence of Christian philanthropy, "These godless Galileans [i.e., Christians] feed not only their own poor but ours, who lack our own care."[44]

In a political system that provided little welfare besides the dole, the Christian Church institutionalized material help to the huge Roman proletariat, all financed by voluntary contributions from believing Christians of all social classes. Churches did not charge fees for their services, a common practice where Egyptian or Greco-Roman gods and goddesses were worshiped. In the second century, Tertullian, one of the most important early historians of Christianity, wrote that unlike other societies and clubs that collected fees to pay for feasts, Christians freely contributed money to support orphans, to provide medicine and care for the sick, and to work with prisoners and slaves.[45]

The sense of community, or *Koinonia*, was also a compelling attraction of Christianity, and the message of human equality had special appeal for women. A fellowship that embraced Jew and gentile, free and slave, men and women, and wealthy and poor, where the "last shall be first," was a radical idea in the highly stratified first-century societies. Christian ethics proclaimed that every person was equal before God and that the rich and powerful had no special claim on God's love. God had taken the form of a modest carpenter far from the centers of power to embody His message. Christians were taught that they must "love another" in order to love God, and Christianity, like the other universal religions, strove to create a universal community.

Removed from centers of power, Christians stood in opposition to the mainstream values of Rome and its worldly concerns. Like Buddhism before it, Christianity combined otherworldly transcendence and social morality. The relationship with local gods had been transactional: The worshiper offered a sacrifice and the particular god under worship was expected to reciprocate by answering the prayers. In Christianity, God's grace came unconditionally, whether or not one offered sacrifices or gifts. In addition, Christianity, unlike pagan religions, insisted that it was the only true way to salvation.

Christianity grew very slowly in the first century. Jesus' disciples and many of the first preachers were relatively well-off artisans and tradespeople who could move from place to place, readily finding work to support their preaching. Christians came from all classes, and the new faith appealed to the poor, especially slaves, and to the moderately wealthy. Christianity also attracted some aristocrats, successful business people, and large numbers of women and soldiers. However, by the late first century, probably no more than one percent of the 60 million people who lived within the Roman Empire thought of themselves as Christians.

Conversions increased during the second century, especially in cities where people lived close together. Word-of-mouth communication was important. Christians explained their new faith to family members, friends, and neighbors. Nonbelievers could see how believers lived, close up and on a daily basis, and the faith spread from neighbor to neighbor as they went about their daily rounds. By the end of the third century, the Christian community had grown to include about five percent of the population.

Although men and women were not equal in the early church, Paul's letters cite many examples of active and prominent Jewish and gentile churchwomen. Paul greets Prisca, Junia, Julia, and Nereus' sister, who worked and traveled as missionaries with their husbands or brothers (Romans 16:3, 7, 15). He explains how Prisca and her husband risked their lives to save him. He praises Junia, a prominent disciple, who had been arrested for her work. He praises Mary and Persis for their efforts (Romans 16:6, 12), and he calls Euodia and Syntyche his "fellow-workers" (Philippians 4:2–3). Paul's letters also mention women leaders of house churches (Apphia in Philemon 2; Prisca in I Corinthians 16:19) and female heads of churches (Acts 16:15) (Colossians 4:15). Many sources identify Mary Magdalene as one of the active followers of Jesus. Many converts were well-to-do woman who often converted their husbands and other members of their families. Large numbers of women also organized food distribution to the hungry and other charities for the poor.

There were few genuine intellectuals among the early Christians, and many contemporary Greek and Roman writers thought Christians

were illiterate folk with little formal education. Paul thought the majority of the Corinthian Christians were ignorant, powerless, and of obscure
birth. However, Christians living in the 20 largest cities present a different picture. They were probably mainly workers and artisans, with a
sprinkling of aristocrats and businessmen. Few farmers who lived in the
countryside joined, which may explain why *pays*, which means "country,"
gradually came to stand for "pagan," or nonbelievers.

MULTIPLE VARIETIES OF THE CHRISTIAN FAITH

Early Christianity, like Buddhism, spawned several groups that held different interpretations of their founder's message. Present-day Christians
probably seldom realize how many interpretations of the new faith flourished in the first centuries C.E. Among the most contentous of these
interpretations were the nature of Jesus, the role of individual experience, how one relates to God, Jesus, and the Holy Spirit, the essence of
Jesus' ethical teachings, and the place of personal mystical experience.
In those early centuries, there was no concept of heresy nor a single
authority that could designate which interpretation was correct.

Gradually, clusters of Christians gathered around individuals such
as Paul and John and groups such as the Jewish Christians, the Gnostics,
the Macionites, and the mainstream Christians. Often the boundaries
separating these and other movements were vague and shifting as
Christian seekers moved freely from one group to another.

PAUL AND JOHN

Paul preached about "the divine son" who lived spiritually within those
who accepted him as their savior. As Paul and the other early believers
took the message outside the Jewish community, they gradually added
the Greek concept of Logos, which meant both "word" and "reason."
John, however, believed that Jesus was "logos made flesh." In the Gospel
of John, Jesus is presented as both Messiah and Logos, one and the same,
omnipotent and eternal. To emphasize this aspect of Jesus' nature, they
called him "the Christ." As John put it: "In the beginning was the word
and the word was with God and the word was God." He hoped that
Jesus the Messiah would be thought of as Jesus the Christ, coeternal
with God.

THE JEWISH CHRISTIANS

The Jewish Christians insisted that Jesus was the messiah who had come
to liberate God's chosen people from Roman social and political

control. They believed that God had adopted Jesus, a righteous human being, to be his chosen son, and God had endowed Jesus with the ability to work miracles and heal the sick. Jesus had willingly sacrificed himself on the cross to atone for all the sins of the world. God then raised his son to heaven to be with him through eternity. In their view Jesus was not the "Christ," equal to God; he was just a man, although the most remarkable man who had ever lived. They believed that making Jesus divine would violate the commandment, "You shall have no other God before me."

Jewish Christians insisted that non-Jewish converts must observe Jewish law, including circumcision, proper dietary rules, and keeping the Sabbath. Many of them disagreed with Paul because he taught that with the coming of the Christ, Jewish law had been replaced by a higher law.

GNOSTIC CHRISTIANS

On the other end of the theological spectrum from the Jewish Christians stood the Gnostic Christians, one of the largest and most radical Christian groups. Their views are reflected in a trove of "secret" documents known as the Nag Hammadi texts, which were written in the generation after Jesus' death and discovered only in 1945. Often identified as the "Gnostic Gospels," these documents reveal a variety of influences beyond Gnosticism, and they emphasize the mystical side of Christianity.

Among the most important of the Gnostic texts is the Gospel of Thomas, a collection of Jesus' sayings to Thomas, one of his disciples. It describes a large group of so-called "Thomas Christians" that flourished in the first century and included many women who were searching for a personal experience of God. Several of these gospels suggest that Mary Magdalene was a favorite of Jesus and the one who truly understood his message.

Gnostic Christians believed Jesus Christ was a transcendent savior, infused with the Divine Spark at his baptism when he became the Christ. Gnostics believed that Jesus Christ revealed "secret knowledge" to a few chosen disciples and that these Jesus "elect" were also pure spiritual beings. Just prior to his death, this Divine Spark departed from Jesus and reunited with the Divine Spirit. For Gnostics, there could be no bodily resurrection. Salvation meant being free of ignorance.

These mystically oriented Christians believed it was possible to have an inner experience of God and even be one with God. Thomas stressed that Jesus' light resides in every person, and that the Second Coming was already here: Jesus' kingdom is not an otherworldly place that comes after death, but rather it is within each person now.

THE MARCIONITES

Marcion, a devout follower of Paul, taught that Paul was the most important apostle and that he alone had a true understanding of Jesus and his message. His followers, known as Marcionites, believed that Christ was the single path to salvation and that Christians should abandon Jewish law completely. They emphasized God's mercy rather than what they saw as the Jewish emphasis on obedience and punishment. They believed God's love as mediated through Jesus Christ was primary, and divine forgiveness should be stressed. The Marcionites, like the Gnostics, believed that Jesus the Christ was true spirit and had no material form. He had only seemed to be human: His body was simply a phantasm. In reality, he was the one true God who had come to bring his people salvation.

THE SYRIAN CHURCH

Saint Thomas and the Gospel of Thomas, along with other Gnostic-leaning writings, became very important in the Syrian (or Coptic) Christian community that developed in Antioch and later in Edessa, in southern Anatolia. Some Christian historians claim that the Syrian Church was started by a Jewish Christian named Addai who came to Edessa sometime in the late first century and persuaded the nobles there to accept Jewish Christianity. Contemporary scholars argue that Thomas introduced Christianity in Edessa and may have composed the Gospel of Thomas there. Thomas's views seem to have taken root in the Syrian Church and there is evidence that he also carried the Christian message to India, where he went seeking work as a carpenter.

By the mid third century, members of the Syrian Christian community, who met on Sunday, had a bishop and elders who presided over their service. Men and women were separated. Deacons were advised to ignore any rich or powerful person who entered the church but to welcome and find seats for poor men or women. Female church members were warned against wearing too much jewelry, fussing too much with their hair, or otherwise trying to improve their looks. All were expected to live simply and be attentive to the needs of the poor, orphaned, and widowed. Syrian missionaries took vows of chastity, poverty, and self-denial, but instead of disengaging from the world, they preached the Good News and served others.

MAINSTREAM CHRISTIANS

The so-called mainstream Christians attempted to synthesize what they saw as the extreme elements of Jewish, Gnostic, and Marcionite

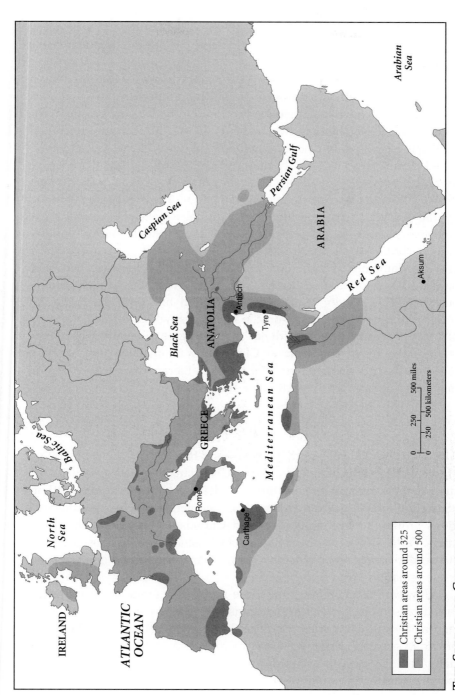

THE SPREAD OF CHRISTIANITY

This map shows the journey of Christianity from its beginnings.

Christian areas around 325

Christian areas around 500

North Sea

Baltic Sea

IRELAND

ATLANTIC OCEAN

Mediterranean Sea

Rome

Carthage

GREECE

Black Sea

ANATOLIA

Caspian Sea

Antioch

Tyre

Persian Gulf

ARABIA

Red Sea

Arabian Sea

Aksum

0   250   500 miles

0   250   500 kilometers

Christianity.[46] By the fourth century, this group had attracted far more converts than all the other branches of early Christianity and was strong enough to crush much of its opposition and declare the others deviants from the true faith.

Walking the tightrope of synthesis, mainstream Christians taught that Jesus was both human and divine. In promoting this dual role, they denied the Jewish Christians version that he was only human, the Gnostic view that he was two beings, and the Marcionite interpretation that he was only divine. For them, the term "Jesus Christ" combined Jesus' divine and human aspects while also affirming a monotheistic God, even if this claim has taxed logical analysis for centuries. They also sought to retain both the ethical teachings stressed by the Jewish Christians and the mystical aspect preferred by the Gnostics, as well as the central place of Paul, which the Marcionites emphasized.

The claimants to orthodoxy insisted that Jesus' message had been handed down to his disciples and accurately recorded, so there should be no argument over what he had intended his followers to do. Of course, interpretations based on the scriptures, which formed the basis of the orthodox position, did not always agree. To gain ascendancy among so many varying views of Christianity, the mainstream Christians relied on the growing strength of the church hierarchy and, after 312, on the powerful support of the Roman emperor.

CHRISTIANITY IN THE LATE ROMAN EMPIRE

Although church leaders grew increasingly troubled by the proliferation of conflicting interpretations, early Christians focused primarily on sharing their message of salvation and dealing with the Roman authorities. The Roman government tended to be tolerant of the numerous religious groups and generally accepted Christianity as one of the many faiths. Far from being subversive, most Christians followed Jesus' advice "to render unto Caesar what is Caesar's" and tried to be good citizens while remaining true to their beliefs.

However, as churches grew more numerous, emperors periodically found reasons to persecute Christians. Christians were acquiring more land and wealth, and their assets could easily be confiscated. Christians provided a ready scapegoat for emperors who governed poorly, especially because the Christians did not fight back. Those who refused to worship the emperor and other state gods and goddesses threatened the government's authority, and soon rulers feared that the crowds of enthusiastic Christians might become rebellious.

As a result, the authorities often spread rumors about Christian practices, exaggerating what went on during the Christian mass and distorting the meaning of the Holy Kiss. Opponents claimed that Christians practiced cannibalism and incest and that their secret rites were filled with bloody rituals. Weak and unstable emperors such as Caligula (37–41), Nero (34–68), and Domitian (81–96) often stirred up violence against Christians to divert attention from their own failures. As one historian of the time explains:

> Therefore, first those were seized who admitted their faith, and then, using the information they provided, a vast multitude were convicted, . . . And perishing they were additionally made into sports: they were killed by dogs by having the hides of beasts attached to them, or they were nailed to crosses or set aflame, and, when the daylight passed away, they were used as nighttime lamps. Nero gave his own gardens for this spectacle.[47]

Emperor Diocletian (284–305) directed Roman authorities to make one last concerted attempt to wipe out Christianity. Roman subjects were required to carry certificates stating they were sacrificing to the local gods. The government ordered churches burned to the ground. Christian scriptures were also to be burned, those who held honored positions were degraded, and household servants who were Christians were to be jailed. Instead of destroying Christianity, however, the systematic persecutions probably strengthened the community. They may also have helped weaken the government and especially the army, which included numerous Christian converts.

Diocletian's reforms, intended to stabilize the economy and check the gradual decline in Roman authority, did little good. After the government decided to establish two major centers of power in Rome and Anatolia, a struggle for the throne between Maxentius (r. 306–312) and Constantine ensued. In the battle between the contending armies, Constantine claimed he saw a cross in the heavens, and he interpreted this incredible sight as evidence that the Christian God favored him and that his political fortunes were tied up with the success of Christianity.

CHRISTIANITY UNDER CONSTANTINE

Constantine assumed control over the eastern half of the empire in 312 and built a second capital at Byzantium, a small Greek town on the Bosporus, which he named Constantinople (Constantine's city). As the western portion of the empire weakened, Constantinople became the "Second Rome" and gradually became the far more powerful, rich, and creative center of power.

In spite of his vision, Constantine did not immediately become a Christian. Unlike his father who had supported Christians, Constantine was a follower of Mithra, as were many of his army officers, and Constantine often shared the Mithraic resurrection feast with them. Even so, in 313 Constantine issued the Edict of Milan, which legalized Christianity throughout the empire and stated that Christians should be tolerated. Constantine also continued to issue coins imprinted with images of the sun god, and he dedicated his triumphal arch to the "Unconquered Sun." Constantine's inclusion of pagan forms is also evident in his order to create an image of the mother-goddess Cybele kneeling in prayer.

As the supreme political power, Constantine not only strengthened the new faith but also conferred major economic and political benefits on the Christian community. He ordered that land confiscated from the Christian Church be returned. Moreover, he gave land to Christians and they began to build churches and cathedrals. He sponsored great basilica churches, such as Saint Peter's and San Giovanni in Laterano and the Church of Holy Sepulchre in Jerusalem. He took church land and the clergy off the tax rolls, exempted many average Christians from paying taxes, and directed that Christians should receive jobs and enjoy other advantages. However, in a significant move toward identifying an "orthodox" Christianity, he was careful to stipulate that these benefits be offered only to "ministers of the lawful and most holy Catholic Religion."[48]

Constantine allowed bishops to decide legal matters that affected church personnel and their decisions became law, and he declared Sunday a public day of rest for all. Constantine also elevated Christians over Jews and ordered that any Jew who forcibly prevented other Jews from converting to Christianity would be burned alive. Constantine's actions brought the Christian church wealth and the ability to expand its membership and power. However, he probably waited to reveal that he was a Christian until he was dying. He may not have wanted to risk offending the local gods and other followers.

Throughout the first three centuries of the Common Era, the different Christian groups continued preaching their own interpretations of church doctrine and arguing over who had the correct understanding of the faith. But as local versions were maturing into schools, many church leaders wanted to establish a single orthodox interpretation, and they developed the concept of heresies: incorrect ideas that should be persecuted.

The desire to establish one orthodox statement of the faith may have been nurtured by Zoroastrian radical dualism, which made it difficult to accept compromise and ambiguities, and also by the tradition of Plato and Aristotle that assumed there was one universal truth that humans could discern. Christians did not want the church to splinter into countless small sects, and they probably believed that having a consistent message would strengthen their ability to compete with local beliefs, particularly the deep-seated commitment to polytheism. In any case, unlike Buddhists leaders, the church hierarchy tried to establish a common core of Christian belief and create an official canon that would apply to all Christians everywhere.

WHO WAS JESUS?   Perhaps the most contentious issue was the true nature of Jesus. By the fourth century, the idea that Jesus had a dual nature, both human and divine, had attracted the most converts. However, a crisis surfaced when Arius (c. 250–336), a well-known teacher and priest in Alexandria, openly proclaimed that Jesus was neither human nor divine, but a demigod placed somewhere between God and humans. His followers were known as Arians. Athanasius (296–373), bishop of Alexandria, insisted that Jesus was the same substance as God, coequal and coeternal, "of one being with God the Father." As a way to eliminate the seeming duality of God/Christ, Athanasius argued for the concept of the Holy Trinity: the unity of God the Father, God the Son, and God the Holy Spirit.

In 325, Constantine convened the Council of Bishops at Nicaea to establish the nature of Jesus once and for all. About 318 attended, and decisions were to be made by majority rule. Christian patriarchs from Rome, Alexandria, Jerusalem, and Antioch, as well as elders of the cults of Mithra, Tammuz, Oannes (Dagon), Ceres, Janus, Bacchus, Apollo, Osiris, Jupiter, and Constantine's personal deity, Sol Invictus, all attended. Constantine wanted all religions to be united into one "catholic" universal church that would include not only Christianity but as many of the Roman religions as possible.

A majority of the delegates voted to condemn Arius and affirm the Holy Trinity. The Council also issued a statement of belief that became known as the Nicene Creed, which is still used in most Christian communities. All Christians were required to accept the Creed or face excommunication, even though it made heretics not only of Aries and his followers, but of about half the Christians in the empire at the time.

No wonder Roman Catholics call Athanasius the "Father of Orthodoxy." He insisted that the church be the only source for interpreting the meaning and intention of each word of scripture. He also convinced the church leaders to accept 27 books as official scripture: The four Gospels, the Acts of the Apostles, and numerous letters to young churches were officially adopted as the "New Testament" that the vast majority of Christian churches use today.

With the completion of the New Testament around 360, the Ortho-dox position was secure. In the Gospel of Matthew, Jesus is presented as the Jewish Messiah. In Luke he is the universal savior of all people. But later, in the Gospel of John, Jesus is the eternal Christ, coterminus with God, who stated, "Before Abraham was, I am." The Acts of the Apostles and Paul's letters to the fledgling churches, which compose the majority of the New Testament, reveal how Christian theology was being practiced. Excluded from the official collection are any of the more mystical gospels associated with Gnosticism.

After the Council of Nicaea, many of the early strands of Christian-ity were labeled heresies and ruthlessly persecuted, not unlike the way Roman authorities had persecuted Christians a short time before. Constantine supported the suppression of heretics, even though his own son, who was the successor to the throne, was an Arian. He forbade members of heretical sects from meeting in private homes and required them to give their church buildings and other common property to "catholic" churches that followed the dictates of Nicaea.

It was a short step from Constantine's recognition of Christianity's right to exist to Emperor Theodosius' proclamation in 380 that Chris-tianity was the official religion of the empire. He ordered statues of other gods destroyed and made it an act of treason to practice any other religion. Perhaps most importantly, he allowed the church to establish its own courts and conduct trials, according it increased power quite independent of the political authority of the empire.

CHRISTIANITY REACHES NUBIA AND AXUM

Even before Christianity became the official religion of the Roman Empire, Christians were carrying the Good News to Africa. The Acts of the Apostles describes how Philip, one of the apostles, met "an Ethiopian eunuch, a court official of the Candace, queen of the Ethiopians, in charge of her entire treasury." The official was secretly reading about the prophet Isaiah in the Bible and he asked Philip to explain the text and then to baptize him (Acts 8:27–38). Because the eunuch came from Meroe in the Upper Nile valley where queens were called Candaces, this passage sug-gests that Christianity was spreading south in Egypt at a very early date.

Christianity reached Axum and Ethiopia during the period of harsh persecutions of Christians that Emperor Dioletian had initiated. Axum encompassed an area of the Upper Nile valley east of Meroe. The kings of Axum accepted Christianity at about the same time that Emperor Con-stantine made Christianity legal in the Roman Empire and probably with the same trepidation lest they offend the local gods.

Trade was a key to Axum's strength, and the city was linked through Red Sea ports to the Mediterranean and the Indian Ocean. Sometime around 320 C.E., two shipwrecked sailors returning from India were given shelter by the king; the elder sailor, Frumentius, soon became the tutor for the princes who ruled as co-kings until about 365 C.E. Frumentius was instrumental in the spread of Christianity in Axum. He publicly baptized the young kings and other members of the royal family, and King Ezana proclaimed Coptic Christianity the official religion.

It was not only Frumentius and his close relationship with the two young kings that account for the spread of Coptic Christianity in Axum. Improving trade opportunities may have been a strong motivation. The Axumite rulers might have hoped that promoting Christianity would result in increased trade between Axum, Constantinople, and other important Christian centers.

Although King Ezana's actions made the Axumites nominal Christians, probably few of his subjects knew anything about the faith or had any chance to participate in its rituals. Christianity did not spread beyond the court until 480, when several missionary monks introduced monasteries, and from there Christianity spread into the countryside. In the fourth and fifth centuries, the northern regions of Africa were among the most devoutly Christian areas in the world.

NESTORIAN CHRISTIANS SPREAD CHRISTIANITY EASTWARD

Although Athanasius had been persuasive at Nicaea, the debate over the nature of Jesus was far from settled. Christians, inspired by the conflicting views of the patriarchs of Alexandria and Antioch, could not agree on this issue. Some argued that the Nicene Creed made Jesus two realities—one human and one divine—and they asked, "What happened to the single unity that is God? How could Jesus be wholly divine and wholly human and still be one?"

In the fifth century, the debate crystallized over the question of whether Mary was the "Mother of God" or the "Mother of man." Nestorius, the patriarch of Constantinople, openly argued that Jesus had two distinct and separate aspects, human and divine. God was the source of his divine nature, and Mary, his mother, of his human nature. Therefore, Nestorius maintained, Mary was not the Mother of God, because she had given birth only to his human aspect. As a compromise, he suggested calling her the "Mother of Christ," but many Christians were accustomed to using "Mother of God," and they turned against Nestorius.

Cyril, then patriarch of Alexandria, led the attack against Nestorius and his followers and publicly accused him of denying the divinity of

Jesus. To resolve the question, the Pope assembled a council at Ephesus in 431. After locking Nestorius's supporters out of the meeting, the proponents of the single nature of Jesus Christ voted unanimously that Nestorius was a heretic and excommunicated him.

Although the followers of Nestorius lost the official debate, Nestorianism continued to spread. Syrian followers had been trying to spread Christianity within the Sasanid Empire that controlled Persia from 226 to 651. The Sasanids had made Zoroastrianism the state religion, although a new faith taught by Mani was also gaining support. In spite of this competition, the Syrian Church had developed a sophisticated organization, and in 484 it adopted the Nestorian version of Christianity. Nestorians were largely responsible for sending missionaries to Central and East Asia, and they spread Nestorianism wherever they traveled. As the Syrian church spread to the east, it was known as the "Persian" Church.

DESERT FATHERS, MOTHERS, AND THE FIRST MONASTERIES

No matter what version of Christianity one accepted, most Christians continued to live in society, performing their jobs, getting married, and raising a family. A significant minority, however, felt they could not live Christian lives if they stayed in society, so they dropped out and lived alone, isolated from all distractions, and devoted their lives to prayer and meditation.

Renunciation was not a new idea. As early as 900 B.C.E., some Hindus were renouncing the world to live in the forest, to practice austerities, to meditate, and to become one with the Divine. The Buddha had renounced his princely life and followed a similar path in search of enlightenment. Some of the Hindus and Buddhists who were living in West Asia during Jesus' lifetime practiced meditation and renunciation. Moreover, Jewish Essenes had also dropped out of society, and Jesus knew of their teachings and may even have participated in their community.

Many of the first Christians who renounced society went to live in the desert in Egypt. They were called "hermits" (from the Greek word for desert) and are known in Christian history as the "Desert Fathers and Mothers." By the fourth century, an impressive number of them were living alone, sometimes in caves. These ascetics often practiced self-flagellation and even mutilation of their bodies. By the fourth century some of the men began joining together in communities of monks. Basil (330–379) was one of the first to organize them into monasteries and he wrote down the first guidelines for monastic life. Asking the lonely hermits, "Whose feet have you washed?" Basil urged them to serve others,

FIGURE 3-2   THE BENEDICTINE MONASTERY AT MONTE CASINO, ITALY
This monastery is one of the oldest and most important monasteries in the Roman
Catholic religion.

and service became the hallmark of many monastic orders. In 529 an
Italian patrician named Benedict founded a community for monks north
of Naples. Benedict's rules also stressed obedience, labor, and devotion,
and Benedictine monks were probably the major agents for the spread
of Christianity to Europe.

With the rise of monasteries in the fifth and sixth centuries, the
Sisters of Christ, not unlike Buddhist women nearly a thousand years
earlier, formed communal orders for cloistered women called nuns. Both
male and female monastic orders copied the family structure. Titles that
indicated the monks' status in the monastery included father and brother
and, for nuns, mother and sister and bride of Christ.

LAY CHRISTIANS AND THE SECULAR CLERGY

Monks and nuns were not the only people who longed to turn away
from society and live a Christian life. Melanias the Elder was born in 342
into one of the richest families in Rome. Her father was both a senator
and a Christian. Melania grew up as a very pious Christian and at age
30, she left for Palestine where she spent 27 years caring for pilgrims,
reading, and praying. She also gave money to found a monastery on the
Mount of Olives. By the time she returned to Rome in 399, she was
famous throughout the Christian world.

Her granddaughter, Melania the Younger, was the only heir to her
family's palace in Rome and their estates in Iberia, Africa, Britain, and

Gaul. Her annual income was about 1,600 pounds of pure gold. She decided to sell all the property, free the family's 8,000 slaves, and donate the proceeds to buy monasteries for monks and nuns whom she provided with generous stipends. The family also gave their expensive clothing, jewels, and other belongings to churches and monasteries and used their silver to build church altars.[49]

Early Christianity, like Buddhism, struggled to work out a satisfactory relationship between those who wanted to withdraw from society and the laity who wanted to marry, have families, and succeed in worldly matters. Tensions between the religious and secular life led to the development of two types of clergy: the regular clergy, who lived in monasteries removed from the pressures of society, and the secular clergy, who performed the rituals in parish churches and tended to the needs of their parishioners. These dual functions provided a practical solution for serving both the spiritual and physical aspects of human experience.

MAKING SENSE OUT OF THE DISINTEGRATION OF THE ROMAN EMPIRE

The division of the Roman Empire in 395 had significantly weakened the western half. As Rome's resources dwindled, its power slipped away and waves of nomads threatened. The government had few resources to back its currency and could not collect taxes. As a result, it could not pay a standing army to maintain order, protect against invasions, or provide services to its subjects. Disease, climatic changes, and the destructive nature of the Germanic invaders all combined to undermine the cohesion of the western half of the Roman Empire.

It is not clear just what role Christianity played in this process. By exempting some Christians and church land from taxation, Emperor Constantine certainly increased the tax burden on others. Moreover, after he made Christianity legal, larger numbers of people became Christians, and many withdrew from society.

Part of the incentive for withdrawing may have been the insecurity and anxiety that accompanied the disintegration of Rome's power. In this era of decline, Augustine of Hippo, in North Africa, who lived from 354 to 430, became perhaps the most gifted and influential of all the church leaders. Faced with the catastrophic sack of Rome in 410 by invading Germanic warriors, Augustine wrote *The City of God*. Separating secular life in Rome from the eternal City of God in heaven, Augustine argued that no human institution could ever be a true expression of God's will. People, said Augustine, must cultivate their spiritual dimension but at the same time support imperfect human institutions. His assurance that faith and love were the best routes to salvation and his scholarly presentation of grace (God's unconditional love) resonated with average people facing impending disaster. Many in and around Rome put their faith in the "City of God" rather than in Rome or any actual city. By 476, the Roman state was so weak that its leaders were forced to accept the German Odoacer as emperor, marking the end of the western Roman Empire.

CONSTANTINOPLE AND BYZANTIUM

The experience in the eastern half of what had been the Roman Empire was quite different from that of the declining western half. As Rome's power weakened, Constantinople became the source of imperial authority throughout the region that became known as the Byzantium Empire, or Byzantium. The Byzantines referred to themselves as "Romans."

From the fourth century onward, Byzantium maintained an increasingly strong and unified political system, supported by prosperous trade, a well-trained and highly motivated army, an efficient bureaucracy, and a strong tax base. Popular factions—the Blues and the Greens—were a characteristic feature of Byzantine life, and their competitions took place in the hippodrome (circus). Emperors used public opinion to bolster their authority and edicts, but popular support proved volatile and fickle. Emperor Justinian I (527–565) played a major role in solidifying the Byzantine Empire's authority. His military campaigns regained significant Roman territory that had been lost to invading Germanic groups, and under his leadership Byzantium achieved its greatest territorial expansion.

Byzantium was a theocracy with Christianity as its official religion. As a result, Christianity became the dominant religion from Anatolia through the Nile Valley. The Byzantine emperor served as God's deputy on earth, the head of both church and state. He often made decisions on church doctrine, and anyone who opposed him was guilty of blasphemy. The Byzantine aristocracy, a self-confident and splendor-loving group of land owners and government servants, embraced Christianity and the empire, ruled by God's chosen vicar.

After the Nika Riots in 532 that destroyed much of Constantinople, Justinian supervised the construction of many new churches, most notably Hagia Sophia, one of the most beautiful churches in the world. For many centuries, Constantinople was the richest, most beautiful, and most cultivated city in Europe and one of the largest in the world. Art was used to convey imperial and religious authority, and the magnificent imperial palace that contained a Christian shrine and many precious relics symbolized the ruler's dual authority.

The Byzantine emperor appointed patriarchs who oversaw all religious matters, and they were directly responsible to him. The relationship between patriarch and emperor was of utmost importance. These two leaders often competed, but they also realized they must cooperate. The "Kiss of Peace" they exchanged at the consecration of Hagia Sophia symbolized their cooperation.

THE GROWING SEPARATION OF THE ROMAN AND EASTERN CHURCHES

In the wake of the power vacuum left by the collapse of Rome's political authority, the Roman Catholic Church[50] attempted to establish itself as the dominant force in Western Europe. The title "pope," from "father," originally referred to any respected individual, but gradually it came to refer exclusively to the patriarch of Rome. That office took on special significance in 440 when Pope Leo (d. 461) argued that his direct succession from St. Peter established his ultimate authority. Leo's fame also resulted from the manner in which he had handled the nomad threat. In 452 Attila and his Hun forces defeated the Roman legions and threatened to destroy Rome. Leo rode out of the defenseless city to meet Attila. No one knows exactly what transpired between the two leaders, but Attila turned away and died soon after. Three years later, Leo also convinced the Vandal chief not to burn Rome.

The Church Council in 381 that had outlawed Arianism and affirmed Catholic Christianity also declared that the patriarchs of Constantinople and Jerusalem had equal authority. Theoretically that was true of all five patriarchs. However, from Leo's time onward, the office of pope grew in stature, and he became the ultimate authority over the Roman Catholic Church. By the late fifth century, the pope had greatly enhanced his authority in the western provinces. By contrast, as Constantinople's political power increased, its emperors, not the patriarchs, were the ones exerting influence over the Byzantine or Eastern Orthodox Church. Emperors and patriarchs of Constantinople were vying for supremacy in church matters with the Roman papacy, alternately fighting, parting, and reconciling.

CHRISTIANITY SPREADS TO IRELAND AND WESTERN EUROPE

With the disintegration of Roman power, the Roman Catholic Church became the only major institution capable of carrying traditional knowledge and services to a vast area of the mostly non-urban, illiterate peoples in western Europe. Monks were the church's most important missionaries. Priests and bishops established courts, controlled elections of city officials, distributed public funds, and provided food and other services to the needy. Monks established cloister schools in their monasteries and it was from these simple schools that aspects of Greco-Roman learning were transmitted to Europe.

In the fourth century, through a series of improbable events, Patrick (385–461) brought the Christian message to Ireland. After that, Christian monasteries spread quickly over remote Irish islands and coastal hills, and a cathedral was constructed in 444. Like Buddhist monasteries in China at about the same time, these monasteries gradually acquired significant land, and towns grew up around them. Irish monasteries also became important educational centers, and because their instruction was superior to anything in Europe at that time, many students from the mainland went to Ireland to study. Besides teaching Christian texts, the monasteries gave instruction in Greek and Roman classics and included mathematics and science in their curricula. From Ireland, monks actively sought to convert the British Isles and take their message to the European mainland. However, popes thought Irish missionaries were straying from orthodox doctrine.

Earlier in the fourth century, Christian missionaries began to take the Good News to Germanic tribes that were trying to adjust to a sedentary lifestyle in western Europe. Between the fifth and eighth centuries, missionaries worked to spread Roman Christianity among tribes of Celts, Anglo Saxons, Franks, West and East Goths, and Lombards. The missionaries concentrated on converting political leaders, especially kings, because leaders brought their followers with them into the church. Some leaders welcomed being associated with Rome's former glory and hoped that association would confer legitimacy on them, not unlike Northern Wei nomadic leaders who embraced Buddhism at about the same time. Missionaries tried to convince Germanic "barbarians" that if they wanted to become part of the "civilized" world, they must give up their polytheistic beliefs and accept Christianity and be baptized.

To enhance their authority, nomadic leaders drew upon existing tribal loyalties and appealed to their ethnic heritage. They also realized that if they were to expand their power, they had to convince their subjects to enlarge their loyalty. Christianity offered an identity that tended to ameliorate potentially divisive tribal loyalties and could be applied to an expanding political loyalty. Moreover, Christianity's nonviolent message might promote greater social stability and be a check on the almost constant tribal warfare.

Theoretically, converting kings meant their subjects also became Christians. In reality, few subjects, like those in Axum, understood what that meant or grasped the fact that their faith had changed. Sometimes they were required to be baptized and to participate in Christian rituals, but they continued to cling to their earlier beliefs and rituals and their daily lives changed little. Paradoxically, that helps explain both the intolerance of many missionaries who feared the converts would quickly slip back to their old beliefs as well as why so many local beliefs and rituals crept into Christianity.

Germanic groups were polytheistic, so at first spreading monotheism was especially difficult. To eliminate polytheistic practices, Christian missionaries often destroyed images of local gods and goddesses, burned sacred groves, and forbade the so-called pagan rituals. Religious intolerance, coupled with a commitment to one orthodox set of beliefs, led to the use of expulsions, excommunication, inquisitions, and heresy trials, all designed to stamp out polytheism and impose a single orthodox system of belief.

At the same time, to win the hearts of the local people, Christians gradually appropriated local cultural forms and adapted them to the new faith. In Ireland, local deities that had been called on to prevent illness and protect towns and travelers were reincarnated as Christian saints. For example, Brigid, an all-powerful and ever-helpful local goddess, became identified with Saint Bridget, a Christian saint, and her festival was celebrated on the same day as Brigid's had been. Sacred pagan sites, including wells and springs, gradually became Christian holy places, and Germanic reverence for trees and light worked its way into Christian practices such as decorating Christmas trees. These adaptations made it easier for the Germanic groups to move from their earlier faith to Christianity even when they had little understanding of its beliefs or theology.

Initially, Arianism attracted a great many converts because many Germanic leaders who were drawn to Christianity and the status it brought did not want to be identified too closely with Rome. Joining the "Arian" wing of Christianity, which the Roman Catholic Church considered a heresy, allowed them to become Christians without being seen as heirs to the Roman Empire.

The Franks, by far the most organized and aggressive of the Germanic tribes, created a small kingdom in present-day France. Clovis (481–511), the first significant Frankish chieftain, had the foresight to try to blend both Germanic and Roman elements and encourage intermarriage. In a dramatic victory for the Roman Catholic Church and a severe blow to Arianism, Clovis converted to Roman Christianity around 495. Because he was a major political leader among Germanic settlers and the founder of a successful royal line, Clovis's conversion formed the basis for the spread of the Roman Catholic Church in western Europe.

By the end of the sixth century much of western Europe, the Nile valley, and Axum, as well as Byzantium, had become part of a general cultural ethos called Christendom. The people in these areas shared a coherent worldview and accepted a common set of Christian values from an understanding of the universe down to the intimate dimensions of personal life. Further, within Christendom there were no serious conflicts between science, humanism, and faith because the church controlled knowledge in all these areas. To be accepted as a full and functioning member of society, one had to be baptized into the Christian faith. Anyone who was excommunicated lost other rights as well. Outsiders, such as Jews, pagans, and dissidents from accepted Christian teaching, were effectively marginalized from mainstream community life.

THE WIDENING SCHISM BETWEEN EAST AND WEST

POPES AND PATRIARCHS

Within Christendom, however, tensions between the Roman Catholic Church and the Byzantine Church, also identified as the Eastern Orthodox or Greek Orthodox Church, continued to escalate. The Roman Catholic Church relied on Latin as its official language both for translations of the Bible and the language of the Mass, while the Eastern Orthodox Church used Greek as its official language. A major cause of the widening schism, however, was the struggle for power between the patriarch of Constantinople and the pope of Rome. The Roman Catholic Church balked when the Fourth Ecumenical Council in 451 agreed that the patriarch of Constantinople was equal in status to the pope. However, the Eastern Orthodox leaders maintained that there was no biblical evidence that Peter had been appointed the first pope, which the Roman Church maintained, and therefore no justification for the pope being the supreme head of the church.

In the seventh and eighth centuries, renewed nomadic threats and the advances of Muslim Arab forces threatened eastern Christendom, and the two churches became increasingly isolated from each other. Attacks from Slavs, Avars, Bulgars, and Muslims gradually diminished Byzantium's territory and effectively isolated Byzantium from western Europe. Because the Bulgars and Ayars had conquered land between the western and eastern parts of Christendom, Byzantine subjects had to travel by sea to reach Rome, and vice versa. Bulgars and Turks were threatening Anatolia, and Muslim forces twice laid siege to Constantinople. In addition, Muslim forces had conquered Antioch, Alexandria, and Jerusalem, leaving only two patriarchies: Constantinople and Rome. At the same time Charlemagne's campaigns in western Europe were threatening to further isolate Constantinople.

THE DEBATE OVER RELICS

A debate about icons in the eighth and ninth centuries increased tensions between the two branches of the church. This time, the issue was over divine intercession in human affairs: Did relics or icons provide the best access to God? At stake as well was the question of where ultimate religious authority lay.

No ritual element contributed more to Christianity's success in Europe than the Cult of Saints and the special power of the relics, such as bones, teeth, fingernails, or strands of hair, that were associated with them. Many early church leaders had been declared saints, and church officials collected their relics and welcomed popular worship at their graves. Bishops used relics to build loyalty and commitment in local communities. Churchmen even dug up the graves of earlier saints hoping to find relics,[51] and parishes stole relics from other churches and reburied them as their own.

The growing veneration of saints was associated with a changing view of the afterlife. The first Christians tended to regard death as polluting, and cemeteries were established far from town centers. However, by the late fourth century, the church had worked out ways that dead saints could intervene with God to help believers attain immortality in heaven. Instead of inspiring fear, burial sites became hallowed ground and a focus of church life. Saints functioned like Mahayana Buddhism's bodhisattvas, and their relics transformed the fear of death into the hope of eternal life in heaven. Heroes and saints were buried underneath churches or in graveyards adjacent to churches. By 500, tombs of saints had become regular pilgrimage sites, and veneration of saints proved to be a major factor in the spread of Christianity throughout Europe.

Further to the east the Byzantine Church also venerated saints, but instead of relics, their worship focused on the adoration of icons: images of Jesus, Mary, and saints that were believed to have spiritual powers. These icons symbolized divine protection. Believers told how, by merely touching an icon, they had miraculously been cured. Merchants hung icons in their shops to protect their goods, and soldiers carried them into battle. The gaze from an icon allowed the worshiper to communicate directly with the saint. Bishops argued that "simple folk" needed them, and that icons helped remind believers of the full humanity of Christ.

In the eighth century as Muslim armies advanced against Byzantium, the icons Christian soldiers in Anatolia carried seemed unable to protect them from Muslim advances, so some Christians lost faith in the icons. After all, Muslims who did not have icons were winning. Others defended their beloved icons.

Despite the deeply honored place that icons had enjoyed, in 730 the Byzantine emperor Leo III (717–741) issued a decree banning them. It stated that the cross, which symbolized the resurrection of Christ, and the Eucharist (the Mass), should be the most important objects of veneration and aspects of worship. Emperor Leo may have been influenced by the Muslim ban on images as well as the Biblical commandment forbidding the worship of "graven images." He may have hoped that exerting his authority over the church in this matter would help restore some of the imperial authority that Muslim expansion was eroding. Moreover, worship of icons that the church had not properly consecrated threatened the church's authority and blurred boundaries between the sacred and profane.

Offended because Emperor Leo III had made this important religious decision on his own, Pope Gregory II refused to accept Leo's iconoclastic doctrines, and his successor, Pope Gregory III, convened a council that openly condemned the "iconoclastic" edict. (Iconoclasm, which initially meant destroying icons, now refers to anyone who tries to destroy familiar ideas and symbols.)

Many Byzantine Christians were also angered by the ban on icons, and arguments raged for more than a hundred years. The Second Nicene Council, called in 787 by Emperor Constantine V's daughter-in-law Irene, reversed the ban and tried to reinstate the use of icons. But when iconoclasm erupted in Byzantium again later in the eighth century, it had a great deal of popular support. Finally, in 843 Empress Theodora, trying to reconcile the factions, reinstated the Second Nicene Council's position allowing icons. Slowly they were restored to their central place in worship.

Two empresses, Irene and Theodora, were instrumental in restoring the veneration of icons. Whether or not women respond better to images, icons, even when they had not been properly consecrated, were important in household worship. Women might well have wanted to be left alone to decide how they would worship, especially within the privacy of their own homes.

THE FRANKS AND CHARLEMAGNE

Emperors, popes, and empresses were not the only ones involved in the iconoclastic controversy and the wider issue of church and imperial authority. The Franks, who occupied much of present-day France and northwestern Germany, were struggling to find a proper balance between the authority of the pope and the growing power of their kingdom.

In 768, Charlemagne (Charles the Great) gained control of the Frankish kingdom that had converted to Christianity under Clovis, and his rule lasted until 814. In an effort to unite his subjects within a single cultural and administrative system, Charlemagne tried to introduce a common coinage and language as well as standard weights and measures. Under his leadership, the church provided community centers for peasants, drafted contracts, aided the poor, protected the weak, nursed the sick, and provided a rough form of law and social justice and performed marriage ceremonies.

Although the vast majority of people in his kingdom, including Charlemagne himself, could not read or write, Charlemagne encouraged churches to sponsor cloister schools to train literate priests and to maintain monasteries in which monks carefully copied major texts, especially the Bible. He invited Irish monks and scholars trained in Muslim science and mathematics and Greek and Roman philosophy to his court. Despite these efforts, the level of learning remained very low, and the majority of even the wealthiest aristocrats were illiterate.

In reality, Charlemagne's kingdom was only loosely held together and contained no large cities. However, his actions were transforming western Europe—which had been a backward, undeveloped area—into a military power that both the Byzantine emperor in Constantinople, the political leaders in Christendom, and the Roman papacy would have to confront. Perhaps as a means of establishing his authority, Charlemagne proposed marriage to the Byzantine empress Irene. Byzantium's recognition of Charlemagne's growing influence is symbolized by the fact that Irene might have accepted Charlemagne's proposal had it not caused her subjects to oust her.

Well aware that the papacy was threatened by Lombards, Muslims, and Byzantines, Pope Leo III (795–816) decided to cast his lot with Charlemagne. In hopes of exerting the church's authority over Charlemagne, even if only symbolically, Leo invited Charlemagne to Rome and on Christmas day 800, he personally placed the crown on Charlemagne's head and prostrated at the new emperor's feet, a custom associated with Roman emperors. Charlemagne was furious that the pope had crowned him. Why was the pope claiming ritual authority over him? Charlemagne said afterward that had he known about the pope's plan, he would have boycotted the celebration.

By crowning Charlemagne, Pope Leo III was undermining the concept of the unity of the Roman/Byzantine Empire. Moreover, Charlemagne's coronation as emperor signaled that Europe was becoming a rival to both Byzantine and Islamic power. It also ushered in a long tradition of both cooperation and competition between the Roman Catholic Church and political sovereigns in Europe. Each institution used the other in the hope of elevating its own status. Kings could offer the church armies, land, and relative order; the church could provide legitimacy for would-be rulers and provide a myriad of services for the king's subjects. Frankish leaders gave the church protection against the Lombards and any expansionist designs that the Byzantine emperor might entertain. Charlemagne and his successors also felt the relationship would help meld a homogeneous population out of the many divisive clans and tribal loyalties across Europe.

The crowning of Charlemagne was only one example of the Roman Catholic Church's growing political power. Besides owning a vast amount of land, bishops were deeply involved in secular affairs. They advised nobles and church officials and acted as judges in trials. They required believers to tithe, which meant giving 10 percent of their income to the church. Carolingian kings and nobles gave the clergy stipends, financed the copying of manuscripts, and supported monasteries. Educated church leaders provided literacy, scientific knowledge, a history, and other trappings of civilization. In return, local warriors and chieftains allowed the church to benefit from their military conquests.

Meanwhile, after the ban on icons was lifted, Byzantium entered a period of renewed intellectual activity: More books were available, including classical works, the result in part of a new script that was easier to copy. Anatolia became semi-independent and was divided into *themes,* military units from which men could be conscripted for the army at any time.

With the precedent of the Roman Catholic Church's deep political involvement with the political powers of western Europe, the schism between the western and eastern churches became irreparable. Although the formal break, initiated by disagreements over the role of the Holy Spirit, did not occur until 1054, by the ninth century, Christianity was already divided into the Eastern Orthodox Catholic Church and the Roman Catholic Church. (Today's Orthodox churches, which are very sacerdotal and mystical, are situated predominantly in Eastern Europe. Like Roman Catholicism, Orthodoxy claims a direct line of succession back to the original apostles, and both churches observe seven sacraments.)

CHRISTIANITY MOVES ACROSS ASIA

INDIA

At the start of the Common Era, an Egyptian pilot of a Roman ship figured out the pattern of the monsoon winds and wrote a sailor's manual that describes their role in navigation in the Indian Ocean. His discovery greatly facilitated travel across the Arabian Sea. The Greek geographer Strabo, who lived around the time of Jesus, reported that as many as 120 ships a year were sailing from Egypt to India.[52]

South Indian Christians believe that the apostle Thomas traveled by sea to India in 52 and established seven churches along the Malabar (western) coast and converted many of the local residents. According to a popular legend, Thomas was killed when he refused to worship the Goddess Kali. Indian churches still celebrate July 3 as the date of his martyrdom.

The Gospel of Thomas reports that Thomas reluctantly accepted Jesus' assignment to go to India. He may have been hired to help build a palace for King Gundaphar.[53] Thomas, in good Christian conscience, is reported to have distributed the building funds to the needy instead and to have told the monarch that he could see his palace after he died.

The Gospel of Thomas also reports that Thomas performed magic and miracles and, after convincing the king that he would live forever in heaven, Thomas was permitted to visit other parts of India and try to convert other princes and rulers. Finally reaching present-day Chennai (Madras) in South India, he converted the queen-to-be and convinced her to remain a virgin. As a result, her angry husband, the king, ordered Thomas executed. (When the Portuguese arrived in South India, they were told that the bones of Saint Thomas were interred in a church in Chennai. Believing that Thomas's remains should rest in a more Christian setting, the Portuguese transported them to Portugal.)

Recently discovered evidence suggests that Thomas could well have traveled to India, but the first tangible evidence of any Indian Christian communities in India is a small group of Nestorian Christian immigrants who settled in Southern India in about 350. Soon after, the Nestorian Christian Church, under Persian ecclesiastical authority, took root in India. It was composed mainly of Persians who used Syriac for their liturgy. There was a report of a Nestorian church in Sri Lanka in the sixth century and also Nestorian communities along the Malabar coast. Hindus identified the Christian community as a separate caste, evidence that Christianity was merging with the local Indian culture. They no doubt spoke Indian languages but continued to use Syriac in the liturgy to keep from being totally absorbed into Hindu culture.

FIGURE 3-3   JESUS STANDING ON LOTUS, ST. THOMAS CATHEDRAL, CHENNAI, INDIA

Note the many Hindu aspects of this statue of Jesus. The lotus is one of the most important Hindu and Buddhist symbols.

Indian Christians lived in separate communities near their churches, although they shared some Hindu customs. *Thoma Marga,* the Christian way of life that gradually developed in India, is a unique combination of Christian ethics and Hindu, Buddhist, Jain, Jewish, Persian, and local south Indian influences all mixed together. *Marga,* Sanskrit for "way," was a Hindu term that meant a pathway to moksha, but the term is commonly used in India to denote any path or means to the divine. By labeling Christianity a marga, the larger Hindu community seems to have accepted the Christian message as one of the many acceptable paths to the divine. Christians were called *margakkar* or *margavasi* ("those of the way").

Perhaps this easy tolerance helps explain why conversions to Christianity in India never reached significant numbers. The Nestorian Christian communities remained firmly within the larger Hindu tradition and culture, retaining caste membership and marrying within their castes. Believers focused their worship on images and continued to observe Hindu dietary practices.

Nestorian rites continued in Indian churches until the sixteenth century when Portuguese Roman Catholicism began to have a powerful impact in the subcontinent. At that time there were about 64 churches and perhaps only about 80,000 Catholic families scattered among 168 Christian villages. The Portuguese, representing Roman Catholicism, disapproved of the Nestorian elements they saw in Indian Christianity and insisted that the South Indian Christians revere the pope as the supreme head of their church.

KIEV AND RUSSIA

The spread of Christianity to present-day Russia was part of the general spread of Byzantine influence to eastern Europe. As trade developed between Kiev on the Dnieper River and Byzantium, an increasing number of Russians traveled to Constantinople. In about 862, the Byzantine emperor sent two brothers, Constantine (later called Cyril) and Methodius, as missionaries to Kevian Rus. They carried translations of the Bible in an alphabet of modified Greek characters adapted to the Greek language that Cyril had developed, and they provided scriptures and liturgy in the local languages. (The Cyrillic alphabet is still used in Russia and parts of eastern Europe.)

An organized Christian community existed at Kiev as early as the first half of the tenth century, and in 957, Olga, the regent of Kiev, was baptized in Constantinople. Olga's grandson Vladimir I (c. 956–1015) the prince of Kiev, considered several possible religious faiths for his people, including Roman Catholicism and Islam. Undoubtedly influenced by his Christian grandmother and by a proposed marriage alliance with the Byzantine imperial family, Vladimir chose Eastern Orthodox Christianity. After he was baptized in 988, he ordered mass baptism for all Kievans, although few of them had any idea about the new faith they were supposed to be adopting. As a result, many continued their earlier practices, which were gradually mixed with Christian doctrines and rituals.

Vladimir preferred the Eastern Orthodox version of Christianity for many reasons. The splendor of the Byzantine court bedazzled visitors from Kiev. They were deeply impressed with the rituals and wanted to become associated with all its grandeur. They appreciated the Eastern Church's acceptance of national languages for the liturgy and its willingness to have the scriptures translated. Vladimir may also have wanted to offset the influence of two strong political rivals, one of whom had chosen Judaism and the other that had instituted Islam. The Russians did not relish Islam's ban on alcohol, and Vladimir feared the power of the Roman Catholic pope. As a result, the fledgling state of Russia began to develop its own Christian institutions based on the Eastern Orthodox model.

Kiev soon become known as the "Jerusalem of Russia" and served as the center of the Christian religion throughout the Slavic region. Within 20 years, St. Sophia's Cathedral was constructed in Kiev, and Christian churches and monasteries were being built all over Russia. Church schools trained clergymen and upper-class children, and the church made provisions to take care of the needy. Metropolitans of Kiev (who after 1328 resided in Moscow) led the Russian Church, and the church hierarchy imitated much of Constantinople's bureaucracy and lavish rituals. Russian Christianity absorbed hundreds of local saints and enthusiastically adopted the use of icons as the centerpiece of popular worship.

The Mongols occupied Russia from the 1220s through the fifteenth century. The Mongols supported the Russian Church and freed it from taxation. By 1448, the Russian bishops were electing their own patriarchs without permission from the Orthodox Church, and the Russian Church became an independent body.

After the Turks conquered Constantinople in 1453 and Islam became the official religion of their empire, the Russians began referring to their kingdom as the "Third Rome." A monk in 1500 wrote the tsar: "Two Romes have fallen. The third stands. And there will not be a fourth. No one will replace your Christian Tsardom!"[54] After the fall of Byzantium, Russia became the most powerful Orthodox Christian state, and the tsars claimed to have succeeded the Byzantine emperor as the rightful ruler of Christendom.

Russia's conversion to Eastern Orthodox Christianity had many long-range effects. It brought Russia into the circle of European Christendom and made her a part of Western civilization and European culture. At the same time, because of the split in the Christian Church in 1054, accepting Eastern Orthodox Christianity isolated Russia from western Europe. The Russian Church remained dependent on Byzantine trade and commerce, and Russian culture was essentially Byzantine in nature.

CENTRAL ASIA

Greeks, Buddhism, Christianity, Zoroastrianism, Manichaeism, and later, Islam, all played a role in shaping the culture of central Asia. Nestorian Christianity, which spread out from monasteries along the silk roads, was the dominant Christian group. Its diaspora communities sheltered monks, merchants, and other travelers.

Sogdians who were living in the Ferghania valley were among the first central Asians to adopt Nestorian Christianity. The Sogdians, the source of "blood sweating horses" that the Chinese coveted, had a reputation as the sharpest traders in central Asia. Sogdian merchants were at home both in Persia and further to the east, and their language was used across the steppe lands. By the mid-seventh century, Sogdiana had a bishop at Samarkand, the major city in the area. Soon there were about 20 Nestorian bishops across central Asia. Because the Persians had advanced medicine, local people often went to their monasteries for medical care. Cemeteries with inscribed burial stones suggest that permanent, literate Christian communities were established.

Besides the Sogdians, Nestorians spread their version of Christianity among Turkish nomadic groups in the steppes. A group of Turks captured as slaves in 580 had crosses tattooed on their foreheads for protection. Periodically, Turkish groups sent requests for bishops, and there were churches in areas now identified as Uzbekistan, Kazakstan, and Tajikistan. Nestorian missionaries sought to convert nomadic chieftains in hopes that the chiefs would bring their followers into the faith.

The Nestorians successfully converted the Kerait and Naiman tribes, even though tribal members had trouble giving up eating meat and dairy products during Lent because normally that was all they ate. According to a letter written around 1000, 200,000 Kerait Turks accepted Christianity, at least nominally. The conversion of the Kerait leaders would later prove significant because they married their royal daughters to Mongol princes.

By the time of the Mongol advance during the thirteenth century, Nestorian Christianity was the largest religious presence in central Asia, although Buddhists, followers of Mani, and Muslims also attracted large numbers of adherents in the region. However, converting to Christianity did not greatly alter the life style of the steppe peoples. All that was required was a profession of faith and baptism. From most accounts, nomadic converts retained most of their earlier religious rituals and practices in which their cherished fermented mare's milk continued to play the central role.

NESTORIANS IN CHINA

Sogdian merchants introduced Nestorian Christianity, identified as the "Persian religion," to China during the early years of the Tang Dynasty (618–906). Many Chinese believed the Persians were the only civilized non-Chinese people, and their sophisticated astronomical and medical knowledge undoubtedly contributed to Christianity's warm welcome in China. So did the fact that initially the Chinese authorities probably thought that Christianity was a Buddhist sect.

A 10-foot high monument erected in 781 in Changan is an important source of information about "Rome Illustrious Religion" in China. A

Maltese cross resting on a Daoist cloud with a Buddhist lotus graces the top of the monument. Under the lotus, the so-called Eight Virtues, which are really the Buddhist Eightfold Path, are enumerated. The monument also has a summary of the Christian faith and tells of the visit of Alopen, a Nestorian monk who arrived in 635 carrying sutras and images. Emperor Taizong (626–649), one of the greatest Chinese emperors, invited him to the court and told him to translate the texts he had brought into Chinese.

Chinese scholars helped Alopen translate the *Jesus-Messiah-Sutra*, a free adaptation of the Christian message. Alopen was careful to point out that nothing in the text threatened Chinese values. He even used the familiar Buddhist term "Sutra" in the title and identified Jesus as "Buddha." Many of the Sutras demonstrate an ingenious blending of Christian and Buddhist concepts. For example:

> The other world can be found by doing acts of karma in this life, by living in this world. This world is like a mother's womb in which you are shaped for the world to come. All creatures should know that the karmic consequences of what is done in this life will shape the next life . . . (2 Sutra 4:16–22)[55]

After reading the scriptures, the emperor issued an edict proclaiming the virtues of the Nestorian faith and commissioned the building of a Nestorian monastery in the western quarter of the capital where Persian and central Asian traders lived. Nestorians installed portraits of Emperor Taizong on the walls of their churches, similar to portraits of Justinian that were painted on the walls of Byzantine churches. According to the monument, Nestorianism "spread throughout the ten provinces . . . [and] monasteries abound in a hundred cities." In reality, probably only about 12 monasteries were actually constructed, and perhaps there were never more than several thousand Chinese Christians.

Empress Wu (690–705), who became known as the "Heavenly Empress," vigorously supported Buddhism, and her patronage of Buddhists and Daoists greatly weakened the Christians. However, soon after, Xuanzong (712–756), one of the most popular of all Chinese emperors, ordered the Nestorian monasteries repaired, welcomed a new delegation of priests, and received a bishop who started a new Nestorian church for foreign merchants living in Canton. Xuanzong also rewarded the Nestorians for helping him crush the An Lushan rebellion. By the end of the eighth century, the Nestorians were becoming absorbed into Chinese culture, using Chinese in their services, and attracting some Chinese converts.

The Tang's policy of religious toleration was evident to an eighth century visitor to Turfan, an important city on the silk roads. He noticed

FIGURE 3-4   NESTORIAN PILLAR AT XIAN, CHINA
This Nestorian pillar contains Buddhist and Daoist symbols as well as a Christian cross.
The text describes the early history of Nestorianism in China.

a mosque, a Buddhist monastery, and a Nestorian church in the same
general location. Most Chinese did not think the various religions were
contending for a single truth or demanding an exclusive following, and
they were tolerant of the many faiths.

During the later years of the Tang Dynasty, however, the territorial
expansion and cultural openness that had characterized early Tang rule

shifted dramatically. During the all-out attack on Buddhism that the emperor launched in 843, other religions that could be labeled foreign also suffered. Christianity and Zoroastrianism were banned, and their foreign leaders were expelled from China. As many as 3,000 of their monks and priests had to return to secular life.

Christianity in China never fully recovered. The few Christian communities became quite sinofied and lost their distinctive Christian identity. Christian merchants traveling to China failed to establish new Christian communities. An Arab in Baghdad in 987 reported that a monk who had gone with a delegation to determine the status of Christianity in China could not find a single Christian there.[56]

By 1279, when the Mongols conquered China and established the Yuan Dynasty, there were small groups of Christians throughout the empire and along the southern seacoast. Marco Polo estimated there were probably only about 1,000–2,000 Christians in cities that had populations of perhaps half a million, and most of them were isolated and unsure of their own history.

The Mongols were remarkably tolerant of all religions. Kublai Khan's mother Sorghaktani, a talented and intelligent woman, was a Nestorian princess. Kublai's protection of the Nestorians no doubt stemmed in part from his wish to honor her memory. In 1289 Kublai established an office of Christian affairs, and in 1291 he selected Isa (Arabic for Jesus), a Syrian Christian, to fill the post and also serve as a minister at court. George ("Korguz" in Turkish), a faithful member of the Nestorian Church, married Kublai Khan's granddaughter. When George gave his life in 1298 in defense of the Grand Khan, the Nestorians were rewarded for their loyalty and given positions with the Mongols, and Nestorians were influential for several generations.

The spread of Christianity across central Asia to India and China followed the pattern Paul had established centuries earlier. Many of the missionaries settled for a simple confession of faith and baptism, leaving converts free to continue their familiar rituals, so Chinese practices continued and foreign Christianity became increasingly sinofied. The Christian impact in this huge area was minimal. Although the Nestorians were active in China, their influence was small compared to Buddhism.

SOMALIA AND ETHIOPIA

As Roman Catholic Christians were solidifying their influence in Europe, and the Nestorians were finding converts in central Asia and China, the Ethiopian Church continued its relationship with the Christian patriarch of Alexandria until 1323 when the Muslims, who had established a dynasty in Egypt, cut them off from any contact with the patriarch of Alexandria. After 1450, Nubia became entirely Muslim.

In response to Muslim pressure to the north, Ethiopia established a series of dynasties and tried to promote their remembered Semitic past. Ethiopians increased their pilgrimages to the Holy Land, and in 1189 several churches in Jerusalem were designated for them. King Lalibela, who ruled in the early thirteenth century, is known for the 11 churches that were constructed during his reign. Unlike most buildings, these churches were started at the top and made by cutting down into solid rock.

In 1270, the Solomonids established a dynasty that they traced back to King Solomon and Makeda, the Queen of Sheba. According to their national epic, Makeda had visited King Solomon's court in the tenth century B.C.E. and adopted his religion. The Solomonids claim she gave birth to King Solomon's son, whom the king later recognized and crowned king of Ethiopia. A uniquely Ethiopian synthesis of the earlier monastic influence and the Solomonid traditions gradually developed. In the fourteenth century, the Ethiopians were ruling the only Christian state in Africa.

By 1200, Christianity in Asia and Africa had receded greatly. Aside from a brief period under the Mongols in China, the number of Christians from west Asia to the borders of China had been reduced as Islam spread through the region. Meanwhile, Roman Catholic Christianity in Europe was entering a more prosperous age as it increased its trade and built towns that could support a more vigorous intellectual and cultural life.

CHRISTIANITY MATURES IN EUROPE, 1000–1550

When compared to conditions in the Byzantine and Muslim empires, Europeans in the eighth to tenth centuries were living in a sparsely populated, illiterate, and relatively poor agricultural society. With the breakup of Charlemagne's kingdom after 843, any semblance of centralized political control in Europe vanished. In this vacuum, local landlords hired soldiers to guard their estates, and farmers, fleeing the insecurity of the countryside, moved to these estates for protection, marking the beginning of European feudalism. For the next 200 years, Viking and Magyar nomadic invaders spread a cloud of fear over Europe and undermined attempts to secure a social order and build a vibrant society.

By 1000, Europe was becoming more urbanized and beginning to participate in the vibrant Eurasian commercial world and gradually moving to a money economy. As specialization of labor and capital increased, the gap between rich and poor widened.

Most Europeans were nominal Christians who attended church only occasionally. Their worship usually focused on miracles, relics, and prayers for immediate personal gain. Many must have felt estranged from the church that was becoming richer and more powerful, demanding contributions and turning into the very "Caesar" that it had initially attacked. Particularly loathsome to the average Christian was the church's insistence that a deceased person's second-most expensive possession be donated to the church. Some churches even claimed up to one-third of a dead man's legacy.

Much of the church leadership was corrupt. Members of the landed aristocracy installed their own relatives as priests and bishops and removed them at their whim. Bishops, beholden to their benefactors, were selected largely for their ability to pay large sums of money for their appointments, not because of their spiritual gifts. They often lived lives of luxury and debauchery. Priests were usually illiterate and most kept concubines. Popes were generally incompetent and corrupt and gained the highest church office because they came from rich, landed families near Rome. For example, John XII, who was selected pope in 955 at age 18, spent much of his nine years in office seducing women and turning the papal headquarters into a brothel.

REFORM MOVEMENTS

These major challenges stimulated a call for reform and renewal in the Roman Catholic Church and an outburst of popular faith. Systematic reforms from about 1050 to 1200 radically redirected church history, and sparked fundamental changes in European society as well. The reform movement had its greatest impact on three major areas: the monastic movement, the papacy, and Christian theology, leading to a popular outbreak of religious fervor.

THE CLUNY MONASTIC REFORMS   The Benedictines, one of the oldest, most powerful, and most influential monastic groups in Christendom, led the eleventh century reforms. Although less corrupt than the secular clergy and local churches, most monasteries depended on the local landed aristocracy for support. To free themselves from the influence of the richest families, the Benedictine monks at Cluny decided to put their monastery directly under the pope's jurisdiction. They also required that the 67 monasteries that joined the Cluny "family" of monasteries observe strict rules.

The Cluny movement launched a vigorous religious revival that swept across Europe. Cluny produced popes, cardinals, and advisors to the leaders in Europe. Its monks were able to persuade secular leaders to institute periods of peace called "Truces of God" and "The Peace of

God." They called for an end to the church's practice of simony (the buy-ing and selling of church offices) and insisted that all church officials—priests, bishops, archbishops, and even the pope—take vows of celibacy. Wealthy landed aristocrats welcomed this call for celibacy because they now had less reason to fear the growing accumulation of land by the sons of church officials. At the same time, aristocrats lost some of their ability to control church appointments.

Several new monastic orders sprang up to address the growing prob-lem of mass poverty. Many were mendicant orders that stressed the vows of poverty and strongly identified with the poor. Many mendicants, which means working with the poor, dressed as the poor and devoted their lives to prayer, silence, and extreme austerity; others honored physical labor and worked as farmers. Friars were one of the mendicant orders.

The two most significant mendicant orders that were founded in the early thirteenth century were the Franciscans, modeled on the life of St. Francis, and the Dominicans, founded in 1216. Both groups took vows of poverty, chastity, and obedience and encouraged monks to serve the needs of the community. These monastic orders infused a sense of human-ity and service to the Roman Catholic Church, and both endure to this day.

PAPAL REFORMS   The second major area of reform was the papacy under Pope Gregory VII (1074–1085). Before then, bishops commonly lived with women and fathered children, whom they called their "nephews" and "nieces." Gregory demanded absolute chastity from his clergy and tried to limit the practice of simony. More importantly, he worked to transform the concept of the Christian life from monastic con-templation to active social engagement dedicated to creating the "right order in the world." Gregory wanted papal supremacy over both church personnel and heads of state, and he treated emperors and kings as infe-riors who should follow his orders.

Under Gregory, the pope's authority increased significantly. In 962 the pope had created the fiction of the Holy Roman Empire with a German prince, supposedly a successor of Charlemagne, as its ruler. These "Holy Roman" emperors appointed the popes. To prevent that practice, in 1059 the church hierarchy had organized the College of Cardinals that was to elect the pope.

After the papacy gained control of the election of the pope, it attacked the practice of investiture, a ceremony where the political leader handed symbols of power such as a staff and ring to newly appointed bishops or abbots. In 1075 Pope Gregory announced the elimination of investiture. In reply, Henry IV of Germany, the most powerful king in Europe, fired Gregory and called for the election of a new pope. Gregory retaliated by refusing to seat the bishops Henry had chosen, ending his privilege of appointing bishops and excommunicating him. In effect, the pope and the king had removed each other from office. When King Henry lost public support as a result, the pope forced him to stand in the snow and ask for forgiveness, a dramatic symbol of the enormous power the church had acquired.

Popes that followed Gregory VII looked for ways to strengthen the church's power by systematically organizing canon law and insisting on the church's right to administer its legal system. Church law covered all aspects of life including registering new births, marriages, deaths, and presiding over inheritance, the rights of widows and orphans, and other civil matters. Administration of law became so important in the latter twelfth century that most popes were trained in canon law.

The church-state struggle symbolized by the investiture debates was temporarily resolved in 1122 when the pope and the Holy Roman Emperor signed the Concordat of Worms. The settlement clearly distinguished between the pope's spiritual responsibilities and his position as a large landholder and vassal of the crown. The clergy was to select bishops and abbots, but the emperor could decide any contested elections. This compromise served only to paper over the real schism that was opening between the papacy and the leaders of the newly emerging nation-states of Europe.

Unlike continental Europe, in England the state asserted its legal right over the church. King Henry II of England (1133–1189) appointed the bishops he wanted and made his close friend Thomas Becket his chief church officer in 1162. However, Becket and Henry disagreed over where offending church clerics should be tried, bringing the secular and sacred legal systems into sharp conflict. Noting a large number of murders committed by church clerics in 1163, Henry was incensed by Becket's lenient treatment of church-affiliated criminals.

Even though most bishops opposed Becket, he was determined to control the legal proceedings of any church-related crime. When King Henry ordered him arrested, Becket chose martyrdom. The conflict was finally resolved when Pope Alexander III agreed to accept Henry's candidates for bishops and supported Henry's move to annex Ireland. The English had strengthened the principle of state control of religion, even as the church canonized Becket and Catholics worshiped his relics.

REFORMS IN THEOLOGY   Theology was the third significant area of reform. European Christians had to respond to the infusion of new ideas and values coming from a variety of sources, including Muslims in Spain and Sicily, returning Crusaders, and especially as a result of the capture of Toledo in 1085. Before that, European Christians were largely unaware of the advances in philosophy, rationalism, scientific thought, and new technologies that the Islamic world was nurturing. Spanish Christians, with major help from Jewish and Muslim linguists, had translated Greek texts and the works of Muslim scholars, especially Averroes' commentaries on Aristotle. The example of Muslim schools (*madrasas*) stimulated the creation of European universities, and the philosophical work of scholars such as Maimonides and Averroes, who both lived in Cordova in the twelfth century, led to dramatic changes in Christian theology.

Stimulated by new insights from Muslim and Jewish scholars, a new generation of Church theologians, especially those working at the University of Paris, created a philosophy called "scholasticism." Scholastics attempted to adjust the church's classic belief that salvation resulted from faith alone to the growing interest in science and reason.

Beginning with Anselm (1033–1109) and Peter Abelard (1079–1142), the scholastic movement culminated in the work of Thomas Aquinas (1225–1274), perhaps the most important Catholic philosopher who championed reason and good works as the means to salvation. In *Summa Theologica,* his most famous work, Aquinas argued that reason is necessary to understand philosophic truths, whereas faith reveals spiritual truths. He further argued that both reason and theology were proper subjects of philosophy. Blending philosophy and theology—faith and reason—was Aquinas's great gift to the maturing theology of the Roman Catholic Church, reducing—if not eliminating—the threat that the growing secular faith in reason was posing for the church.

The transition from the Augustinian worldview based on faith and love to Thomas Aquinas's theology based on faith and reason demonstrates fundamental changes that had taken place in European society between 500 and 1200. Augustine had lived during the demise of the Roman Empire; his world was capricious, disorderly, and harsh, so it is little wonder that his theology stressed faith and salvation in heaven. By the time of Aquinas, Europeans were building towns and enjoying the fruits of a cosmopolitan commercial network. Aquinas's stress on good government, justice, order, and the use of reason were values well suited to the new age. His emphasis on good works better prepared the church to deal with more complex political and social realities and to accept the expanding values of merchants and traders.

RENEWED RELIGIOUS ENTHUSIASM IN EUROPE

As ordinary Christians witnessed the genuine efforts at reform being carried out by church leaders such as Thomas Aquinas and Pope

Gregory VII, a popular religious revival swept across Europe. One of the most important aspects of this revival was the elevation of the Virgin Mary to the threshold of the Holy Trinity. The centuries-long fascination with and worship of saints and their relics gave way to the cult of Mary. Reformed monasteries, seeking to reduce the burgeoning number of saints, officially acknowledged only two: St Peter, credited with founding the papacy, and St. Mary, whom Roman Catholics consider the Mother of God.

The consecration of the Eucharist became the major focus of worship, and the doctrine of transubstantiation, when the wine and bread become the body and blood of Jesus, was officially proclaimed in 1215. Priests began to celebrate the Mass publicly so all could witness and participate in this greatest of church rituals.

FIGURE 3-5   MARY, QUEEN OF HEAVEN
This painting expresses the importance of Mary in the Christian tradition.

Popes did not want to thwart the rising spiritual energies that were reviving a moribund Christian faith, but neither did they want to lose control of the popular movements that a growing number of charismatic reformers were leading. The church hierarchy tried to manage these spiritual enthusiasms, sometimes legitimating new zealous groups and at other times declaring that their leaders were heretics. For example, Pope Innocent III (1198–1216) launched a crusade against the Albigensians, a group that flourished in southern France in the twelfth and thirteenth centuries. They were accused of reviving older Gnostic and Manichean beliefs that the Church considered heresies, and the pope ordered inquisitions to judge individual heretics. At the same time he supported the friars who were wandering through the countryside tending the sick, helping the poor, and spreading the word of God.

Under Innocent III (1198–1216), the church reached the height of its power and influence in Europe. By consolidating church lands around Rome, he created the basis for the papal states. He often intervened in European politics and sometimes disciplined leaders who did not heed his advice. Innocent III crushed what he considered heretical opposition, but at the same time patronized idealistic religious orders that pledged their obedience to the pope.

The church developed a sophisticated administrative system that was superior to any state governments at that time. The streamlined bureaucracy increased the church's ability to collect revenues efficiently and to involve itself at every level of human life, and these reforms made the church far more wealthy and worldly. The church hierarchy enjoyed vast incomes from feudal dues, tribute from monasteries, and the first year's income of appointed churchmen, and the papacy took a large percentage of all church income to support the lavish court in Rome. Popes maintained impressive armies that enabled the church to interfere in the affairs of many European states. As new towns and cities developed from feudal fiefs, churchmen actively participated in the rising commercialization and many became astute businessmen.

As a result, the church became extremely wealthy. By the thirteenth century, it controlled nearly one-third of the land in Europe and wielded enormous economic and political influence. By 1400 in England, church officials, who composed only 1 percent of the population, controlled about 25 percent of the nation's wealth. The French and German churches were equally prosperous and in some areas owned nearly half the land.

THE CHURCH IN CRISIS

By the end of the fourteenth century, the church began to embrace the commercial revolution, but the alliance proved toxic. The church's increased involvement in worldly affairs tended to corrupt its leaders, who once again started to sink in the public's esteem. Moreover, merchants in Italy and other western European cities were seeking a place in the ecclesiastical and political power structure and some, like the wealthy Medicis of Florence, were striving to install their own family members as popes.

Church officials often managed their land holdings as if they were secular estates, maintaining serfs and knights and focusing on maximizing their power and profits. Cathedrals that had symbolized the deepest values of Roman Christianity gradually became another source of income. Rich patrons could purchase a complete burial there, including silk robes that had once been reserved only for saints and martyrs, and naves were lengthened and chapels were added to accommodate their tombs. It was not uncommon for cathedral priests to receive payments for performing tens of thousands of commemorative masses each year.

Church officials also sold indulgences to help finance building new cathedrals. An indulgence originally meant a kindness or favor, but it came to mean remission of a tax or debt, then God's mercy, and finally the remission of punishment for sin and the assurance of forgiveness. The church, as the earthly agent of God, could grant anyone an indulgence. Church officials found it increasingly tempting to offer believers instant salvation in exchange for cash. The church seemed to be saying: "The meek shall inherit the earth—providing they have the money to pay for it."

Besides internal corruption, strong monarchies were ruling the newly formed nation-states. These kings, some of whom claimed a "divine right" to rule, relentlessly threatened the church's authority. Symbolic of the weakening of papal authority was the fact that from 1309 to 1378, the popes, largely subservient to the French kings, lived in splendor in Avignon in France rather than in their historic home in Rome. During this so called "Babylonian Captivity," all seven pontiffs were French. For the next 31 years, two rival popes plotted to gain sole power.

The church was unable to match the power of the emerging nation states, especially England, France, and Spain. Supported by a growing number of artisans and a rising middle class of merchants and bankers, state governments collected increasing tax revenues and mustered large armies that could enforce their will. With the rapid rise of the commercial classes and the growing power of the emerging nation-states, a new wave of religious reformers launched revolutionary movements against the established church and in the process helped transform the face of Europe.

A NEW WAVE OF REFORM

The political machinations of the church hierarchy, coupled with the church's vulgar pursuit of material and political power, spawned a second period of reform, this one in the fourteenth and fifteenth centuries. As feudalism crumbled and literacy expanded, peasants, left out of the new prosperity that increased commercialization was creating, rushed to join the call for reform.

A new wave of European writers also added their voices. Petrarch, the great humanist writer, called the Avignon papacy "the whore of Babylon." The Italian writer Dante found a special place for popes in his literary hells, and the writers of French fables pictured the clergy as a dishonest collection of seducers and tricksters. Perhaps the most devastating satire of the decline of the church can be found in the pages of Geoffrey Chaucer's *Canterbury Tales*.

Reformers condemned the church's commercial activities, especially the open marketing of salvation, calling such practices "mechanical Christianity." Incessant fund-raising drives usually fell hardest on the lay community that increasingly resented the pressure, and more people simply stopped tithing. Reformers also directed their wrath at the popes who were often embroiled in personal power struggles that threatened to split the church.

John Wycliffe (1224–1384), a brilliant scholar and administrator, spoke for many of the reformers. He believed God's will was revealed in scriptures, not through church leaders, and he wanted to replace church-centered Christianity with a Bible-centered faith. Like the Buddha 1,500 years earlier, he wanted the message to be available in languages average believers could understand, His devoted followers, known as "Lollards," set out to translate the Bible into English. Wycliffe further alienated himself from the church when he questioned the literal truth of the act of transubstantiation.

In 1402, John Huss of Bohem (1369–1415), a staunch follower of Wycliffe, publicly proclaimed that Christians need not obey an unworthy pope. As Huss was burning at the stake for his heresy, he prophesized, "In 100 years, God will raise up a man whose calls for reform cannot be suppressed." In 1517, almost exactly 100 years later, his prophesy came true.

Savonarola (1452–1498), a Dominican friar, insisted that the local friars in Florence should study languages, learn history, and read the Bible for themselves. He also led the "burning of vanities" in an effort to end their luxurious life styles. Later, with the pope's blessing, Savonarola was also burned at the stake.

Meanwhile, a wave of mystical enthusiasts was sweeping across Europe. The greatest of these mystical teachers was Meister Eckhart, a German Dominican. Eckhart argued that knowledge of God must be intuitive and can never be purely rational because with every statement one makes about God, its opposite may also be true. We can know God, he preached, only by experiencing his presence in our deepest being. Another group that gained many followers was the Flagellants, who practiced self-mutilation. They reemphasized the message of Paul and many others who believed that the End of Time was near if people did not repent and change their evil ways.

A major mystical movement developed in Wursburg, Germany, where people testified that an image of Virgin Mary had appeared and Hans Bohm started preaching to the pilgrims who came to see the image. Bohm attacked the church for oppressing peasants and condoning the enormous disparity between the opulent lives of people in and out of the church and the teachings of the Gospel. He threatened both church and state when he counseled everyone to refuse to pay both taxes and tithes. The church fathers had him burned as a heretic.

Popular reform movements also included women's groups that accepted poverty and chastity and gathered to pray, meditate, and carry on good works. Some bishops tolerated these women's groups, but the church leadership banned most of them.

Thomas Kempis (1379–1471), a German monk and reformer, sought to combine traditional rituals, mysticism, and the core ethics of Jesus' teaching. In his *Imitation of Christ,* written in 1427 and translated into most European languages, Kempis urged his readers not only to observe the sacrament of the Eucharist, but to focus on their inner spiritual condition. Most importantly, he preached that each Christian should become a "partner" of Jesus by meditating on his or her own spiritual condition and living a simple, moral life. This slender text was immediately popular and over the next few centuries, it probably became the most admired Christian book after the Bible.

In an age of both enormous church power and the growing muscle of the emerging nation-states, these reformers directed their venom against both political leaders and the church hierarchy. In turn, both church and political leaders fought to preserve the status quo and were often united in condemning many of the reformers to death. However, these early reformers paved the way for the final break Luther and Calvin initiated in the sixteenth century that culminated in the Protestant Reformation.

THE BREAKUP OF THE ROMAN CATHOLIC CHURCH: THE PROTESTANT REFORMATION

At the center of what began as a fundamental critique of the growing Catholic abuses stood Martin Luther (1483–1546), a German priest, and John Calvin (1509–1564), who studied to be a priest but turned instead to law. By Luther's time, the sale of indulgences had grown into a full-blown sale of one-way tickets straight to heaven. When Tetzel—a corrupt Dominican friar who came to Germany to hawk indulgences to raise money for the pope and the Archbishop of Mainz—set up his bargain basement indulgence shop in Wittenberg, many of the poor and illiterate lined up to buy. Luther's 95 Theses, the grievances that he nailed on that famous door of the Wittenberg Cathedral in 1517, were directed primarily at Tetzel.

Luther, hailed as a leader sent from God, spoke for the countless number of people who were appalled at the church's denigration of heaven. His bold public act against the pope's chief salesman resulted in a public revolt that drove Tetzel out of the country. However, Pope Leo X, suddenly cut off from an important source of income, moved quickly against Luther and his followers.

In 1518 Leo ordered Luther to recant, but, energized by his growing German following, Luther refused the pope's order and stated that the sale of indulgences was a distortion of Christian values and teaching. In the ensuing debates, Luther realized that his theology clashed seriously with much of the church's teachings and activities. When the pope gave him 60 days to recant or be dealt with as a heretic, Luther's response was to publicly burn the pope's order. He was quickly excommunicated.

Friendly princes helped Luther avoid capture by the pope's soldiers, and until his death in 1546 Luther labored to create a new German church. Although he kept many of the Roman Catholic Church's practices, he boldly eliminated the pope, bishops, and priests, dismantling the entire church hierarchy. He observed only two sacraments—baptism and Holy Communion (the Eucharist)—but dismissed the concept of transubstantiation, arguing that no priest had the power to change wine and bread into the blood and body of Christ. He married and began a family and encouraged priests to follow his example.

Returning to the teachings of Augustine, Luther insisted that humans were saved by God's grace alone and could not earn heaven by good works. Further, he ended important traditional practices such as the veneration of saints and the cult of relics. He worked with scholars to translate the Bible into German and he conducted services in German. Finally, Luther denied the superiority of the church over the state, paving the way for the creation of national religions that would soon accompany the newly forming European nation-states.

Luther's religious rebellion was an important part of a series of economic and social rebellions against the large landholders and newly emerging capitalists. Luther's pronouncement that every man should "be his own priest" not only encouraged individuals to read and interpret the Bible for themselves, but also seemed to suggest a greater equality in all spheres of human experience. However, Luther's loyalties lay mostly with the princes who supported him rather than with the poorer majority, whose uprisings were, in part, motivated by his teachings.

Luther's Protestant movement quickly spread from Germany to most of Europe. Ulrich Zwingli (1484–1531) led the anti-Catholic forces in Northern Switzerland where, by 1528, a majority had left the Roman Catholic Church. The Protestant fever soon reached the city of Geneva where the people overthrew both the political leader and the bishop and declared the city a republic. Preachers streamed into the city to convert the people to the new religion.

John Calvin (1509–1564), a charismatic French lawyer and preacher, won the hearts and minds of Geneva, and Geneva's republic soon became a theocracy with Calvin at its head. Supported by a council of elders, he circulated a constitution that merged church and state and added the death penalty for blasphemy, dancing, playing cards, and attending the theater, as well as for murder.

Like Luther, Calvin believed that only through God's grace could someone be saved and that God had predestined some to be saved and condemned most others to hell. Nothing that humans did could change this inevitable truth. The "elect," those God had chosen for salvation, would live an exemplary Christian life, and their good conduct would be a sign, but not a guarantee, of salvation. Other signs were participating in religious services and making a public confession of faith.

Although they shared a common concept of grace and predestination, Calvin differed from Luther in several ways. As a trained lawyer, Calvin was deeply influenced by the Old Testament and emphasized the supremacy of law, whereas Luther stressed individual conscience. God, for Calvin, was a mighty lawgiver who had set down a body of rules to be carefully followed.

The lives of the two major Protestant reformers were also dramatically different. German princes gave Luther his strongest support. He did not admire the newly rising capitalists and often assailed their greed and materialism. Calvin, on the other hand, embraced the bourgeoisie of Geneva and his theology reflected mercantile values of thrift, investment, and, above all, hard work. It is no accident that Calvinism took root in the Netherlands and Scotland and among the commercial classes of France. (Nearly 400 years later his commercial bias would form the basis of Max Weber's famous work, *The Protestant Ethic and the Spirit of Capitalism*.) Finally, Calvin was far more hostile to Roman Catholic practices, and he labored to purge his brand of Protestantism of any residue of that faith. Worship was to be held in simple buildings without art, stained glass windows, or music.

The rift between the various wings of Protestantism and Roman Catholicism quickly segued into a rash of European conflicts that lasted for nearly 150 years. Sometimes these wars were state against state, and some were internal battles to determine which faith would be the official state religion. The concept of a single religion in each nation-state served to reinforce nationalism as a rival faith to Christianity. Among the implications of this double loyalty would be kings appealing to Divine Right to rule and national armies marching into battle with God on their side. Catholic Spanish conquistadors would conquer Spain for God and English Protestants would soon attempt to establish a "New Jerusalem" in North America.

CONCLUSION

The early Christian churches took three centuries to gain political support at the highest levels of the Roman Empire and to become the major institution that carried classical Mediterranean civilization to the western frontiers of Eurasia. Christians in India who made St. Thomas an important part of their remembered past were never able to compete effectively with Buddhism and Hinduism or attract significant numbers to their community. Although Nestorian Christianity enjoyed a long and somewhat successful expansion in central Asia, it was never a significant presence in China. Roman Catholicism flourished in Ethiopia, but Christianity was all but absent in other areas of Africa. The spread of Islamic political control, followed by large-scale conversion to Islam, also inhibited Christianity's success in the vast area from Turkey to Southeast Asia.

Christianity fared far better in the Mediterranean basin and reached its height in Byzantium and western Europe. The Byzantine Empire had a strong central government, but Europe had virtually no political unity from 500 to 800. In both these areas, the Christian faith provided a common bond of surpassing strength. Although politically divided, the whole of northwest Eurasia was a spiritual commonwealth—a quasi-real, quasi-ideal entity called Christendom.

As it spread in Europe, the Christian Church challenged the political authority of would-be emperors and kings. From 800 to 1300, the Roman Catholic Church enjoyed great power and in 1000 was stronger than the majority of its contemporary political states. However, as commerce increased and nation-states formed in western Europe, powerful new political and business classes successfully challenged the power of the church and gradually forced it into a defensive posture. Even so, new states such as England, France, Spain, and Portugal, infused with a zealous Protestantism or a renewed and vigorous Roman Catholicism, did not abandon their Christian mission but would continue to spread the faith to the Western Hemisphere and beyond.

By 1300 the Roman Catholic Church had grown very worldly, controlling nearly a quarter of Europe's land and amassing huge wealth, and it was accused of forgetting its mission of service to the poor. Church leaders lived in luxury and practiced politics similar to their secular counterparts. As popular disenchantment with the church reached historical heights, a number of reformers tried to redeem the church's promise. In the process, the church was weakened even more as it faced major schisms.

The rise of new nation-states in Europe and the new concept of "nationalism" severely undermined the ideal of a single universal empire and church. Accompanying the new commercial revolution in Europe was a much higher rate of literacy and a growing demand for books. Many of the religious reforms focused on an individual's right to read the Bible, a demand that seriously undermined the church's authority as the final arbiter of God's will.

The rapid growth of the middle class, the expanding power of the new nation-states coupled with the massive corruption of the church led to a reform cycle in the fifteenth and sixteenth centuries. These challenges opened the way for the development of a series of national churches and a proliferation of sects too numerous to count. By 1550 the Roman Catholic Church's monopoly on the Christian faith in Europe had been shattered beyond recognition.

The westernization of Christianity, built on the Greco-Roman foundation, provided a crucial ingredient in the making of the modern "West." More than 1,000 years of the European people's interaction with their Christian teachers had created a new social order, and this synthesis, by the mid-sixteenth century, had led to the rise of nation-states, a rebirth of commercial activity, and a revival of Christian zeal, all of which would help propel Europe to the forefront of world power.

CHAPTER FOUR

THE WIDENING REACH OF
DAR AL-ISLAM

> **GETTING STARTED ON CHAPTER FOUR:** What challenges and achievements characterized the Period of the Rightly Guided Caliphs? How did Muslims relate to people of other faiths? How did Muslims encourage and support the brotherhood of all believers and what factors challenged that unity? What were the relationships between religious leaders and political authority? What enabled Islam to spread so rapidly and widely beyond its Arabian heartland and what role did urbanization play in the process of Islamization? To what groups in particular did Islam appeal and why? How did dar al-Islam succeed in incorporating a variety of diverse cultural traditions? What held that vast Islamic world together?

Islam was forged out of the nomadic Bedouin culture of the Arabian Peninsula as Muhammad brought revelation from Allah to his fellow Arabs. He called on them to submit to Allah and follow the revelations he had received, and he worked unrelentingly to unite Arabs living on the peninsula into a brotherhood of all believers, in large part by transforming their loyalty from clan and tribal bloodlines to a shared faith in Allah.

STRENGTHENING THE COMMUNITY

Belonging to a community of believers that incorporated and transcended tribal loyalties was extremely important in the initial spread of Islam among Arabs. Unlike the Buddha and Jesus, who established relatively small and isolated communities of believers, Muhammad's goal was far more ambitious: he sought to unite all the tribes in the Arabian Peninsula into one brotherhood. To accomplish that end he tried to replace blood loyalties based on family, clan, and tribe with the higher allegiance to Islam and submitting to the will of Allah. His brotherhood would be a fellowship (*ummah*) that transcended tribal ties.

The core Muslim practices, which became known as the Five Pillars, strengthen and sustain the sense of unity and brotherhood. The First Pillar is the *Shahada*, the affirmation of faith: "There is no God but God, and Muhammad is his prophet." The Second Pillar is *Adan*, prayers that Muslims are to perform in unison at five fixed times during each day. At first, the faithful faced Jerusalem, the third holiest Muslim shrine in Islam after Mecca and Medina, but in 624, after the hegira, Muhammad directed his followers to pray facing Mecca. Some of the prayers are set; some are personal prayers. The first mosque (a "place for prostration") was Muhammad's courtyard, and it became the prototype for all mosques: an open courtyard with a fountain that provided water for ritual ablutions. Mosques also often have a covered arcade. The only other requirement is a marker indicating the direction of Mecca, which all Muslims are to face when they pray. Friday became the Muslims' sacred day, and when possible, Muslims are to perform the noon-hour prayer in a mosque together with other Muslims.

The Third Pillar, *Zakat*, giving alms to the poor, reflects one's responsibility for the welfare of the community. Muslims are expected to contribute one-fortieth of their wealth as an annual donation, much like a tax. The Fourth Pillar, *Sawn*, fasting, is observed during the holy month of Ramadan. Every year during Ramadan all Muslims refrain from taking food and liquids from dawn until sundown. Participating in the fast is an act of humility and compassion that also helps unite Muslims. The Fifth Pillar is making the hajj, the pilgrimage to the Ka'ba in Mecca, at least once. In Mecca, pilgrims take off their clothes and drape themselves in white sheets, symbolizing their equality and solidarity.

Equality and social justice are fundamental tenets of Islam, and Muhammad stressed equality among members of the community. The daily prayers and the Friday communal prayers that Muslims most often perform in mosques include bowing, prostrations, and prayers said in unison. They have a mesmerizing effect that bond the believers closer together. Giving alms affirms the importance of supporting fellow Muslims and promotes economic equality. Fasting during Ramadan gives everyone a shared experience of devotion and deprivation. Fasting is not undertaken to atone for one's sins, as in Christianity, but is a way of gaining God's mercy for oneself and the whole community. Eid al-fatr, the celebration ending Ramadan, includes sharing with poorer members.

The hajj brings Muslims together from all over the world during this transformative experience. The white sheets hide regional or class distinctions and help pilgrims experience the racial and spiritual equality of the vast community to which they belong. Sharing ideas and learning from one another during the hajj encourages people in far-flung areas to worship in similar ways.

The Quran, the revelations that Muhammad received, stresses the importance of equality. In several places the Quran directly addresses women, and several statements explicitly establish the absolute moral and spiritual equality of men and women. For example:

> Lo! Men who surrender unto Allah and women who surrender, and men who believe and women who believe, and men who obey and women who obey, and men who speak the truth and women who speak the truth, and men who persevere [in righteousness] and women who persevere, and men who are humble and women who are humble, and men who give alms and women who give alms, and men who fast and women who fast, and men who guard their modesty and women who guard [their modesty], and men who remember Allah much and women who remember—Allah hath prepared for them forgiveness and a vast reward. (Sura 33:35)

By the time Muhammad died, most of the tribal leaders in the Arabian Peninsula had pledged their allegiance to him, and the Muslim community was securely established in Mecca; however, its future remained uncertain. It faced two immediate challenges: finding a successor who could legitimately adopt the mantle of leadership and keeping members of the brotherhood from leaving the community. Muhammad had been both a religious and military leader, and his earliest followers had to address both spiritual concerns and institutional issues that the early followers of the other faiths had not been required to confront.

The revelations Muhammad received gave him enormous legitimacy, but, like the Buddha, he never named a successor or explained how the community should choose its leaders. He had appointed Abu Bakr, a close Companion and the father of his favorite wife, Aisha, to lead Friday prayers, so the elders chose him to be Muhammad's deputy (caliph). It may have helped that Abu Bakr was not a member of either of the two major clans. Following traditional methods for selecting clan leaders, elders also chose the next three caliphs based on their personal connection to Muhammad and their loyalty to Islam. These early leaders became known as the "Rightly Guided Caliphs."

THE ERA OF THE RIGHTLY GUIDED CALIPHS

Abu Bakr's most daunting challenge was trying to maintain the unity of the community. He did not claim to have divine authority to rule. As a deputy of the Prophet, he pledged to try and follow Muhammad's example, and he labored diligently during his two years as caliph to keep the tribes united. Most of them had sworn allegiance to Muhammad, but after he died, many felt their obligations had ended and they were free to transfer their loyalty and allegiance to some other leader. Abu Bakr did not permit tribes that were already part of the brotherhood to leave the community, and he proclaimed that Muhammad was the last or "Seal of the Prophets" so they would not look for another prophet. He required the entire community to obey him as long as he was faithful to the Prophet's example, and he did not hesitate to use armed force to prevent dissenting tribes from breaking away.

After Abu Bakr's death, the elders choose Umar, another Companion of the Prophet, as the second caliph. Umar served from 634 to 644, and under his leadership Muslim Arab forces began to expand into present-day Iraq and Palestine. At first these military excursions resembled traditional raids against rival clans and were not aimed at occupying territory. But the victory against the Byzantine army in 634 may have inspired the Muslim Arab forces to keep on the offensive. After this surprisingly easy triumph, the forces went on to defeat the Sasanid army at the battle of Qadisiya in 637, effectively destroying Sasanid power, although they still had to subdue remote areas in Iran before they could claim to control all of the Sasanid territory. Because of these dramatic military advances, Caliph Umar added "Commander of the Faithful" to his titles.

Umar segregated his military forces, requiring them to stay together in garrisons (*amsar*) in Kufa and Basra in Iraq and Fustat (Cairo) in Egypt. He wanted to keep his men from harassing the indigenous people, and he may also have feared they would be corrupted by the extravagant lifestyles of the people living in the urban areas they had conquered. To prevent clan rivalries and hostilities while offering the security of one's own clan, members of each tribe lived together within the garrisons and had their own burial ground. Tribal areas were separated by wide avenues. Smaller tribes were stationed together in separate sections of the garrison.

In an attempt to strengthen unity under the banner of Islam, there was a large area where the troops drilled together and where everyone could pray together. Soldiers rested in these garrisons after battles, and they drilled and also planned upcoming campaigns. Isolating the troops

FIGURE 4-1   THE MOSQUE OF IBN TULUN, CAIRO, EGYPT
This is one of the oldest mosques in Islam.

prevented them from either losing their will to fight or assimilating foreign ways. Moreover, it prevented tribal groups from embarking on their own raiding parties and claiming spoils or territory for their tribes.

In spite of its impressive military successes, early tensions threatened to split the Muslim brotherhood apart. One of the first arguments was over who should be given positions in the new government. One faction, the "Muslim group," was composed of early converts who had been Companions of the Prophet and had supported Muhammad's initial initiatives. The other main faction, the "Arab" contingent, composed predominately of members of the important Quraysh clan, had initially opposed Muhammad and had converted only after his forces took Mecca.

Caliph Umar favored the Muslim group and gave governorships, generalships, and administrative offices to Companions of the Prophet and other members of the clans that had supported Muhammad's early rise to power. Members of the Quraysh aristocracy and other Arabs who had not initially supported the Prophet resented this favoritism and so did later converts who migrated to the garrison towns to live.

This potential schism in the brotherhood made it difficult to select the third caliph. In an attempt to quell contention over succession, Umar established a committee to choose the caliphs. When he died in 644, the selection committee opted for Uthman, a member of the prominent Umayyad clan that had initially opposed Muhammad.

Uthman increased the power of the caliph, in part by taking more control over the collection of revenue and by giving the newly converted Arab clans greater power. He increased the caliph's religious authority as well by supervising the completion of the official written version of the Quran, the revelations Muhammad had received from Allah, which Companions of the Prophet had written down.

Despite his many achievements, opposition to Uthman grew. He angered the Prophet's early supporters by favoring Arabian tribal aristocrats and giving coveted positions to members of his own clan. Members of the army increasingly resisted being confined to their garrisons. Dissent grew and members of the anti-Uthman groups, empowered by their rising resentment, assassinated him in 656.

Ali, Muhammad's first cousin and his daughter Fatimah's husband, had long claimed the right to lead the community. He was, after all, directly related to Muhammad, which many believed gave him a special right to rule. He had opposed Uthman's attempt to centralize power in the caliph's hands and wanted to ensure that the spoils of war were shared equally among all the Arab forces.

Although Ali was chosen as the fourth caliph, tensions between the early Muslim and Arab factions continued, and two inconclusive uprisings erupted. Aisha, Muhammad's favorite wife, along with several of the Prophet's close companions, were among the prominent leaders of an unsuccessful uprising against Ali and his forces at the Battle of the Camel in 656, named for the camel which Aisha rode. Muawiya, a kinsman of Uthman and the governor of Syria, led a second uprising. Arbitrators then judged that Uthman had been unjustly killed and that Ali should not have accepted leadership. Shortly after, Ali was assassinated. His death brought an end to the period of the Rightly Guided Caliphs, during which the Muslim community (*ummah*) took shape. However, the dispute over who should lead remained unresolved.

ACCOMPLISHMENTS UNDER THE RIGHTLY GUIDED CALIPHS

Important Islamic principles were firmly established during the Rightly Guided Caliph period. Besides the strict monotheism and the importance of Muhammad, proclaimed in the affirmation of faith "There is no God but Allah and Muhammad is his prophet," Muslims believe in the Last Day, a final judgment, and heaven and hell. The sacredness of the Quran, the written record of the divine revelations given to Muhammad in

Arabic, is another fundament belief of Islam. The Quran is literally the word of God for Muslims. Its importance for Muslims can be compared to that of Jesus for Christians. The Quran was compiled in its present form in 651 under Caliph Uthman, and Muslims resist translating any part of this sacred scripture for fear they may obscure or distort its meaning or spoil its poetry.

Several factors help explain the increasing strength of the Muslim community during this period. A major reason was that the leadership was able to build on and reinforce existing beliefs and practices. Identification with and loyalty to one's clan had long been paramount values in Bedouin society. The Rightly Guided Caliphs continually tried to balance traditional blood loyalties with a growing identification with a united brotherhood of believers, and they convinced Muslims that being true to their tribal values enhanced their faithfulness to Allah. The Quran's repeated affirmation of equality also echoed a fundamental value of the nomadic society.

Expanding clan membership beyond blood relatives was increasing at the same time that Muslims were being encouraged to widen their loyalties. Clans used the pre-Islamic Arab practice of "clientship" to absorb Arabs from diverse backgrounds. A client (*mawala*) was considered to be an inferior person, often a former slave, whom a clan adopted. *Mawali* gave loyalty to the clan in exchange for the promise of protection. As warfare resulted in more slaves who became mawali, clans gradually ceased to be exclusive kinship groups. This shift in the clan's composition may have made it easier for loyalty to the ummah to replace the longstanding commitment to one's clan and for tribal groups to fight for the larger community. Increasingly, the ummah assumed the responsibility for punishing violation of honor or transgression of traditional rules.

Muslims identified the caliph with the traditional concept of a *shaykh*, the leader who arbitrated issues. Courage in battle and bravery in defending one's tribe were transformed into dedication to the brotherhood. Determination and patience in face of adversity became faith in God when facing hardships. Generosity to clan members now meant giving alms and caring for weaker members of the larger Muslim community. In addition, believers who had been accustomed to following tribal traditions (*sunna*) could continue their adherence to tradition by following the example of the Prophet.

REASONS FOR THE MILITARY VICTORIES Under the leadership of the Rightly Guided Caliphs, Muslim Arab armies made impressive conquests of Syria, Egypt, and the entire Sasanid realm. Early military achievements of Muslim Arab forces may have been enhanced because Byzantium and Sasanian Persia had exhausted each other with 300 years of warfare. In addition, their constant hostilities had inhibited the flow of commerce, especially between their two empires. As a result, their subject populations, overtaxed, impoverished, and weary of seemingly meaningless and unending fighting, had become disaffected and may even have welcomed the invading Muslim Arab forces.

It is probably true that the many Eastern Orthodox Christians, Copts (Egyptian Christians), and Nestorians who were living under Byzantine control, as well as Zoroastrians and Manicheans, did not have any great affection for Byzantine rule and resented being forced to fight. Taxes required to support military expenditures were burdensome and some in west Asia may have considered the Muslim Arab warriors liberators from oppressive Byzantine rule. However, most had no idea about the faith of the invaders, so Islam could hardly have influenced their attitudes.

The superior military skill of the Muslim Arab forces helps explain their rapid expansion. Although many Bedouins lived sedentary lives and assisted with the caravan trade rather than raiding caravans, the austerity of Bedouin life helped prepare them for the hardships of military life. Horsemen honed their skills protecting their herds from wild animals, raiding other clans, and participating in the huge hunting expeditions that were similar to military campaigns. Arab horsemen, standing in stirrups while firing arrows at close range, could decimate attacking infantrymen. Added to their military superiority was the motivation of the Muslim Arab troops, especially for the spoils of war.

Although many of the invading soldiers were expert warriors, they did not view their campaigns as a way to spread Islam. Some may have thought that their victories offered proof that Allah was on their side, but most of the soldiers had little knowledge about the faith, so it could not have been a compelling reason why they fought. Furthermore, they did not expect non-Arabs to convert.

One eminent scholar suggests two important reasons why the Muslim Arab leadership carefully planned military campaigns outside the Arabian Peninsula.[57] For one, in order to support their expanding community, the leaders had to secure food and other resources that were not available in Arabia. Because Muslims were forbidden to attack or plunder fellow believers, the community was forced to seek resources in non-Muslim areas. The promise of plunder won in war was certainly a strong motivation for the troops, and spoils from the richer, more urbanized areas they conquered were very attractive to soldiers who normally had little hope of getting rich. The army was guaranteed the majority of

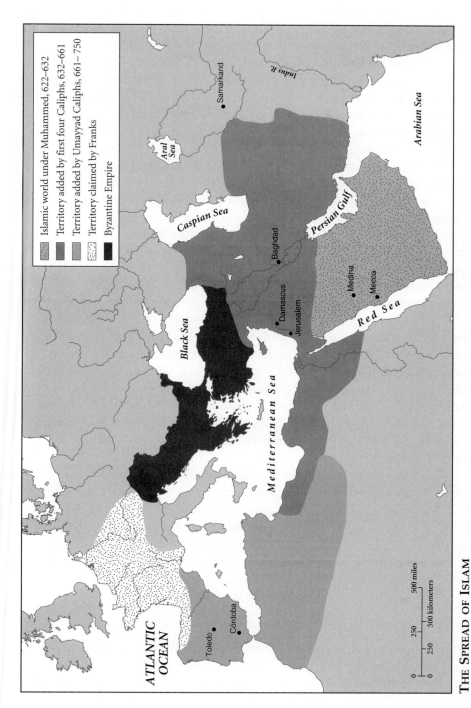

THE SPREAD OF ISLAM

This map shows the journey of Islam from its beginnings.

Islamic world under Muhammed, 622–632
Territory added by first four Caliphs, 632–661
Territory added by Umayyad Caliphs, 661–750
Territory claimed by Franks
Byzantine Empire

ATLANTIC OCEAN

Toledo
Córdoba

Black Sea

Caspian Sea

Aral Sea

Samarkand

Indus R.

Mediterranean Sea

Baghdad

Damascus
Jerusalem

Persian Gulf

Red Sea

Medina
Mecca

Arabian Sea

0   250   500 miles
0   250   500 kilometers

the spoils from these campaigns, and leaders tried to ensure that it was divided equally among the Arab troops. Sharing the rewards of conquest also contributed to the sense of equality and brotherhood.

A second reason for the successful military expansion may have been "the political need to contain and channel the tremendous energies released by the Prophet's socioreligious revolution."[58] Embarking on constant military campaigns kept the various tribes from fighting among themselves, so commanders strove either to keep their men engaged in warfare or preparing for battle.

The tolerant treatment of the conquered populations may have been another reason for the impressive success of the Muslim Arabs. Because the troops were isolated in garrisons, soldiers had few opportunities to harass the local people or otherwise threaten their way of life. Their sudden, dramatic military victories meant the caliph and his advisors and armies now had extensive areas to govern. Because they had had no experience in administering complex urban areas, they depended on local leaders, leaving existing officials in their jobs even though few of them converted to Islam.

In theory, non-Muslims were not to have jobs that gave them authority over Muslims, but this stipulation was not enforced. In the conquered areas, local scribes, accountants, chiefs, and headmen retained their positions. Most people had had little or no contact with the earlier rulers, and they were hardly aware of any change in the government that traditionally was very remote from their daily lives. Muslim Arab governors limited themselves to overseeing the collection of taxes and tribute, supervising the distribution of revenues to troops, and leading their forces in battle.

The system for collecting tribute that the invaders followed also minimized the negative effects on conquered areas. Instead of demanding gold, jewels, lands, and other tangible valuables, soldiers received a stipend taken from the taxes peasants and townspeople paid so that spoils were distributed more systematically and equitably. Further, troops moving into newly subdued areas were instructed not to damage agricultural lands, so much cultivated land was not pillaged.

WHAT DID MUSLIMS THINK OF NON-MUSLIMS?

In the early stages of expansion, Muslims made little or no effort to convert non-Arabs. Initially, Islam was a religion for Arabs and a mark of their unity and superiority. Jews already had their prophets and the Torah, and Christians had Jesus and the New Testament. Muhammad was the prophet for Arabs. Muslims were not to pressure anyone to surrender to Allah. The Quran states, "There is no compulsion in religion." (2:256) However, Arabs were expected to convert and after they surrendered to Allah, they were not to leave the faith, on pain of death.

Muslims were not responsible if those who heard the message did not surrender. The Quran explains:

> And say unto those who have received the Scripture and those who read not: Have ye (too) surrendered? If they surrender, then truly they are rightly guided; and if they turn away, then it is thy duty only to convey the message (unto them), . . (3:20)

> Leave me to deal with the deniers . . ." (73:11)

Muslims tended to be tolerant of their non-Muslim, non-Arab subjects, especially Christians and Jews who were already monotheists and who, they believed, were worshiping the same God. The Quran states:

> Say, O Muslims. We believe in God that was revealed unto us and that which was revealed unto Abraham, Ishmael, Isaac and Jacob, and the tribes, and that which Moses and Jesus received, and that which the Prophets received from their Lord. We make no distinction between any of them, and unto Him we have surrendered. (2:136)

Muslims were far more tolerant of their non-Christian and non-Zoroastrian subjects than either Byzantine or Sasanid rulers had been, and they were certainly more tolerant than the early Christians who tried to spread Christianity among predominately polytheistic peoples. Muslims revere the major Jewish patriarchs and prophets. They also believe that Jesus' message was essentially correct, but that his followers mistakenly claim he is divine. They think of him as a great prophet but not the Christ.

Muslims referred to Christians and Jews as "People of the Book." (During the early years of conquest, Zoroastrians, while not officially People of the Book, were often included in the category because their faith is also based in scripture.) People of the Book became members of a "protected" group (*dhimmi*); they had to obey the rules, pay the poll tax (which theoretically covered the cost of protection), and not try to revolt. The Quran states:

> And argue not with the People of the Scripture unless it be in (a way) that is better, save with such of them as do wrong; and say: We believe in that which hath been revealed unto us and revealed unto you; our God and your God is One, and unto Him we surrender. (29:46)

Jihads were not initiated to spread the faith. The Muslim concept of jihad means "struggle," not "holy war," and Muslims teach that there are two kinds of struggles. One is the individual's effort to try to live as

Allah wants people to live. This means struggling against selfishness, egotism, jealousy, and all the other emotions that keep a person from experiencing inner peace. The second jihad is the struggle against enemies, especially those who threaten the community.

Muslims are expected to fight for a righteous cause and to defend the faith and the faithful with force, if necessary:

> Fight in the way of Allah against those who fight against you, but begin not hostilities, Lo! Allah loveth not aggressors. And slay them wherever you find them, and drive them out of the places whence they drove you out, for persecution is worse than slaughter . . . But if they desist, then lo! Allah is forgiving, Merciful. (2: 190–192)

Non-Arabs who wanted to gain status in the Muslim community might try to copy Arab customs, a process called "Arabization." When Arab clans offered "protection" to non-Arabs who converted to Islam, these converts became clients (*mawali*) of the clans, but they could not become full members of the Arab kinship-based society and they, like other mawali, were considered inferior to Muslim Arabs.

HOW WAS ISLAM CHANGING WOMEN'S LIVES?

Women experienced significant changes during the Rightly Guided Caliph period. Many different marriage customs and a variety of attitudes toward the appropriate roles for women existed in pre-Islamic Arabian society. Both matrilineal family arrangements, where descent goes through the mother and the wife stays with her own family, as well as patrilineal arrangements, where descent goes from the father and wives join their husbands' families, were widely practiced. In addition, examples of polyandry, where the woman has several husbands, polygamy, where the man has several wives, and monogamy, only one wife or husband, existed. Female infanticide was not uncommon, but grown women in the Jahilia period participated actively in society, unlike most women in the neighboring Sasanid and Byzantine empires. As one scholar reminds us:

> Jahilia women were priests, soothsayers, prophets, participants in warfare, and nurses on the battlefield. They were fearlessly outspoken, defiant critics of men; authors of satirical verse aimed at formidable male opponents; keepers, in some unclear capacity, of the keys of the holiest shrine in Mecca; rebels and leaders of rebellions that included men; and individuals who initiated and terminated marriages at will.[59]

Pre-Islamic marriage customs varied with different Arabian groups, but in general women had a great deal of autonomy. There is evidence of both matriliny and polyandry and knowing the child's paternity was not always important. In general, women had much more control over their sexual lives: They could propose marriage, initiate divorce, insist on monogamy, and remarry. Several reforms such as outlawing female infanticide were instituted during the period of the Right Guarded Caliphs. However, a patrilineal marriage structure where men controlled women's sexuality was starting to become the only legitimate form of marriage.

The changes taking place in the lives of women are dramatically reflected in the experience of Khadija and Aisha, Muhammad's two favorite wives.[60] Khadija, his first wife, was an independent, prosperous businesswoman who hired Muhammad to work for her. Fifteen years his senior, Khadija, a widow, proposed marriage to Muhammad, and she was his only wife until she died, 25 years later. Aisha, by contrast, was only about six years old when her father, Abu Bakr, suggested to Muhammad that he take her as a bride. They probably consummated the marriage when she was nine or ten. Although he had other wives and concubines, Aisha was his favorite and he insisted on being in her room when he died, and he was buried there.

The attitude toward the veiling and seclusion of women was gradually changing. Because Muhammad and his wives lived close to the courtyard and mosque where he carried out his activities and where large numbers of travelers prayed and camped out, Asiha and the other wives were secluded and were advised to cover themselves when they went out. However, during Muhammad's lifetime these restrictions applied only to his wives.

In spite of the greater restrictions placed on Asiha, pre-Islamic attitudes can be detected in many of her actions. She played an important role in the Muslim community, especially after Muhammad's death. She was the source of much of the information about Muhammad's activities and thoughts, proving that at that time the elders gave credence to a woman's testimony. After Uthman was assassinated, she spoke in the mosque, publicly rejecting the selection of Ali as caliph, and she participated in the Battle of the Camel that opposed his succession.

THE UMAYYAD CALIPHATE

Muawiya became caliph in 661, and his rule, which lasted until 680, marked the beginning of the Umayyad Caliphate. Caliph Muawiya consolidated power under the caliphate, but he continued to stress personal client-patron relationships and was able to motivate tribal leaders to cooperate without offending their dignity.

The earlier split between the first Muslim supporters of Muhammad and Arab tribes that had joined the community later continued to have bearing on who had the right to lead. Although Muawiya claimed to believe in treating all Arabs equally rather than favoring Muhammad's early supporters in Medina, he moved the capital to Damascus, which symbolically distanced the community from the world of the Prophet and reduced the importance of the earliest supporters.

Tension over leadership remained: The three main groups were those who supported tribal identities and accepted Muawiya and members of the Umayyad clan as the legitimate leaders; Ali's supporters, and others who believed that only descendants of the Prophet could be rightful leaders; and the pious Kharijis who believed they were the only true Muslims and wanted to move the government back to Medina. When Muawiya designated his son Yazid as his successor, establishing the precedent for hereditary rule rather than selection based on the consensus of the community or relationship to Muhammad, many protested, arguing that hereditary rule violated long-standing traditions.

When Muawiya died in 680, civil war again broke out over the issue of succession. Ali's followers formed the Party of Ali (Shi'a) and encouraged Husayn, Ali's surviving son, to fight for his right to be caliph. Umayyad forces surrounded Husayn's small contingent of soldiers at Karbala, in present day Iraq, and when none of Husayn's other supporters came to his aid, Yazid's forces easily killed Husayn and his remaining troops, and Umayyad leaders prevailed.

As the years passed, Husayn's supporters, Shi'i Muslims, became extremely remorseful over what they interpreted as Husayn's martyrdom and their own failure to try to rescue him. Every year, during Muhurram, Shi'i Muslims, a relatively small but important part of the total Muslim community, perform acts of self-mutilation for what they believe was their betrayal of Husayn; this ritual is called Muhurram. At the same time, other Shi'a remember Hasan, Ali's other son, who had retired to Medina to devote the rest of his life to spiritual practices. Thus Shi'a, who now make up about 10 percent of all Muslims, revere both the aggressive and the mystical aspects of Islam. The present cities of Najaf and Karballa in Iraq, associated with Ali and Husayn, are the holiest sites for Shi'a.

The vast majority of Muslims continued to believe that the caliph should be selected by the consensus of the community and not because of one's relationship to the family of Muhammad and Ali. They are known as Sunni Muslims. Sunni Muslims follow the *Sunnah*, a term which emerged in the ninth century. Sunnah means custom, method, path, or example, and it refers particularly to the example of the Prophet.

The Shi'a and Sunni have remained the two major schools (wings, sects) of Islam, although there have been many offshoots from both of these groups.

ACHIEVEMENTS OF THE UMAYYAD CALIPHATE

The Umayyad Caliphate achieved impressive military success. Instead of the annual military campaigns the Right Guided Caliphs had sent out from garrison cities, the caliphate launched planned attacks organized from the imperial court, and the spoils of war paid most of the army's expenses. Muslim Arab forces spread relatively quickly across North Africa, conquering tribal groups known as Berbers (from the Greek word "barbari" for "savage"). Although many Berbers initially resisted Arab advances, the area was sparely populated so they could not wage a vigorous defense.

Caliph Abd al-Malik (685–705) demilitarized the Arab garrisons in Iraq and began including Syrian forces in the army. Berber converts to Islam who crossed the Strait of Gibraltar in 711 to invade Spain were known as Moors. (Although "Moor," a Greek word meaning "dark," initially referred to inhabitants of North Africa, it now usually refers to any Muslim—whether from North Africa or west Asia—who lived in Spain.) By 719, Arab-led Algerian and Moroccan Berbers had conquered much of the Iberian Peninsula, and a band of Muslims even crossed the Pyrenees Mountains. After the Franks defeated this small contingent at Tours in 732, the Muslim army had little incentive to try to invade sparsely settled northern Europe, where the absence of significant settlements, not to mention cities, meant spoils would be meager at best.

In 711, Arab Muslim forces also entered Sind, the southern portion of the Indus River valley. By 750, only 128 years after Muhammad's death, the Muslims controlled the territory from the Pyrenees bordering Spain, across North Africa, western Asia, and as far east as the Indus Valley in the Indian subcontinent, and in 751 they defeated Chinese forces near the Talas River. Their victories opened up commercial opportunities across this huge area and contributed to the wealth of the caliphate.

Umayyad leaders modeled their administration on the efficient bureaucratic organization of the Sasanians and Byzantines, and they continued to take advantage of the expertise and experience of local government officials by allowing them to remain in their jobs. Virtually the same officials collected the same amount of taxes, only the payments of money or goods now went to the Umayyads instead of to Byzantine or Sasanid courts. State support for religion was similar to Byzantine practices, and

building impressive mosques echoed the Byzantine example of constructing elaborate churches.

THE ULAMA AND SUFIS

Although the caliphate had significant political and military power,
caliphs did not have ultimate religious authority. Anyone could read the
Quran, the source of religious insight; Islam has no priests, popes, clergy,
or organizational hierarchy, and Muslims appeal directly to Allah.
Instead, a separate religious elite formed known as the *ulama,* "those
who possess knowledge," and are learned in religion and the law. These
religious scholars were schooled in the Quran and they could interpret
its true meaning. The ulama and other particularly religious persons
were considered the true authorities on Islam. In an effort to align their
rule with Islam, Umayyad leaders became patrons of the ulama and supported the construction of mosques and schools.

Equality had been relatively easy to maintain in Bedouin communities where blood loyalty, not wealth, determined one's status. However,
as the years passed, the Umayyad clan members who had received the
best government positions became wealthier, and the gap between the
rich and poor dramatically widened. Many Muslims were offended by
the court's opulence and wasteful practices and its obvious violation of
the commitment to equality, a central principle of Islam.

As a result, some individuals renounced wealth and tried to focus
on a direct personal experience of God, who often seemed inaccessi-
ble. In the beginning of the ninth century, some of these individuals,
who stood apart from both pious Muslims and scholars who were
more concerned with the law, became known as Sufis. (The name may
come from the wool (*suf*) robe early ascetics wore to symbolize their
commitment to a life of poverty.) Sufis wanted to reclaim the purity
of the early faith, shorn of the imperial trappings that political and
military success had brought. They also sought to dig beneath the
ulama's legalism to experience the spiritual essence of the faith. Sufis
longed for a personal transformation, and they wanted to erase the
ego and experience oneness with God. Like Christian Desert Fathers
and Mothers, many withdrew from society and practiced various
forms of asceticism including prayer, fasting, and purification.[61] The
Quran stated "There is no God but Allah," or, as Sufis say: "Wherever
you turn, there is the face of Allah."

Like Buddhist and Christian monks, Sufis stressed asceticism, renunciation of material goods or money that one did not earn, and celibacy.
They focused on the inner, spiritual meaning of the Quran. Sufi

communities included many women, and some became important voices, often expressing ideas that went against the dominant view of gender relations. Rabi'a (Raiah, d. 801), a famous Sufi saint, spoke of the mystical experience of the love of God. She is said to have gone through the streets of Basra with a torch and pitcher of water, intending to burn paradise and pour water on the fires of hell. Instead of desiring the one or fearing the other, she taught, one should concentrate on loving God. Instead of relying on law, respond to God's call.

Rumi (1207–1273), one of the most famous Sufi poets, wrote:

One went to the door of the Beloved and
knocked. A voice asked, "Who is there?"
He answered, "It is I."

The voice said, "There is no room for Me and Thee."
The door was shut.

After a year of solitude and deprivation he returned and knocked.
A voice from within asked, "Who is there?"
The man said, 'It is Thee.'
The door was opened for him."[62]

Although their numbers were relatively small at first, the ulama feared that Sufis would undermine their religious authority and, as their numbers grew, might compete with the larger Islamic brotherhood.[63] Sufis responded by saying that they were going back to the "divine source itself" and trying to imitate the example of the Prophet. Sufis also hoped to reduce the tensions between Sunni and the Shi'i factions. Gradually Sufism became an increasingly important religious movement, and average Muslims looked to both the ulama and Sufis, not to the caliphs, for moral instruction and religious guidance.

INITIAL CONVERSIONS

Initially, Arabs considered Islam their own special faith and almost all converts were Arabs. Conversions were almost all voluntary, occurring informally through social interaction and intermarriage. All one had to do to become a Muslim was declare with sincere conviction that Allah is the only God and Muhammad is his prophet. Many of those who professed faith in Allah probably had only a vague idea of what Islam was all about, although the promise of salvation after death must have been appealing.

Arabs living in Syria who did not follow the retreating Byzantine forces tended to convert. In the social hierarchy Arab Muslims enjoyed the highest status, half-Arab Muslims came next, followed by the *mawali*, non-Arabs who had converted and been adopted by a clan. Non-Muslims were consigned to the bottom of the social hierarchy.

Barring some emotional experience or revelation, most people do not convert to another faith unless conversion improves their standing in the society.[64] Some non-Arabs were probably motivated to surrender to Allah for political, social, and economic reasons. Because non-Arabs who converted were considered mawali, that is, inferiors, most of the initial non-Arab converts were former slaves or individuals with a very low standing in the society who would improve their status if they converted. Non-Muslims captured in battle who became slaves soon learned that conversion increased their chances of becoming freedmen because Muslims were forbidden to enslave fellow Muslims. Converts who came from the lower ranks of the society were often attracted to some of the more emotional sects of Islam such as the Kharijis that seemed to offer them improved status. Cavalry officers who joined the Muslim army might convert because they were promised handsome stipends and a chance to maintain their privileged status as warriors.

Avoiding the head tax might have been an incentive for conversion, although the obligation to pay alms for the community's welfare (*zakat*) amounted to a tax. Some converted to take advantage of different rates of taxation. For example, tax rates the Umayyad administration imposed in Egypt favored Muslim immigrants and Egyptian converts. Some non-Muslim bureaucrats serving in the conquered areas converted to ensure that they kept their government jobs. Those in conquered areas who experienced Allah's majesty might be moved to surrender. In addition, the Umayyad Caliphate attracted many who wanted to be a part of something so impressive.

In spite of these factors, during the first century and a half, military conquests were not usually followed by conversions, and by 750 no more than 10 percent of the indigenous population that was under Muslim control had surrendered to Allah.[65] Muslim forces wanted to control territory, not win converts, and conversion, forced or voluntary, was rare.

WHAT INTERNAL TENSIONS WEAKENED THE UMAYYAD CALIPHATE?

The hereditary monarchy Muawiya had instituted was very different from the example of the Rightly Guided Caliphs. Centralized government might be very effective, but the devout who remembered the earlier idealized period resisted its authority and feared that investing so much power in one person was unwise. Resentment at the growing inequality, mingled with bitterness against the wealthy Umayyad clan that initially had opposed Muhammad, eventually developed into open hostility against the Umayyads. Early supporters of Muhammad and devout Muslims had always considered the Umayyads outsiders, and the secularism and corruption of the caliphate only increased the sense of the caliphate's illegitimacy.

Heightened tensions between Arab Muslims, and half-Arab and non-Arab converts grew increasingly divisive, and discontent over the growing inequalities led to intense reform efforts. Non-Arab converts who were increasingly resentful over their unequal status and no longer wanting to be considered mawali, joined the calls for reform. Many Arab soldiers had married local women, and their children, who were raised as Muslims, were demanding to be treated as equals. So were the children of Muslim men and their non-Muslim concubines. In addition, Shi'a resented the prominence of Sunnis in the government.

Caliph Umar II (717–20) attempted to lessen tensions between Arabs and non-Arabs and he sought to make Arab, half-Arab, and non-Arab Muslims equal. However, his efforts did not prevent disgruntled Muslims from staging a successful revolt. The Umayyads were overthrown, and in 750 the Abbasids took control.

THE ABBASID CALIPHATE

The Abbasids claimed to be descendents of Abbas, Muhammad's uncle, but they did little to forward the Shi'i cause. To distance themselves from the Umayyads and eliminate any suspicion that they favored Arab Muslims, al-Mansur, the second Abbasid caliph who ruled from 754 to 775, ordered a new city built by the Tigris River, near the former Sasanid capital. Creating a new capital that symbolized the government's power was a long-standing west Asian tradition.

Baghdad (Madinat al-Salam—City of Peace) was laid out as a cosmic city, an earthly replica of the ruler's vision of the cosmos. This new city was arranged in three concentric circles with the caliph's palace at the center and the Friday Mosque to one side. A large plaza for commercial activities and troop review surrounded the palace and mosque. Four prominent streets radiated out from the center in the four cardinal directions.[66]

Rulers and administrators found it difficult to entirely give up the earlier policies of personal ties, but the practice of making non-Arab converts mawali was discontinued, and, as the government became increasingly impersonal and professional, the term lost its association with inferiority. The Abbasids consciously recruited administrative and military leaders from all over the empire. Although Arabs remained

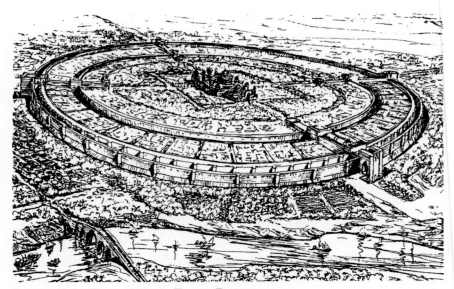

FIGURE 4-2   DIAGRAM OF EARLY BAGHDAD
This demonstrates the layout of Baghdad as a well with the sacred center.

important at all levels, bureaucrats might be Copts, Syrians, Persians, Nestorian Christians or Jews, as well as Muslims. The common commitment to Islam as an overarching system of belief and a common culture undergirded the transition from governance by an ethnic elite to a more open and pluralistic system.

The Abbasids were not primarily interested in conquest. They focused more on consolidation, commerce, and development of the arts and literature. Building on the wealth and sophisticated culture of the earlier Sasanid and Persian empires, the new capital quickly became a metropolitan center. By 800, its population had reached more than 700,000, making it the second-largest city in the world at that time, 10 times larger than the Sasanian capital of Ctesiphon that had been the largest west Asian city up to that time. (Constantinople had only about 200,000.) By 900, Baghdad may have had as many as 900,000 people, and Changan in China probably had about 750,000.[67]

Baghdad became a major commercial center. The Umayyads had introduced standard silver and gold coins engraved with Arabic phrases but no images, and these coins were soon being used from Morocco to the borders of China. Baghdad's textile, leather, paper, and other industries flourished. It was also a center of international trade. Its founder, Caliph al-Mansur, stated: "There is no obstacle between us and China; everything on the sea can come to us,"[68] By the ninth century, an Arab geographer would identify the area around the Persian Gulf as "the center of the world or the navel of the earth."[69]

Baghdad's renowned prosperity during the rule of Caliph Harun al-Rashid (786–809) came from trade, commerce, industry, and agriculture, not from conquest. He is immortalized in the fictional tales *The Thousand and One Nights*. Stories such as Sinbad the Sailor illustrate the vibrant commerce that existed in the Indian Ocean, which Muslim shippers and merchants dominated.

Baghdad's heterogeneous, cosmopolitan character was its most important characteristic. Baghdad residents became patrons of the arts and culture. Its diverse population was integrated into a single society that was infused with the Islamic religion. Its culture began to trickle down to an increasing number of subject peoples who hankered to partake of the power and glory of this extremely sophisticated urban culture.

ISLAMIZATION

With the founding of Baghdad and the increased participation of non-Arabs in all aspects of government, Muslims began to reformulate their conception of Islam's relationship to the non-Arab world. Instead of claiming the revelations were meant exclusively for Arabs, as many had assumed initially, they proclaimed that Allah was the God of all humanity. With this shift in consciousness, Islam truly became universal, and religious conversion began to increase dramatically within Dar al-Islam, the areas under Muslim control or those with a Muslim cultural ethos.

Conversion is often assumed to mean a personal decision individuals make to accept specific religious precepts. But most so-called conversions come about gradually as people begin to shift their habits and actions. This was certainly true with Islam. This change was really a process of Islamization: a gradual acceptance of a broader Islamic way of life that resulted from living in an Islamic urban environment and having contact with Muslims and Islamic communal institutions. This process of gradually internalizing new habits of heart and mind lasted for decades and even centuries.

At the same time, Islam changed as well, as it became well-established in new environments. Local attitudes and customs were adopted, making adherence to the faith much easier for the non-Muslim populations. These adaptations took place most often in urban centers as Arabs, accustomed to a nomadic life, settled down and became farmers and traders.

THE IMPORTANCE OF CITIES

Cities played a prominent role in the process of Islamization. Urbanization and Islamization went hand in hand. In spite of its origin in rural Arabia, Islam, like Christianity, quickly became an urban religion, and up until the sixteenth century the majority of Muslims lived in cities. Unlike Christian Europe where cities were largely absent until the thirteenth century, Islamic cities were centers of learning and social activities almost from the start of the faith.

Urban life helped shape Islamic society, and many Muslim religious and communal institutions first developed in urban settings. As one eminent scholar has stressed, cities were the true locus of Islam's civilizational greatness, and life in cities molded society more forcefully than caliph or philosopher.[70] The Islamic ambiance of cosmopolitan communities had a profound influence for centuries. Even when newcomers eventually outnumbered the initial Arab settlers, the cities retained their Muslim character.

The influx of newcomers from the countryside, especially during the ninth century, contributed to the growth of important Iranian cities including Nishapur, Marv, Isfahan, Balkh, Herat, Shiraz, and Hamadan. Rural converts to Islam often felt isolated or shunned in their local communities, and they were drawn to cities where being a Muslim was an asset, not a liability. Nonbelievers living in the cities seldom tried to convince them to renounce their new faith, as often happened in rural communities where there were few Muslims. In cities, they could copy the way their Muslims neighbors acted and gain insights about the faith from them. Non-Muslim rural artisans and farmers who migrated to towns and cities learned Arabic and gradually become Islamized by imitating the way Muslims dressed and acted.

Arabic, already the language of poetry for Arabs, played an important role in the process of Islamization and its spread helped maintain the Islamic character of cities. Arabic was central to the faith because Allah's revelations were given in Arabic and, unlike Buddhist and Christian sacred texts, the Quran was not to be translated. Arabic united the vast Muslim communities and it became the language of administration, business, law, and trade.

Memorizing the Quran was the basis of education and the bedrock of the faith. Learning Arabic allowed nonbelievers to become familiar with the Quran and opened up the world of Islamic literature to them. By the ninth century, Arabic was the language of international scholarship as well as divine truth, and from Spain to the borders of India, Arabic became the main language of the arts, sciences, and diplomacy, much as Latin had become in Europe. Muslims could travel all across Afro-Eurasia and find people who spoke Arabic and shared a common worldview.

Economic, political, social, and religious factors all contributed to the impressive movement from rural to urban areas. Sharing a common faith facilitated commercial opportunities. Merchants tended to trust those who held common values and were usually more willing to take credit risks from fellow Muslims, even if they were strangers. Additionally, many merchants became nominal Muslims to enhance their business opportunities or advance their political fortunes with the ruling elites.

Merchants were especially sympathetic to Islam's message. Muhammad had been a trader, and using Arabic as the language of commerce enabled Muslim traders to establish commercial links throughout Dar al-Islam. Traders had played a crucial role in the spread of Buddhism, and commercial contacts, more than any other factor, took Islam to new areas. Between the eighth and tenth centuries, Arabs brought many new agricultural plants from India to Europe, including staples such as "hard wheat, rice, sugarcane, and new varieties of sorghum; fruits such as banana, sour orange, lemon, lime, mango, watermelon, and the coconut palm; vegetables such as spinach, artichoke, and eggplant, and the key industrial crop, cotton."[71]

Muslim traders' skill as salesmen was well documented, and there is even evidence of "singing commercials," such as this one to encourage the sale of black veils:

> Go ask the lovely one in the black veil
> What have you done to a devout monk?
> He had already dressed for his prayers
> Until you appeared to him by the door of the mosque.[72]

While farmers are usually loyal to local deities associated with the land, long-distance traders, accustomed to coming in contact with a variety of new ideas and beliefs, often found the universal message of Islam appealing. Traders carried Islam to central Asia, China, sub-Saharan and East Africa, and, eventually, Indonesia. Long-distance traders also established diaspora communities that provided services for merchants while they were far from home and facilitated their business transactions in far-off lands. These small communities helped keep these Muslims from losing their faith and made information about Islam available in new areas. Non-Muslims who settled in or near diasporic communities and wanted to have commercial dealings with Muslims often experienced the same gradual process of Islamization.

Negative incentives also stimulated conversion. In al-Andalus (Muslim Spain) non-Muslims, who were considered inferior, were required to wear certain distinctive articles of clothing that identified their inferior status, and they were expected to step aside when they passed a Muslim in the street. They were forbidden from making any public display of their faith, including participating in religious processions. Muslims did not take their evidence in court as seriously as evidence from fellow believers. As a result, non-Muslims might adapt local customs in an effort to "pass," but as they aped Islamic ways, they became Islamized.[73]

When the Abbasids took over the caliphate, perhaps only 10 percent of the population was Muslim. From 750 to the start of the eleventh century, the percentage of Muslims increased to about 80 percent of the population. Most of these conversions resulted from the gradual process of Islamization, not because of missionary activity or other types of pressure.

THE ROLE OF THE *SHARIAH*

Because Islam dictates how people should act, average Muslims rely on their faith to learn what they are supposed to do. They often consult readers of the Quran, Sufis, or members of the ulama, the most trusted authorities on Islam who offer them advice. Besides following the instructions in the Quran, Muslims also sought to imitate Muhammad's example even in the smallest details, such as how he ate, washed, spoke, and prayed, in order to be able to surrender totally to God and to give their lives a sense of sacred transcendence.[74]

Records of what Muhammad had said and done are known as *hadith*. At first, hadith were transmitted orally. Scholars began to collect and compile them soon after he died, and Aisha was an important source for perhaps 2,000 of them.[75] By the ninth century, Muslim scholars realized it was imperative to separate authentic hadith from what, by then, had become hundreds of thousands of statements. In an effort to sift out the spurious ones, scholars tried to identify a chain of persons, starting with someone who had had direct knowledge of the Prophet, who could authenticate any given statement. This involved evaluating each individual in the chain.

When a scholar recited a hadith, he would also state: "I learned this from so-and-so who learned it from so-and-so . . ." all the way back to the person who had heard or seen what Muhammad had done or said. Scholars also had to judge the subject matter of the hadith to make sure that it was reasonable and did not contradict the Quran. Between 870 and 896, six authoritative collections of hadith were compiled. This literature is also an important record of the early history and development of Islamic belief and practice.[76]

The Quran was the most essential guide to action, and Muslims tried to live by its instructions. But some of the Quran's statements seemed to contradict or modify established customs and tribal laws. As a result, starting in the eighth century, legal scholars attempted to figure out how to apply general moral principles to specific situations and how to adjust local practices so that they reflected the Quran's moral standards. Family, commercial, and criminal law, administrative regulations, Sasanian, Byzantine, and Hellenistic popular maxims, the canon law of the Orthodox Church, Talmudic, Rabbinic, and old Babylonian law all had to conform to God's will.[77]

In this effort, the ulama developed numerous centers for the study of Islamic law. By the tenth century, the ulama had developed a total corpus of law known as the *Shariah,* which literally means "a path to the watering place." Besides the growing scholarship related to the Quran, the Shariah was to reflect the customs and practices of Muhammad as reported in the hadith, the actions of the community, and the consensus of the scholars.

Scholars who studied the law (*faqiha*) were to give their unbiased opinion on legal matters, and their opinions became law. However, faqiha did not always agree, and individuals bringing cases were free to consult more than one faqih for an opinion. By 1075, four main schools of law (*madhhab*) had developed. They were named after their founders: al-Shafi, Ibn-Hanbal, Malik b. Anas, and Abu-Hanifah. None of these schools became dominant because ultimately "Allah alone knows."

The caliphate remained the administrative and executive head of state and the symbol of Islamic unity, but in most areas scholars and legalists who interpreted the Shariah, together with Sufi leaders, defined religious belief and practice. Making laws is usually the ongoing prerogative of rulers, but by the late tenth century, Islamic scholars interpreted the text and tradition and determined what was to be done. From then on, governmental institutions and cosmopolitan culture would evolve along one path while Islamic religious institutions, values, and practices would move along another. Unlike Christianity, in Islam no church or clergy was to intervene between the practicing Muslim and God, and Islam had no heresy trials comparable to the disputes Christians have had over the personhood of Jesus or the Trinity. The major issues separating them have been over the source of caliph's legitimacy and the quality of one's faith, not doctrinal issues.

WOMEN'S LIVES

Under the Abbasids in the ninth century, as schools of law developed, attitudes toward the roles of women, marriage regulations, and concubines solidified. It became impossible to imagine women participating actively on the battlefield as Aisha had done. In fact, her role in the unsuccessful Battle of the Camel may have led to a curtailing of women's participation in such actions, as well as the fact that captured female soldiers were humiliated and exposed naked. Although Aisha and several other wives of Muhammad had been the source of numerous hadith and their opinions had been highly respected, women gradually were excluded from religious discussions or any gatherings that men other than family members might attend. Marrying a nonvirgin was considered shameful, and women could no longer initiate marriage or divorce.

The Quran states that men can have four wives if they can treat them all equally. Because this requirement is virtually impossible to fulfill, many assumed that statement supported monogamy, and they pointed out that Muhammad had only one wife while he was married to Khadija. By Abbasid times, men could have four wives and numerous concubines, and husbands, not the courts, were left to determine whether they treated their wives equally. Further, the financial support an ex-husband was expected to give his wife was not enforced by the courts.

The rapid urbanization taking place in Islamic territories under the Abbasids contributed to significantly changing the status of women. The ethical statements that proclaimed gender equality contrasted dramatically with the social hierarchy common in urban settings into which Islam spread. Muslims had to balance the ethical vision of equality with the more restrictive traditions and social mores in the territories that their armies had conquered. Potentially ambiguous Quranic statements interpreted in the early Arabian context often sounded very different when they were read in urban communities in Syria and Palestine. As a result, statements in the Quran proclaiming gender equality tended to get overlooked or ignored.

Increased trade may help to explain why Muslims promoted a patriarchal family structure and greatly restricted the freedom and influence of women. Within the tribal society where property was held in common, identifying paternity was not critical. However, with increasing commercialization and the acquisition of individual wealth, men wanted to know who their children were in order to be able to pass on their wealth to them. As a result, patriarchy and polygamy became the accepted norms.

Increased prosperity meant that many men could afford to buy slaves and support numerous concubines as well as several wives. Prostitutes and concubines were readily available, and men could easily satisfy their sexual passions outside of marriage. Women were often viewed as another commodity to be bought, enjoyed, or sold. At the same time, wives and female family members were required to be secluded in the home and to cover and veil themselves when they went outside. As time passed, these restrictions were mistakenly assumed to have originated with Muhammad, and the debates about them were forgotten or censured.

SOLDIERS AND MAMLUKS

The composition of the army also changed significantly during the Abbasid Caliphate, especially as areas under Muslim control extended well beyond the caliphate's direct political authority. It proved difficult to effectively rule the vast and diverse area that stretched from the Iberian Peninsula to the Indian subcontinent. By the ninth century, an increasing number of areas were only loosely under the Abbasids, and various factions, including Shi'a and Sufis as well as regional leaders, were all vying for power.

In an effort to check the fragmentation of Abbasid authority, al-Ma'mun, caliph from 813 to 833, supported several important military and cultural innovations. One was using slaves called *Mamluks* (meaning one who is owned) in the army. These professional soldiers helped keep the peace, patrolled the huge expanse of empire, and served as palace guards. Before long, Turkish and Iranian slaves made up most of the armed forces in the east. Berbers and Slavs filled most of the slave armies of Europe, augmented by some Africans. Some of these slaves were captured in war, but most were purchased and then given military training. Slave soldiers were often offered opportunities for advancement; some became officers and a few even became commanders and rulers.

Many Islamic rulers favored using Mamluks in their armies because they believed they could rely on their absolute obedience. Mamluks had no family ties or loyalty to any local area and no potential power base. Moreover, Muslims believed they were exceptionally strong, equipped with martial skills and a military mind-set.[78] Ibn Khaldum, the famous fourteenth century Muslim historian, wrote that slaves come

> . . . with nomadic virtues unsullied by debased nature, unadulterated by the filth of pleasure, undefiled by ways of civilized living, with their ardor unbroken by the profusion of luxury. . . . Thus one intake comes

after another and generation follows generation, and Islam rejoices in the benefits which it gains through them, and the branches of the kingdom flourishes with the freshness of youth.[79]

Besides transforming the armed forces, Caliph al-Mam'un also patronized Greek, Indian, and Arabic scholarship. Byzantine emperors sent him works of Plato, Aristotle, Hippocrates, Galen, Euclid, and Ptolemy, and he gave them rich gifts in return. Indian scholars introduced place numbers, decimals, algorithms, and the concept of zero, later known in Europe as "Arabic numerals." Ma'mun started the famous House of Wisdom (*Bayt al-Hikma*) in Baghdad and brought the most experienced translators there, and he urged his subjects to read the translations they made. Scholars had high status, and the caliph surrounded himself with learned men, legal experts, and a wide range of scholars.[80]

FIGURE 4-3   THE OBSERVATORY OF MURAD III, ISTANBUL, TURKEY
This picture demonstrates the high level of Islamic science.

Scholars at the House of Wisdom and other centers of learning were among the most learned in all of Eurasia. They collected, translated, and commented on the works of Plato and Aristotle as well as Indian mathematicians and scientists and produced lively, innovative, and creative science, mathematics, and philosophy. Long before Christian theologians turned to Greek rationalism, Islamic scholars had forged a synthesis of faith and reason and had accepted the existence of a rationally ordered universe that could be known through human reason. Although the court encouraged the new learning, the ulama made an effort to carefully select those aspects of Hellenistic culture that they believed would reinforce their own moral and religious positions.

Even though Caliph al-Ma'mun's innovations were important and the Abbasids continued to claim ultimate power over Dar al-Islam, the caliphate in west Asia broke into several independent entities. The Fatamids took control over most of Egypt. By the time the Saljuk Turks migrated into Anatolia, most of them were nominal Muslims. They overran Baghdad in 1055, but the kingdom they established had fragmented by the end of that century. A further blow to any united Muslim empire was the Mongol invasion of Baghdad in 1258. The Mongols allowed a caliph to remain as the symbolic religious leader, but the sultan they installed had the real political power.

Although political control was fragmented, strong religious, cultural, and trading networks survived, preserving and even enhancing an overarching sense of Islamic unity. Islamic societies from west Asia to the borders of the Indian subcontinent conformed to general Islamic principles. Common religious values, common institutions, and a common worldview held Dar al-Islam together. The art, literature, philosophy, education, and sciences all reflected Islamic values and forms.

THE SPREAD OF DAR AL-ISLAM

AL-ANDALUS

One Muslim area that was never part of the Abbasid caliphate was al-Andalus, the Arabic name for land south of the Pyrenees Mountains that the Muslims controlled. By about 716, Muslims had conquered all of the Iberian Peninsula. When the Abbasids overthrew the Umayyad Caliphate in 750, Abd al-Rahman, a young Umayyad prince, fled across North Africa, reaching the Iberian Peninsula in 756. His forces united the various factions and established an Islamic emirate there. In 929, Abd al-Rahman III proclaimed that the emirate was an autonomous caliphate, rivaling Baghdad, and he ushered in its Golden Age.

Al-Andalus quickly became a very cosmopolitan area. During the tenth century, Cordoba was perhaps the largest city in the world. Estimates of its population range from 300,000 to nearly a million. Al-Maqqari, a seventeenth century Arab historian, wrote: ". . . in four things Cordoba surpasses the capitals of the world. Among them are the bridge over the river and the mosque. These are the first two; the third is the Madinat al-Zahra [a palace city about five kilometers outside of Cordoba]; but the greatest of all things is knowledge—and that is the fourth."[81]

Cordoba's Great Mosque (*mezquita*), the third largest mosque in the Islamic world, symbolizes Muslim hegemony in al-Andalus. It was a famous center for higher learning and supported the earliest university in Europe. Madinat al-Zahra was built under the direction of Abd al-Rahman III in 936/324. Its magnificent buildings are said to have bedazzled visitors and impressed them with the caliphate's power.

Cordoba was home to 70 libraries. Caliph al-Hakim's library may have had as many as 400,000 books. At the same time, one of northern Europe's major libraries had only 600 books. Cordoba's inhabitants had the reputation of enthusiastically caring for their libraries, and their collections were regarded as status symbols. The city was a center of intellectual life for Jews, Christians, and Muslims, many of whom were bilingual in Arabic and the local dialect. Female copyists worked in the Cordoba book markets, and women worked as teachers, secretaries, and librarians, and some practiced law and medicine.

Subsequently, weak leaders and internal disputes crippled the caliphate and by 1031, it had fragmented into 30 small states. Rivalries among these states further weakened the area, allowing two fundamentalists Muslim groups from North Africa to successfully invade. In addition, by 1212 Christian rulers, who controlled the northern part of the peninsula, launched the *reconquista,* a campaign to conquer the entire peninsula. By 1248 the Nasrid kingdom of Granada was the last vestige of Islamic power in Iberia.

The Alhambra was the Nasrid's impressive royal city. Two exquisite palaces are still standing: the Palace of Comrades, intended for official and ceremonial use, and the Palace of the Lions, the private chambers for the royal family's enjoyment. The spectacular cupola that comprises the ceiling of the Hall of the Two Sisters, with about 5,000 niches cascading downward, symbolizes the rotation of the skies in Islamic cosmology. The walls of the room are covered with poetic inscriptions such as: "The stars would gladly descend from their zones of light, and wish they lived in this hall instead of in heaven."[82] No wonder the Alhambra

FIGURE 4-4   CUPOLA, HALL OF TWO SISTERS AT AL HAMBRA
Cascading niches in the dome in the Hall of Two Sisters.

is one of the most often visited historic sites in the world. As an exile from Granada wrote:

> The city of Granada finds her equal
> Not in Cairo, nor Damascus, nor Iraq.
> She is the bride unveiled,
> While others are just the dowry.[83]

AFRICA

Gradual Islamization characterized the spread of Islam in West Africa. Muslim Berbers carried Islam across the Sahara Desert to the Soninke people in the Sahel, who then spread it further south to Malinke-speaking traders on the fringes of the rain forest. Traders, urbanization, and strong centralized states facilitated Islam's spread.

West African leaders welcomed Muslim traders as long as they did not seem to pose a political threat. In Ghana in the mid-eleventh century, Muslims lived peacefully in a separate town bordering the main city. Although most Muslims were foreigners, the gold trade brought African merchants into contact with Islamic culture in towns or diasporic communities along the trade routes. European travelers and traders remarked on the quantity of the beautiful gold jewelry that people wore, and gold that Europeans acquired through trade from West Africa became Europe's currency and was largely responsible for financing European development at this time.

While Muslims stayed isolated from the rest of the population, the faith made little impact on the wider community. The vast majority of the population worshiped a collection of different spirits, gods, and goddesses. Rural farmers had almost no way of finding out about Islam and little incentive to convert. Local residents considered Muslims synonymous with traders.

Leaders who claimed to have converted to Islam found that they could more readily attract Muslim traders. Those facing challenges to their legitimacy frequently sought supernatural assistance, particularly in wartime. When prayers to Allah brought victory, they may have been glad to add worship of Allah to their other prayers and may even have gradually considered that Allah was more powerful than the local gods.

A leader might try to introduce certain Muslim rituals, but usually the vast majority of his subjects continued to perform their traditional rituals and, although they might add some Muslim prayers, they resented any seeming neglect of established traditions. As a result, leaders often supported both Muslim and local rituals at court, and the Islam that Muslims in West Africa practiced was a synthesis of local traditions and the ulama's teaching.

Sundiata, who helped established the West African kingdom of Mali in the mid-thirteenth century, is a good example of a ruler who blended Muslim and indigenous beliefs. The Malinke people had nominally accepted Islam as a result of their close contact with traders along the Sahel and across the Sahara. *Griots* (storytellers and keepers of legends and history) depict Sundiata as a great Malinke hunter and magician who had become a Muslim. However, at the critical turning point in the battle to defend his kingdom, Sundiata appealed to the local spirits for support, and he believed their magical powers helped him defeat the enemy.

Mali reached its golden age in the early fourteenth century under Mansa Musa (1312–1337), who distributed so much gold during his famous pilgrimage to Mecca in 1325 that its value dropped. By that time, Mali was considered a Muslim kingdom, even though its pre-Islamic heritage remained vital. Ibn Battuta, a famous Moroccan Muslim scholar and traveler, visited Mali in 1352–3 and reported that public prayers and preaching about Islam were accompanied by masked dancers and recitations by local griots. He noted with approval the careful observation of the times of prayer and the effort put into memorizing the Quran, but dismissed the griots' recitations.

The ulama that Mansu Musa took to Timbuktu, and other scholars who settled in commercial West African towns, carried on the scholarly

FIGURE 4-5   THE MOSQUE AT JENNE-JENO, GHANA, AFRICA
From Aramco World, November–December, 1990.

tradition by observing the law and studying the Quran. For a time, books were probably the best-selling commodity in that city. The vast majority of Muslim converts in West Africa, however, practiced a very African-ized version of Islam. They thought prayer was the most important reli-gious ritual they performed, and they viewed the Quran as a source of blessing rather than as a revelation of divine instruction.

Although Islam had difficulty penetrating Ethiopian society that traced its origins back to fifth-century Axum and that was experienc-ing a Christian revival, it spread along the east coast of Africa and to neighboring islands. East Africans supported themselves mostly by agriculture and by participating in the lively Indian Ocean commerce. Bantu-speaking Africans had settled in East African coastal areas long before Muslim traders introduced Islam to the area. Arab Muslim traders seeking goods and markets settled in towns along the coast, including Mogadishu and Kilwa, bringing information about their reli-gion with them. Kilwa, the southernmost point that the monsoon winds propelled ships, became a prosperous trading port handling goods from Zimbabwe, which was farther south.

By the thirteenth century, about 36 towns between Mogadishu and Kilwa were involved in Indian Ocean commerce. Contact between the local people and immigrant Muslims, many of whom settled in the com-mercial towns and married local women, led to the creation of an East

African Islamic way of life known as Swahili culture. Swahili means "coast-dwellers" and their language, a mixture of Bantu and Arabic, was written in the Arabic script. It is not difficult to see Islam's appeal. It must have seemed as though all the successful people, many of them traders, were Muslims, and their prosperity served as an advertisement for the faith.[84] The Islamic ambiance and culture of the independent Swahili city-states resulted in a gradual Islamization of the whole society. To be Swahili meant being a Muslim.

SOUTHEAST ASIA

A tolerant attitude toward religions prevailed throughout most of Southeast Asia where indigenous, Hindu, and Buddhist beliefs and practices had mixed together. Muslims merchants, prominent in Indian Ocean commerce, spread their faith along the Straits of Melacca between Sumatra and the Malay Peninsula, where several small states had developed after the fall of Srivijaya in the twelfth century. Starting in the later thirteenth century, Indian and Arab Sufis introduced their form of Islam there. Sufi saints impressed influential members of these communities by stressing similarities between their faith and local beliefs and by making people feel part of the wider Muslim community. Sufi mysticism, with its emphasis on loving God, resonated with local beliefs as well as aspects of Hinduism. As a result, local residents often became disciples of various Sufi saints.

The fourteenth century marks the introduction of Islam to Java, where a tolerant attitude also existed. Kings of the Hindu-Buddhist court of Majapahit, situated in the interior, did not object to Sufis spreading information about their faith. Religion was looked upon as a means of exerting spiritual power, so local leaders, who appear to have considered Islam as another source of that power, incorporated some Islamic rituals.

Unlike the interior that was relatively isolated, a series of comparatively new trading ports that were part of the trade from the Spice Islands to the Mediterranean developed along the northern coast of Java. Merchants coming to these ports had regular contact with Muslim centers in South India and west Asia, and the majority of them were Muslim. Leaders in the port cities were more interested in attracting traders then in paying tribute to Majapahit, and they used Islam to counter its authority. As a result, by the end of the fifteenth century the port cities had become predominately Muslim.

Because many of the initial leaders in the ports had come from other areas and were already Muslim, these leaders went through a process of

Javanization rather than Islamization. Their subjects may have become nominal Muslims because their leaders were, and Islam gradually became entrenched along the coast and became a way to rally the coastal population.

Islam's spread to Malacca was also largely a result of trade. After defeating the Yuan Dynasty in China, the newly installed Ming leaders wanted to reestablish China's hegemony over neighboring areas and regain its influence in the Indian Ocean. Between 1405 and 1433, the Ming emperor commissioned large, impressive "treasure ships" that made seven voyages intended to showcase China's prestige. The Chinese hoped that as a result of the third voyage (1409–11), China would gain control of the Straits of Malacca.

Local leaders were vying for power in the Straits region, and during the power struggle, Parameshvara, a Hindu prince who claimed to be related to the Srivijayan royal family, escaped to Malacca, a small fishing village with an excellent harbor near the southern end of the straits. When the third Ming voyage reached his village, Zheng He, the commander, stated that Melacca was a vassal state of China and Parameshvara was its legitimate leader. Assuming this meant he would play an important role in trade with China, Parameshvara went on a tribute mission to the Ming emperor.

But 12 years later, the Ming emperor decided to end the voyages, recall the ships, and withdraw the fleet. This decision meant Chinese traders would no longer come to Malacca. To secure trade, Parameshvara would have to attract Muslim merchants who were stopping at neighboring ports where Muslim rulers welcomed them. Parameshvara soon converted to Islam, and before long Malacca was a critical part of the profitable Indian Ocean trading network that Muslims dominated. Melacca's importance led a European traveler in 1520 to remark, "Whoever is lord of Malacca has his hands on the throat of Venice."[85]

By the sixteenth century, Islam had become an important—but not the exclusive—source of spiritual energy in Southeast Asia. Indigenous pre-Islamic culture continued and pre-Islamic legacies, such as shadow puppet performances, which featured the Hindu epics, and belief in many spirits and also the Oneness of all existence, retained their influence and importance in part by incorporating Islamic elements.

CHINA

Muslims made official contact with the Chinese in 651 when Uthman, the Third Rightly Guided Caliph, sent a diplomatic mission to the Tang court. The Chinese decided that the delegation's ignorance as barbarians explained their refusal to kow-tow to anything but Allah. In fact, they looked upon the Muslims as foreign "barbarians" who had come to pay tribute, not as members of a foreign religion.[86] In 751, Muslim forces defeated the Chinese army at the Talis River, but instead of advancing further, they stopped fighting and returned home to participate in the transfer of power from the Umayyads to the Abbasids.

A few years later, in large part because Muslims helped the Tang put down the An-Lushan rebellion, they were allowed to settle in China. Even so, the Islamic presence in China was limited to various Muslim groups who settled along the western frontiers, a scattering of soldiers and advisors who served in the Chinese court, and diasporic communities of Muslim traders who lived in large Chinese cities and along the seacoast. Instead of trying to proselytize as the Buddhists and Christians had done, Muslims lived in separate enclaves and did not try to convert others or adapt Chinese ways and assimilate. Instead, they strove to maintain their Islamic way of life.

Very gradually a two-way process took place: the Sinicization of Islam and Islamization of some of the Chinese who came in contact with Muslims. Their mosques began to look like Chinese buildings and usually did not have minarets. Muslims adapted Chinese clothing, speech, names, and patterns of behavior, but they maintained their Islamic beliefs: they were Muslim in private and Chinese in public, and their main loyalty remained with Muslim rulers in their home countries.

FIGURE 4-6   THE MOSQUE AT XIAN, CHINA
This mosque is very much in the Chinese architectural style.

To gain some status in Chinese eyes, the Muslims tried to associate Islam with early Chinese history. In one story they claimed that the first legendary ruler of China was a descendant of Adam and that scholars before the Hsia Dynasty (the first legendary Chinese dynasty) were all Muslims.[87] A Ming-era monument links Muhammad and Confucius and presents Muslim practices, such as ablutions before prayer and fasting, as expressions of the Neo-Confucian value of self-cultivation and the Buddhist teaching to reduce wants and passions. The monument reads in part:

> Though separated by ages and countries, they had the same mind and truth. . . . The Great Western sage ['s] . . . . teaching were: to purify one's self in bathing, to nourish one's mind by diminishing one's wants, to restrict one's passions by fasting, to eliminate one's faults as the essential element in self-cultivation, to be true and honest as the basis for convincing others, to assist at marriages and to be present at funerals."[88]

Some Muslims received important assignments at the Ming court. Zheng He, the "Three Jeweled" eunuch who commanded the famous Ming naval expeditions, was a Muslim, and he and some of his sailors may have made the hajj during one of the voyages. However, when the Ming cut itself off from foreign contact, starting in the mid-fifteenth century, the Muslim communities lost contact with their homelands and increasingly married Chinese women and adopted Chinese customs.

ANATOLIA

In the tenth century, Turkish groups began to migrate into Anatolia. Many of them became nominal Muslims as a result of earlier Arab conquests as well as the presence of Muslim traders and Sufi saints who had migrated into Central Asia.

In 1055, nomadic Seljuk Turks conquered Baghdad and controlled an empire that stretched from Iraq to Khurasan. Saljuk sultans adopted the Persian bureaucratic organization and used the Persian language at the court, and residents of Konya and other cities adopted an Islamic cosmopolitan life style. The cities attracted Sunni scholars from former Abbasid-held lands, who then established colleges. Sufis, whom the local people respected, served as intermediaries and allies. Sufi *babas* (holy men) mobilized warrior bands that protected travelers, mediated tribal disputes, established schools, and helped create order in rural areas. Sufis also helped settle newcomers and supported agriculture. Sufis were tolerant of Christians and tried to synthesize Christian and Muslim beliefs in an effort to facilitate conversion.

The Saljuk victory over the Byzantine forces at the battle of Manzikart in 1071 effectively ended the Byzantine defense system on its eastern frontier and opened all of Anatolia to the Turks. After 1095, numerous Turkish groups entered the former Saljuk Empire that had splintered into numerous petty states. Small bands of Turkish *ghazia* (warriors of the faith) led by chiefs or Sufi holy men, attacked the "infidels" in hopes of getting booty or martyrdom. The fighting spoiled much of the agricultural land in Anatolia and isolated cities from their supporting hinterland.

The Osmanlis (Ottomans) were one of the warring frontier groups. They established small enclaves in Anatolia, west of the former Saljuk strongholds, and in 1326 they made Bursa, near the Black Sea, their capital. They encouraged Turkish migration into Anatolia and the Balkans and formulated plans to take Constantinople. Over the next 200 years, they launched repeated attacks against Byzantium and captured territory both east and west of Constantinople. In 1453, the Ottomans launched a successful surprise attack against the city. The conquest of Constantinople marked the end of the nearly 1,000-year-old Byzantine Empire and dramatically increased Muslim power in the eastern Mediterranean.

The success of both the Ottoman expansion and subsequent Islamization of Anatolia resulted in large part because of the internal weakness of Byzantium and its Christian communities. Because the Byzantine government appointed church officials, the Ottomans suspected they might be agents of the emperor, so they tried to prevent the clergy from reaching their congregations. Because travel was dangerous, many had difficulty getting to their parishes. By the early-fourteenth century, Christians in the area, bereft of any strong Byzantine presence or leadership from the Orthodox Church, had little or no support. The Greek Orthodox Church in Anatolia was extremely weak, and gradually the Ottomans took over whatever revenue the church had.

Churches, which the first Christian missionaries had built over pagan temples, were now transformed into mosques. One of the grandest of all Christian cathedrals, Hagai Sofia in Constantinople, was converted into a mosque, and four minarets were added. Churches in Anatolia, shorn of income, could no longer provide services such as hospitals, orphanages, and monasteries, and organized Christianity nearly disappeared. Christians were reduced to poverty; their congregations dwindled as their members fled, or were taken into slavery, or converted to Islam. Gradually, Christians were drawn to Muslim services and to the increasingly Islamicized urban centers. Many willingly began to copy Islamic customs and convert. Some probably wondered whether the Muslim victories were signs that God favored Islam. Intermarriages furthered the integration of some Christian and Muslim rites and beliefs. Sufis, trying to stress similarities between Christianity and Islam, emphasized the mystical aspects of both faiths. The members of the Byzantine upper class were no doubt tempted to convert so they could become part of the Ottoman aristocracy, obtain government appointments, and keep their estates.

As disastrous as their conquest had been for Christians in the area, the Turks brought new security to the war-wracked area. In place of moribund Christian communities, the Ottomans built mosques, opened madrasas (schools), caravansaries, and hospitals. They invited Persian and Arabic scholars to assist in creating a vibrant Islamic culture on the ruins of what had been Byzantium.

Toward the end of the fourteenth century, Ottoman rulers established a core of soldiers known as *janissaries*. At first, the janissary ranks were filled by slaves, prisoners, and volunteers, but in 1395 the Ottomans initiated the *devshirme* system. When more soldiers were needed, the Turks took young Christian boys from their families in Anatolia and made them slaves of the Sultan. Totally dependent on the Sultan for their survival and forbidden to marry, the janissaries were trained in the art of war. Those who showed promise were given additional training as officers or scholars. Although they all were expected to convert to Islam, many remained sympathetic to the Christian communities, especially in the areas from which they had come, so they helped reduce tensions between the Ottoman rulers and their Christian subjects.

By the early sixteenth century, Anatolia had become Turkish speaking and was 90 percent Muslim,[89] although for many, conversion meant little more than circumcision, getting new clothes, and following the Sharia.[90] By contrast, in the census taken from 1520–30, 19 percent of the Balkans was Muslim, 81 percent Christian, and there was also a small Jewish minority. Fewer Christians in the Balkans adopted Islam because there were fewer Muslims in that area whom the Christians could emulate than there were in Anatolia. In addition, after conquering the area, the Ottomans quickly granted the Christian dhimmi (protected) status and gave the subject groups autonomy. Each group, identified as a *milet*, had its own social, religious, and communal life, so there was little incentive to convert. Christianity remained vital in the Balkins and the Eastern Orthodox and Armenian churches were two of the main millets.[91]

The Ottoman Empire offers an excellent example of gradual adaptation to the dominant culture. The ongoing absorption of Christians into Ottoman society in large part meant becoming "Osmanli." Members of the Ottoman ruling elite who were considered Osmanli were not necessarily Turks or even Muslims. Many were Bosnians, Albanians, Greeks, Jews, and others. Being Osmanli was more a matter of style: One had to speak Turkish in a certain way and exhibit the manners and actions of the culture of the court. Individuals could become part of the elite if they were able to emulate the life style of those in the inner circle.[92] Many Christians did just that, and gradually, sometimes without even realizing what was happening, they became Muslims as well.

THE INDIAN SUBCONTINENT

Islam first came to the Indian subcontinent in 644 when an Arab commander reached Sind in what is now Pakistan. He reported: "water is scarce, the fruits are poor, and the robbers are bold . . ."[93] In 711, when pirates looted an Arab ship near Sind, the Umayyad governor in Baghdad sent an army against the Sind rulers. The army established a small enclave in Sind so they could protect their merchant fleets in the area, but they had no intention of moving further inland. It was only in the tenth century, as the Abbasid Empire splintered into smaller sultanates, that Islamic military forces marched deeper into the subcontinent.

Muslim Turkish sultanates in Afghanistan lived mostly by raiding settled areas on the eastern side of the Khyber Pass that leads into the subcontinent. Afghan Turks were often tempted to pillage India and carry back some of its vast wealth. The Ghaznavids, who established a kingdom in present-day Afghanistan that lasted for about 200 years, had converted to Islam in the early eleventh century. Their most famous leader, Sultan Mahmud of Ghazni (971–1030), led numerous raids into northern India, Gujarat, and Sind, and he even made forays into the center of the subcontinent. He regarded Hindus as idolaters, not "People of the Book," and he launched a series of annual raids, ostensibly to smash what he considered the infidels' idols, and his forces captured Lahore in present-day Pakistan. Mahmud used the treasures his troops brought back to transform eleventh century Ghazni into a major center of Islamic culture, the home of Al-Biruni (b. 973) one of Islam's greatest scholars, and the Persian poet Firdawsi, the author of the famous epic the *Shah-name.*

A hundred years after Mahmud's death, Muhammad of Ghur, another Afghan sultan, and his slave general Gutb-ud-din Aybak led an invasion into North India and soon captured Lahore and Delhi, the gateway cities to the Gangetic Plain and one of the world's richest and most densely populated areas at the time. The Turkish warriors, firing crossbows from their galloping horses, vanquished the Hindu troops fighting from elephants, although it took years for them to defeat the Rajputs in western India. Muhammad of Ghur returned home and soon died, but his talented slave general whom he had left in Delhi quickly declared himself the Sultan of Delhi, beginning Islam's permanent presence in the subcontinent.

FIGURE 4-7   THE QUTAB MINAR, DELHI, INDIA

The Delhi-based Muslim Turkish armies swept across north India, defeating Hindu kings from Delhi to Bengal in the east. In the process, they destroyed most of the Hindu temples in North India, 26 in the Delhi area alone. They also destroyed Nalanda, the world's major Buddhist University where 10,000 monks studied, effectively ending Buddhism's influence in the land of its birth. From 1206 until the Mughal conquest of 1526, five Delhi sultanates controlled North India. They were able to keep the Mongols out of India and generally permitted Hindus rajas (kings) to serve in the government by recognizing them as dhimmi.

The early Muslim sultans were enthusiastic builders. They established several cities in the Delhi area alone. Their initial cities were crude and hastily built, often constructed with material from temples they had razed. Hindu architects were not familiar with the arch or dome and had had no tradition of burial monuments, mainstays in Islamic architecture. As a result, initially they found it difficult to construct the mosques and tombs their Muslim patrons demanded.

The Islam and Hindu worldviews are so different that it is hard to imagine how people practicing these two faiths would ever be able to coexist. Hindus worship a large number of gods and goddesses, whereas

Muslims are strict monotheists. Hindus revere a seemingly infinite array of images, whereas such symbolism is forbidden in Islam. Muslims champion equality, but Hindu society is hierarchical. Hindus consider eating beef a taboo, and Muslims will not eat pork. Hindus rely on priests to help them worship, whereas Muslims pray directly to God. The differences go on and on.

Even so, some Indians began to be drawn to Islam, especially as Muslim scholars, scribes, and Sufis migrated into the area. Gradually, Indianization and Islamization resulted in a synthesis of cultures. Muslim leaders copied pre-Islamic concepts of kingship, including lavish public displays, to underscore their authority. They ordered the building of impressive mosques, tombs, forts, and caravansaries that advertised their power. Local peasants and literate workers provided labor to maintain the mosques and schools, but few Hindus converted. Those who did, less than 25 percent of the population, were mainly from the lower castes. Most of the converts lived in the Indus Valley, northwest India, and Bengal. Harsh Hindu rule in Bengal caused thousands to turn to Islam, and many members of the lower castes and other disenchanted Hindus in northern India also converted. Because few Muslims settled in the area, Islam had little success in South India.

Sufi poets and saints who appealed to Hindus with songs of love for the divine played a prominent role in most of the conversions. Countless Hindus had already embraced Bhakti, a devotional form of worship that stresses surrender to and love of divinity. Bhakti was especially appealing to lower-caste Hindus, and most Bhakti saints were non-brahmins. Bhakti and Sufism were similar. Both sang of love and union with divinity. Undoubtedly, many Hindus must have believed Sufi poets were singing Bhakti hymns. The similarities made it easy to go from one faith to the other. In fact, when reading the works of great poets such as Kabir, it is difficult to tell whether they are writing Sufi or Bhakti poetry.

In 1526, another group of Turks from Central Asia under their skillful leader Babar plunged into the Indian heartland and established the Mughal dynasty. During the next 200 years, it moved to the forefront of Islamic civilizations. The succession of Mughal emperors varied in their treatment of the majority Hindu population. The most successful, Emperor Akbar (1542–1605), was tolerant of Hinduism and even attempted to create a synthesis of Islam and Hinduism. However, Aurangzeb (1618–1707) not only dissipated the empire's wealth in constant warfare but also persecuted Hindus.

For many living in the Mughal Empire, the boundaries between Islam and Hinduism were blurred. It was common for Muslims to celebrate Hindu festivals and worship at Hindu shrines. It was even more common for Hindus to worship at tombs of Sufi saints. Muslim marriages included many Hindu features. Surprisingly, Muslims in India gradually adopted the caste system, a startling departure from the Islamic stress on equality. In villages, Muslims often became just another caste or group of castes. Hindu and Islamic architectural forms blended into a distinctly beautiful Indo-Islamic style exemplified by the Taj Mahal.

In spite of Islam's political power and the Islamization and conversions that took place, the majority of the subcontinent remained Hindu. Muslim rulers utilized Hindus in their administrations, but outside of their centers of power, local political systems based on caste hierarchy continued unchanged. Hindu-Muslim tensions periodically flared into violence, but in most areas Hindus and Muslims lived side by side without incident. Whether the relationship between these two major religions resulted in violent struggle or creative synthesis, there is no doubt that Islam's long history in the subcontinent became a vital part of Indian history and culture.

CONCLUSION

The Islamic experience across the hemisphere varied. As a result of the slow process of Islamization, most people in Indonesia and East Asia eventually converted to the faith, while India and the Balkans remained largely non-Muslim. In all cases, Islam, like Buddhism and Christianity before it, adjusted, adapted, and merged with local cultures and traditions. In northwest India and the East African coast, a person took on a new cultural identify when becoming a Muslim: Muslim and Turk in Northwest India; Swahili in East Africa. By contrast, syncretism was key to Islamization in Bengal and Java. Individual conversion was far less significant than the transformation of the society in Anatolia where nearly the entire population became Muslim or was assumed to be Muslim. However, even in those areas where people became nominal Muslims, traditional ways survived.

The enormous reach of Islam created a vast commercial network, and communication back and forth among west Asia and south, southeast and east Asia was greatly facilitated. Although Dar al-Islam was divided into many separate kingdoms, Islamic societies conformed to general Islamic principles. Art, literature, philosophy, education, and sciences all reflected Islamic values and forms. Common religious values, common institutions, and a common worldview held this vast area together. As the distinguished Islamic scholar John Voll has pithily observed, post-Abbasid Islam, though politically fragmented, functioned something like a modern "newsgroup" that facilitated interaction and exchange over vast areas.[94]

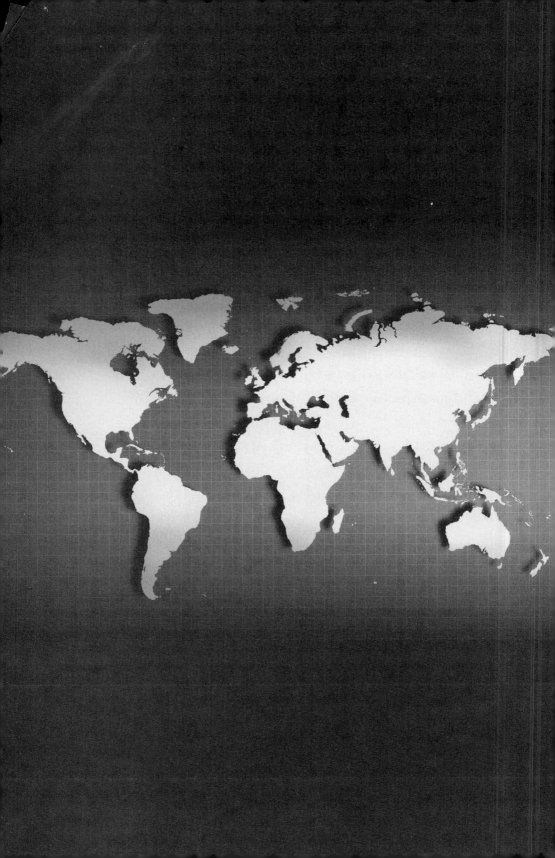

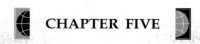

CHAPTER FIVE

COMPARISONS, CONTRASTS, AND SYNTHESES

GETTING STARTED ON CHAPTER FIVE: Believers generally present their religious traditions as unchanging and eternal. How might a historian respond to such a perspective? What does it mean to say that Manicheanism was a "syncretic faith"? What broad similarities can you identify among these three universal religions? And what distinguished them from one another? Consider, for example, their ethical systems, their relationship to political authority, the ways they spread, their understanding of history (time), their attitude toward sexuality, the role of women, and attitudes toward commerce. In what ways did the centuries of encounters among the three religions include times of conflict and periods of peaceful exchanges and cultural borrowing? Why did the Mongols practice religious tolerance during their age of empire? The interaction between the world of Christendom and the world of Islam represents one of the great cultural encounters of world history. In what ways has this relationship been both symbiotic and contentious?

At first glance Buddhism, Christianity, and Islam might seem very different. Each faith was shaped by the culture and historical events in the areas where it first emerged and all were profoundly influenced by the new and diverse cultural contexts into which they spread. The leaders of these faiths formulated their own unique answers to the profound questions of meaning that humans face. However, in spite of the significant differences in origins, practices, and histories, many striking similarities as well as significant differences among these faiths become apparent.

THE GRADUAL PROCESS OF CONVERSION

Buddhism's long career began in a highly sophisticated urbanized context, and its spread was mostly to other large cities in southeast and east Asia. Although the Buddha's father was a local ruler far removed from the center of Indian civilization, the future Buddha left home to begin his spiritual mission in the urbanized region of North India, and Buddhism spread in city after city along the eastern Gangetic Plain. The faith was welcomed outside India in the royal courts and strongholds of local rulers in Sri Lanka and Southeast Asia long before it spread to average people. Even though the nomadic Wei rulers in northern China utilized Buddhism to shore up their authority, its real reception came from the elite members of Chinese cities. Elites in Korea and Japan also promoted the faith. Only gradually did it percolate into the countryside.

Christianity originated in a predominately herding culture in the Judean countryside, but it quickly spread to urban centers such as Jerusalem, Antioch, Alexandria, Rome, and then Constantinople. For the first three centuries, Christianity found followers in the highly urbanized and Hellenized Roman Empire. However, its major thrust and eventual greatest success was among the newly settled peoples along the rural frontiers of western Europe where there were almost no cities. Islam, by contrast, started among nomadic tribes and some of its most enduring values reflect their worldview. However, Islam quickly became an urban religion, and the process of Islamization by which it spread took place primarily in cities.

Adopting a new faith is often thought of as a dramatic personal decision to profess a new set of beliefs and practices. More often, conversion results when kings, princes, and chieftains proclaim that their subjects must accept a new faith, but these commands only gradually permeate among their subjects. Examples abound, such as the Axum king Edzna's conversion to Christianity and Charlemagne's support of Christianity. In Southeast Asia, rulers appropriated aspects of Hinduism and Buddhism, but it was several centuries before their subjects internalized the new faiths.

In general, the process of large numbers of people adopting a different faith is often very slow and subtle. Instead of sudden conversion, the three universal religions more often spread by what can be identified as Buddhazation, Christianization, and Islamization. This process, an underlying theme of this book, is a gradual and not always conscious internalizing of new values, beliefs, and practices that occurs over time as cultural contact and borrowing take place. The process is illustrated by a comment made by a Christian chaplain writing about crusaders who had stayed on to live in the Holy Land after the first crusade: "For we who were Occidentals have now become Orientals. He who was a Roman or a Frank has in this land been made into a Galilean or a Palestinian. . . ."[95]

Urbanization was a key factor in this process of gradually adapting to a new faith. The cultural ethos in cities that expresses the "long-lasting moods and motivations" of the dominant religious group can be seen as a kind of magnetic cosmopolitanism, and the spread of religion is in no small part fueled by the response to that attraction. Cities are by definition pluralistic and support a wide variety of cultural practices, but major cities often reflect one dominant worldview, and minorities often want to copy the majority culture. Outsiders looking for work or coming to trade find themselves drawn into the city's ambiance. Perhaps unconsciously imitating people around them, they gradually adopt some of their beliefs.

Assimilation often becomes a ticket to a more profitable, exciting, and satisfying life. The highly sophisticated cultural life in cities like Patalputra in third-century India, Jerusalem, Rome, or Byzantine Constantinople and Baghdad during the Abbasids and tenth century Cordova, lured newcomers to adapt many aspects of their cultures so as to take advantage of the benefits that being a member of the dominant culture conferred. That often included participating in some of the religious practices, which in the long run could result in gradually accepting the religion as well. Those who came explicitly to learn about a new faith could find many people who would answer their questions and whose actions they could imitate.

Language was important in this process. Knowing the dominant language of the faith makes it possible to understand the tenets of the faith, to converse with its followers, and to read its scriptures and literature. Learning a language is enhanced by living in cities where many people speak it. Moreover, language fluency increases one's opportunities to work for members of the dominant culture, expands educational prospects, and offers participation in a community of believers that crosses many political boundaries.

Urban life has its own particular demands that may have made the message of the universal religions more attractive. Agricultural peoples are challenged by nature, and their religions often deal with propitiating natural forces such as nature spirits, nagas, and kami. In the expanding urban areas, people increasingly looked for faiths that dealt more with human relationships and social issues.

Urban life is capricious, and chance and unexpected results are common. Urbanites are more likely to experience major difficulties with other people—bosses, money lenders, thieves, muggers, armed policemen, armies, and megalomaniacal and erratic rulers. They need a religion that helps them deal with the unpredictability and contingencies of everyday life and the accompanying suffering that seems to punctuate their daily rounds. All three universal religions offered ways to make meaning in the face of contingency, when cause and effect seemed unrelated, so it is understandable that cities provided fertile ground in which the messages of the universal religions flourished.

Cities rely on trade and support diasporic communities, and these factors also contributed to the gradual adaptation of a new faith. Although the merchant groups in the areas where Buddhism, Christianity, and Islam developed were small by contemporary standards, they represented an important development. Cross-cultural trade facilitates the spread of ideas and beliefs, and diasporic communities, common in cities, all provided information about the new faiths that had originated far away.

In urbanized areas people were increasingly mobile, especially those engaged in commerce. The universal religions provided a common identity that transcended tribal and local loyalties, and they facilitated extended zones of peaceful interaction. Interconnected diasporic trading centers all across Afro-Eurasia allowed traders to feel at home wherever they went and were important sources for renewing their faiths. Merchants could use religion to cement loyalty in these diasporic communities. The prosperity that accompanied increased commerce also provided support for the elaborate building projects that graced all three religions, and these magnificent temples, churches, mosques, and tombs attracted even more people to the faiths.

CONTACT AND BORROWING

Another underlying theme throughout this study has been the role and importance of cross-cultural contacts and exchanges. During the first two centuries of the Common Era, after sailors figured out the monsoon patterns, India and the Mediterranean world were in constant contact. Saint Thomas was not the only Christian who went to India; there was lots of traffic across the Arabian Sea. In the middle of the third century B.C.E., Emperor Ashoka had sent Buddhist missionaries "beyond the borders of his kingdom, even as far as six hundred *yeans* (about 3,000 miles) to where the Greek king and kings of Syria, Egypt, Macedonia, Cymene and Epirus ruled."[96] During the Hellenistic Age, India and West Asia enjoyed lively contacts, and Greek scholars also regularly met with Indian scholars in Persia. A Roman geographer writing around the time of Jesus reported seeing as many as 120 ships a year at an Egyptian port, preparing to sail for India.

Contacts between Buddhists from India and philosophers in the Mediterranean world of the first century C.E. are suggested by similarities between Stoic philosophy, Buddhism, and Karma Yoga in Hinduism. All three philosophies suggest that controlling one's thoughts is the best means for achieving peace of mind and advocate working without concern for the result of one's labor. Doing one's duty is the highest calling, they say, whether you endure praise or censure as a result.

In the Indian Bhagavad Gita, Lord Krishna advises:

> Be intent on action,
> not on the fruits of action:
> Avoid attraction to the fruits
> and attachment to inaction.
>
> Perform actions, firm in discipline,
> relinquishing attachment;
> be impartial to failure and success —
> this equanimity is called discipline.[97]

The Buddha taught:

> Whatever deed, monks, has been performed without greed,
> without hatred and free from delusion . . . after greed,
> hatred and delusion were done away with—this deed is
> annihilated, cut off at the root, made similar to a rooted-out palm tree. . . .[98]

The Stoic Epictetus (50–130) advises:

> My life is worthwhile and meaningful to the extent that I am happy,
> and I am happy only when I am not frustrated or disappointed. But
> there are many things that I might desire (such as wealth, power,
> beauty, and health) over which I have little or no control; so I should
> refrain from such desires. Since the only things I am totally in control
> of are my desires, I should desire only those things I am certain to get.
> The easiest way to do that is to stop desiring altogether; that way, I
> will never be disappointed.
>
> I can control whether I am virtuous and whether I let the things over
> which I have no control (e.g., death) bother me. So if I want to be
> happy, I should do my best to do my duty and not to be disturbed by
> things I have no power over.[99]

Buddhism and Jain[100] influences are suggested in the Christian Gnostic concept of liberation from the trap of matter. The Jains believe that all matter contains *jivas* (souls) that are weighted down by karmic matter, but that appropriate human actions could liberate the jivas. In a similar vein, Gnostics taught that the proper actions could release sparks of creative light embedded in humans.

Buddhists, and probably Hindus as well, most likely brought their concept of renunciation of the world and several forms of meditation and yoga to west Asia, where these ideas may have influenced Egyptian priests, Greek Pythagoreans, and Christian Desert Fathers and Mothers. Plontinus (204–270), the founder of Neo-Platonism, a philosophy that significantly influenced early Christianity, traveled to Persia explicitly to study with Hindu philosophers.

At the same time, Greek and Roman influences on Buddhist art are obvious in some of the first anthropomorphic representations of The Buddha. Indian sculptors in Mathura had had a long tradition of making anthropomorphic images of nature deities, but initially they eschewed depicting the Buddha. After Greek and Roman images of gods and goddesses reached Taxila and other trading cities near India, and Buddhists traveling in west Asia saw similar images, Indian sculptors began creating statues of the Buddha.

The first intense interaction between Buddhism and Christianity took place during the Kushan Empire (c. 100 B.C.E–200 C.E.). Buddhists and Christians share certain stories, although the interpretations each makes about them are different. The story of the prodigal son was a Buddhist parable long before Jesus also told about the return of a wayward son. The parable of the mustard seed and walking on water were familiar legends told by both Buddhists and Christians. The Christian philosopher Clement of Alexandria (150–218) even accused his fellow Mediterranean philosophers of stealing their philosophy from the "barbarians," by whom he meant Indians. (By the nineteenth century a Buddhist parable warning against being deceived and entrapped by the five senses had traveled to Africa and then to the United States and reappeared in the Uncle Remus Tar Baby story, where the fox's feet, hands, and head get stuck to a tarred doll.)

As recently as the nineteenth century, Leo Tolstoi recounted that he was suddenly drawn to the Christian faith when he read a fable in the *Lives of Saints*[101] about a man who fell in a well. As he falls, he grasps frantically for a root to keep from tumbling into the jaws of a flaming dragon crouching at the bottom of the well. To make matters worse, black and white mice are gnawing on the very root to which he clings. Tolstoi felt that this fable reflected a basic truth about the human condition.[102]

This fable originated among the Jains in India sometime after the sixth century B.C.E. In the original Jain version, as the mice, which represent day and night or a human's life span, gnaw away, a honeybee, buzzing around the head of the poor struggling man, drops a bit of honey onto his tongue. For a fleeting second he thinks, "How sweet." Although the human condition is dire, and man's days are fleeting, humans long to hold on to life.

In the Kushan Empire during the first century C.E., Mahayana Buddhists developed the concept of the bodhisattva as an intermediary between humans and salvation. Bodhisattvas take away sin and bad karma, serve as intermediaries between humans and more remote gods, and help devotees experience nirvana. The role of the bodhisattva has much in common with Jesus' role in Christianity, and the Buddhist concept may have been informed in part by their knowledge of Jesus. In fact, it is not uncommon for some early Buddhists to identify Jesus as a bodhisattva.

Unlike the influences between Buddhism and Christianity that scholars must infer from circumstantial evidence, Muslims readily acknowledge their roots in both Judaism and Christianity. Muslims recognize that the three faiths share a common Judeo-Christian-Islamic heritage that began with Abraham. The Quran explicitly mentions Abraham and Moses, other Jewish prophets, Jesus, and many ideas from Judaism and Christianity.

The Muslim ban on images rests solidly on the second commandment in the Torah against making "a graven image, or any likeness of anything that is in heaven above or that is in earth beneath or that is in the water under the earth." (Deuteronomy 5:6–21) Muslims are not to have any images in mosques because they might distract worshipers while they prayed. Instead, mosque walls are to be decorated with calligraphy consisting mainly of quotes from the Quran and of geometric shapes and arabesques, which symbolize the tension between cosmic order and creativity, and mosques were often surrounded by gardens that can impart the same message. Christian concern over icons and the resulting iconoclastic controversy may have arisen in part from the Christians' sense that Muslims were better than they were at keeping the commandment forbidding the use of images in worship.

The concept of jihad also seems to have influenced Christians, especially in their call for crusades against the "infidel." Although the Muslim concept of jihad refers to both an individual's internal struggle against destructive impulses and fighting those who threatened the Muslim community, Christians focused on the later meaning. Muslims' conquests in west Asia stimulated Christians to talk of "holy" wars to rescue Spain and especially the "Holy Land" from the infidels, and in 1095, Christians launched a series of preemptive strikes against Muslims.

Mysticism has pervaded all three universal religions. Buddhist ideas such as the oneness of all creation and seeking to experience oneness with the Ultimate through meditation may have influenced Desert Fathers and Mothers. Although becoming one with God was suspect in Christianity, Christian saints and mystics such as St. John of the Cross, Meister Eickhardt, and St. Theresa, have striven for that goal. Sufi saints also seek to experience oneness with divinity, and their intimate interaction with Hindu Bhakti devotees in India may have influenced their emphasis on God's love. Muslims may also have been influenced by contact with Christian mystics. In turn, the development of European romantic poetry after the thirteenth century probably owed much to contact between Sufi saints in al-Andalus, who expressed their longing for union with the divine, and troubadours in southern France who sang of a different kind of union—one between a man and a woman.

RELIGIOUS TOLERATION UNDER THE MONGOLS

Central Asia was an important staging area for the exchange of ideas across Eurasia as travelers from both ends of the hemisphere continually passed through that area. Most of the time these exchanges were peaceful and a variety of diasporic communities existed side by side. Religious toleration was the norm, and the conflicts that did occur were not over religion. In fact, the Mongol Empire, known for its militarism, offers a dramatic example of the peaceful coexistence of many faiths, including Buddhism, Christianity, and Islam.

About the time of the last crusades, the Mongols, who came from the northeastern part of the Asian steppes, were expanding and consolidating an empire that would eventually stretch from west Asia to the Pacific Ocean. Most Mongols followed the ancient shamanistic religion of their ancestors. They believed in a high god known as Tangri (Eternal Heaven) and revered their leader as his representative on earth. Mongol law stated that all people should believe in Tangri, but it did not prescribe any specific creed or practice. Shaman burial rites included the sacrifice of both horses and young women. Purification rituals involved passing through fire; leather dolls were used for exorcism and other rites. Shamans gave advice and accompanied warriors during their military campaigns.

Most of the Mongols' early military victories were over other central Asian nomadic groups who shared their belief in a single sky god. The first contacts they had with the universal religions were with Nestorian Christians and Buddhists who did not try to pressure the far more powerful Mongols to accept their own religious visions. In any case, there was a strong resonance between the nomadic Sky God Tengri and the Nestorian God, and the Buddhists were not very concerned about describing divinity.

Under the leadership of Temujin (1162–1227), who took the title Chinggis Khan (Universal Ruler), the Mongols subdued a coalition of tribal groups, including the Keraits who were nominal Christians. In an attempt to assimilate them into his group, Chinggis Khan gave several Kerait women to his sons as wives. Chinggis's youngest son Tolui married Sorghanghtani, a Nestorian Christian, and their three sons later became great khans: Mongke (1251), Kublai (1260), and Hulagu (who founded the Il-Khanate in Persia that lasted until 1335). Sorghanghtani encouraged her sons to be tolerant of all religions, and a wide variety of religious leaders including Buddhist priests, Manichean teachers, Muslims, and Nestorians were welcome at Chinggis Khan's camp.

Instead of resisting the foreign faiths or adopting one of them, Mongol leaders expertly used religion in an instrumental way as a means of controlling large areas and numbers of diverse people. Because their empire included Nestorian and Greek Orthodox Christians, Manicheans, Buddhists, and Muslims, their tolerance and support of all these faiths was understandable. The Mongols realized that toleration would help keep members of these communities from rebelling, and they offered tax benefits to them to win their support.

Like the northern Wei before them, the Mongols were wary of appointing Chinese administrators whose loyalty they questioned. Non-Chinese, on the other hand, seemed more trustworthy, so the Mongols appointed some Christians to administer the regions they had conquered and also used them as interpreters. They hired Muslim traders, in part because the information they picked up during their travels could help the Mongols plan military campaigns. The Mongols had no written languages, so the Uighurs, many of whom were Christian monks and priests, wrote the Mongol language using Uighur letters. Moreover, the Mongols admired Buddhist and Islamic advances in medicine and astronomy.

From 1236 to 1241, Ogodei and his Mongol forces conquered most of Russia and parts of Hungary and Poland, and a Mongol army Hulagu led sacked Baghdad in 1258. Word of the Mongol advances alarmed Pope Innocent IV. Realizing the Mongols had attacked Muslims, the pope thought he might be able to use them as allies against the Muslims, and he sent several missions to Karakorum, Chinggis Khan's capital, not only to try to spread Christianity, but also to explore the possibility of forming an alliance with the Great Khan.

John of Plano Carpini (1180–1252), a Franciscan monk, led a delegation that departed in 1245. It reached Karakorum just in time for the coronation of Guyug, the third Great Khan. John presented two letters to Guyug: one explained that the Christians wished to spread their faith in his empire and the other stated that the Mongols must end their military campaigns or face the wrath of God.[103] In response, the Great Khan ordered the pope and princes of Europe to come serve him as vassals. He rejected any thought of being baptized and stated that Mongol victories were a sign of Tangri's support of their efforts to bring the whole world under Mongol law.

Guyug informed the Franciscans that, ". . . you men of the West believe that you alone are Christians and despise others. But how can you know to whom God deigns to confer His grace?"[104] The Khan then stated that if the pope did not believe this, the Khan would take it as an act of war. The pope, recognizing his own weakness compared to the Mongol armies, replied that he had not meant to declare war but had only wished to offer the Mongols salvation.

Mongke, the fourth Great Khan, continued the Mongol policy of religious toleration. He supported all the major religions and subsidized mosques and Buddhist monasteries.[105] He hired Muslims as financial advisors and, perhaps unfamiliar with affirmative action, seemed surprised when so many Muslims appeared in lower posts in the financial administration. A Persian historian noted that he "showed most honor and respect to the Muslims and bestowed the largest amount of gifts and alms upon them."[106] Both his mother and his favorite wife were Nestorian Christians, so he sometimes went to church. Leaders of each faith routinely blessed him. He also continued to participate in shaman rituals and relied on the advice of soothsayers. Before making any important decision, he would have a shaman burn the shoulder blade of a sheep to determine the omens.

In 1254 another Franciscan monk, William of Rubrick, traveled to Karakorum where he encountered Buddhists for the first time and identified them as fallen-away Christians. Mongke staged an interreligious debate in his gold-lined tent that involved William, Nestorians, Muslims, and Chinese Buddhists. Each was ordered to show respect to the representatives of the other faiths or face death. The clerics debated whether the world was created, what happens after death, and the nature of God. Introducing the debate, Mongke said, "Here you are, Christians, Saracens, and twins [Buddhist priests], and each of you claims that his religions is superior and that his writings or books contains more truth."[107] Before William left the Khan's court, Monkge told him:

> We Mongols believe that there is only one God, through whom we
> have life and through whom we die, and towards him we direct our
> hearts. . . . But just as God has given the hand several fingers, so he
> has given mankind several paths. To you God has given the Scriptures
> and you Christians do not observe them.[108]

In 1258 Mongke convened another debate, similar to the one William had witnessed. This one was between competing Daoists and Buddhists.

Mongke asked his younger brother Kublai to preside and determine the outcome. Kublai decided in favor of the Buddhists. Mongke then spoke of his preference for Buddhism, explaining that Buddhism was the palm of the hand and the other religions were the fingers.[109]

Kublai became Great Khan in 1260, and in 1279 he conquered China and established the Yuan Dynasty. Ruling China, Kublai Khan tried to continue the policy of religious toleration that informed Mongol leadership and had been a major reason for the Mongols' success. In an effort to pacify Chinese scholar-officials, most of whom had lost their positions under Yuan rule, he kept some government offices such as the Academy of Worthies, the Director for the Diffusion of Confucian texts, and the Archives and the Imperial Diarists' Office.[110] He maintained rituals associated with reverence for ancestors, ordering the construction of the Great Temple where they were to be performed. He also supported altars and ceremonies intended to gain the assistance of various forces of nature and a shrine honoring Confucius.

Kublai Khan was especially impressed with Tibetan schools of Buddhism and recruited a number of Tibetan Buddhists. He granted Buddhist monks tax-exempt status and contributed funds for new temples. Monasteries became important economic centers. A later Chinese source claimed:

> Thus he [Khubilai] made the sun of religion to shine on the dark land
> of Mongolia and invited a Buddha image of veneration from India,
> relics of the Buddha . . . He conducted a government of the ten
> meritorious doctrines, and stabilized the world . . . in this wise he
> became famous in all directions as the wise Cakravartan King who
> turns the thousand golden wheels . . .[111]

Although probably more sympathetic to Buddhism than Daoism, Kublai was fascinated by Daoist magic and its ability to call spirits and ghosts. Daoism was popular among poorer Chinese, so providing funds to build Daoist temples helped him win over Daoist members of Chinese society. Kublai also granted privileges to Muslims and hired them to work in the civil service, especially as tax collectors and administrators. At the same time, he continued to practice shamanism.

According to Marco Polo, Kublai welcomed him and his father to the Chinese court, asked them many questions about Christianity, and wanted the pope to send him 100 learned Christians. Polo mistakenly thought that the emperor had been drawn to Christianity. Kublai Khan also invited Persian Muslim scholars to China to set up an observatory and assist in developing a more accurate calendar, and he invited Persian Muslim doctors who established an Office for Muslim Medicine. A number of mosques were constructed in China during his reign.

Gradually, Kublai began to abandon the long-standing policy of religious toleration. This may have resulted in part because of the economic crisis the government was facing, accompanied by increasing popular unrest. Kublai may have feared Muslims were gaining too much influence in the government, so when some Muslim guests refused to eat the meat he served at a banquet because the animals had been slaughtered by hitting them and not slitting their throat as Muslim law required, Kublai issued an edict that forbade slaughtering animals by slitting their throats. The penalty for disobeying was death. He also outlawed circumcision, an important Muslim rite of passage. These edicts and other anti-Muslim rules were lifted in 1287 in an effort, probably, to attract more Muslim traders to China.

When it was discovered that Daoists were still circulating the two texts that had been banned in 1258, Kublai was furious. In 1281 he ordered all Daoist books except the Dao De Jing burned, and he banned the sale of Daoist charms and forced many Daoists to convert to Buddhism. From 1282 to 1291 a Buddhist monk from Tibet was put in charge of Buddhist teaching in south China. In hopes of strengthening Buddhism, he oversaw the building and support of Buddhist monasteries and temples, in large part by stripping Daoist temples, Song tombs and graves, and Confucians altars of all their wealth. These actions infuriated many in south China. Balancing the interests of the various religions had been a major reason for Mongol success. Abandoning the policy of toleration significantly weakened the Yuan dynasty.

New Syncretic Faiths Develop

The Mongols' religious tolerance allowed many diverse faiths to exist side by side. In other areas, the interaction of diverse faiths sometimes produced a new religion that sought to integrate and synthesize seemingly conflicting worldviews. This process of synthesis usually occurred along the fault lines where two or more major religions met and mingled. Manicheanism, one of the boldest attempts to create a hybrid religion, liberally drew from Hinduism, Buddhism, Christianity, Gnostic Christian sects, and Zoroastrian influences.

MANICHEANISM

Mani, the founder of Manicheanism, was born in 216 C.E. to Parthian parents in the zone between the Greek ruled Seleucid kingdom in Syria and the Parthian kingdom that controlled the Iranian plateau until 224. He also spent time in what was left of the Kushan Empire in northern India where he became familiar with Jainism, Hinduism, and Mahayana Buddhism.

Mani was an avid dualist, and he affirmed the concept of the cosmic battle between Light and Dark that had originated in Zoroastrianism and had spread to Judaism, Christianity, and Gnosticism. Mani taught that darkness holds particles of Light, and Light yearns to escape from out of darkness and come to the fore, a concept very close to Indian Jainism. As a result, God sends prophets to call upon the Light.

Like the Gnostics, Mani preached that all matter, especially human flesh, was an abomination. He accepted the concept of the transmigration of souls from Buddhism and Hinduism and believed that the ascetic path, which was similar to Buddhist and Christian meditation and renunciation, was the true path to God and the best way to release the Light within. Echoing part of the Buddha's Eightfold Path, Mani forbad killing, sex intended only for pleasure, and eating meat and drinking wine and milk. He borrowed the Buddhist concept of the Sangha and accepted women as well as men as his elect. Those who practiced abstinence from sex mirrored Buddhist arhats and Christian monks. Manichean monks and nuns were totally dependent on lay followers, as were Buddhist monks and nuns. They were even forbidden to cook because preparing meals would damage particles of Light in the food.

Presaging Muhammad, Mani believed he was the last prophet. He considered Jesus the most important prophet and claimed Jesus had taken three forms: Jesus the Man, Jesus the Living Soul, and Jesus the Splendor who would return at the end of time. He also accepted the veneration of images, as Hindus, Buddhists, and Christians did.

Mani's eclectic synthesis found converts among Syrian Christians and in the Sasanid Empire, especially among the soldiers. Augustine, one of the most eminent Christian fathers, was a devout Manichean for 14 years before he converted to Christianity. Mani also converted two Sasanid princes, and they allowed him to preach even though the Sasanid court officially embraced Zoroastrianism. His message obviously competed with the more nationalistic Zoroastrianism, and eventually Zoroastrian priests demanded Mani's arrest. He was condemned and crucified sometime between 273 and 276. His skin was hung on the city gates at Ctesiphon, and many of his followers were also killed.

Even so, Mani's teachings spread to Central Asia and from 640 to 763 Manicheanism was adopted as the official religion of the Uighur Turks on the Siberian steppe. Central Asian Buddhists often referred to Buddhas and bodhisattvas as "great caravan leaders," and they applied that term to Mani as well.

At first the Chinese thought Manicheanism was a school of Buddhism, and so they called Mani a "Buddha of Light." Identifying Mani's faith as a "barbarian" religion, they designated it a protected faith as long as only foreigners practiced it. After the Uighurs supported the Tang emperor during the An Lushan rebellion, many Uighers settled in China and built Manichean temples there.

Daoists tended to tolerate Manicheanism, but Buddhists were wary of this new faith, warning: "Talking about accepting Buddha, one should think of converting to which Buddha; not Mani Buddha, not to Nestorian Buddha, nor Zoroastrian Buddha, but Sakyamuni Buddha."[112]

As part of the Tang anti-Buddhist and anti-foreign persecutions in 843, Manichean property was confiscated, its temples were burned, and about 70 Manichean nuns in Changan were killed. Manicheans then went underground in China but they would surface from time to time to support peasant rebellions. The only surviving Manichean shrine in China features a relief of Mani as the "Buddha of Light."

THE RISE OF SIKHISM

Sikhism, a hybrid faith that combined Islam and Hinduism, developed in the Indian subcontinent during a time when an increasing number of Hindus were growing disenchanted with Hinduism's emphasis on rituals and with the brahmins who dominated orthodox Hinduism and kept many low-caste Hindus from access to temples and their inner sanctums. Many Indians felt that Hinduism had lost much of its ability to cultivate the inner human spirit.

The effort to merge with the divine was a common theme with Sufis and Hindu bhakti saints, who both offered total devotion to God. Bhakti worshipers sang love songs to a chosen deity, usually Shiva, Vishnu, or Devi, the Great Goddess, and danced until they experienced a sacred ecstasy, practices also common in Sufism. Waves of Bhakti worshipers and their hymns flowed north from South India, and by the fourteenth century, bhakti was widely popular in North India. At the same time Muslim Sufi singers were spreading a similar doctrine of love and surrender clothed in Islamic symbols and beliefs across North India.

Sikhism developed along with the growing popularity of both bhakti and Sufi devotion. Sikhism, which began with Guru Nanak, who lived from 1469 to 1539, combined elements from both Hinduism and Islam while also trying to correct some of their perceived faults. Sikhs took the Hindu term for teacher, a "guru," and gave it a new meaning. For Sikhs "guru" is composed of two words: "GU," meaning darkness, and "RU," meaning light. Thus, "guru" means the light that dispels all darkness. Nanak was the first Sikh guru. He was born in a family of Muslim weavers, but he was raised by a famous bhakti poet and guru, and he wrote poetry that resonated with both Hindus and Muslims. Out of his teachings a new religion, rooted in both Islam and Hinduism, emerged. Nine additional gurus followed, ending with Gobind Singh (1675–1708), whom Sikhs believe is the last or seal of the gurus. Some Sikhs refer to the Sikh Holy Scripture as the most authoritative guru of all.

Sikhism, like Gnosticism and Christianity, recognizes the existence of heavenly light in every human being, no matter what his caste, class, gender, creed or ethnic background might be. The faith, unlike Hinduism, eschews fasts, rituals, renunciation of this world, yoga, and self-mortification. However, the first Sikh gurus followed Hindu and Buddhist teaching of non-violence, and Sikhs, like Hindus, believe in rebirth and karma. The departed soul may pass through animal lives, suffering harsh agonies. However, humans have consciousness and can strive to achieve the highest point of spiritual understanding.

Sikhism, like Islam, is strictly monotheistic. Sikhs focus on NAM, the name of God, which is the cure for all sufferings and the sustainer of all beings. Salvation is attained by meditating deeply on NAM. Sikhs are encouraged to repeat prayers several times each day, but they reject images, statues, and pictures of divinity. Their houses of worship, called Gurdwaras, are open on all four sides. Any person is welcome to worship in a Gurdwara.

FIGURE 5-1   SIKH AT PRAYER IN A GURDWARA

Sikhism developed in the Punjab, where invading Turkish and Mughal forces often clashed with Hindus, and Sikhs were often subject to brutal treatment at the hands of the Muslim military. The fifth guru was tortured and killed on the orders of the Mughal emperor. Because of his violent death, succeeding gurus developed an army and since then, Sikhs have relied on the sword to protect their religion. All Sikh men are expected to carry or wear the Five Ks: *Kesh*, long hair, *Kachha*, a special kind of underwear; *Kangah*, a comb; *Karra*, a metal bracelet; and *Kirpan*, a sword. The five Ks identify Sikhs and also symbolize the community's readiness to defend itself.

Manicheanism and Sikhism were not the only hybrid faiths that developed during this period. The Druzes in west Asia were an offshoot of Islam that developed in the eleventh century and they were also heavily influenced by Christianity. Baha'i is a more recent example of eclectic religious synthesis. Sikhism and Baha'i both continue to this day, whereas Manicheanism thrives most prominently in scholarly works and Web site chat rooms.

SIMILARITIES AND DIFFERENCES AMONG THE UNIVERSAL RELIGIONS

Given the many ways that Buddhism, Christianity, and Islam influenced one another, it is not surprising that there are many similarities among them. There are certain aspects that all three faiths share and others that are common to only two of them. There are also major differences.

SIMILARITIES

All three universal religions focus on divinity, although initially Buddhism did not postulate a transcendent divinity. They all promise salvation to those who believe in their message of devotion and surrender to divinity, and the heaven that they promise, whether temporary or eternal, sounds quite similar. Further, each offers believers assistance along the path to salvation. In the Pure Land School of Buddhism in east Asia, Amitabha Buddha promises salvation to those who have faith and offer devotion. In the Augustinian tradition of Christianity, one achieves salvation through faith and God's grace. Islam makes surrender to Allah the paramount requirement for salvation. And, most obviously, they are all open to anyone.

Besides the qualities that identify a universal faith, Buddhism, Christianity, and Islam have additional things in common, especially in their ethical systems. All three promote equality among all people and provide charity for the needy. They all rail against selfishness and luxurious waste. Buddhism cautions against accumulating wealth for its own sake, and it advocates renunciation of worldly goods. In the gospels, Jesus addresses the distressing gap between the rich and the poor more often than any other topic. Equality is a centerpiece of Islam. Muslims are obligated to take care of their fellow believers and are expected to support the community with annual gifts. All three faiths attempted to elevate the status of women, slaves, and other members of the most dispossessed groups in society.

All three religions labored to moderate cut-throat competition for worldly success and the increasing use of violence. The Buddha's basic message was that desire—whether for power or physical goods and pleasures—is the root of suffering. Jesus taught his followers to clothe the poor and feed the hungry, assuring them if they did this to the poorest members of society, they did it to him. Charity is a basic imperative in Islam, and devout Muslims try to give something to those in need each day.

Islam grew out of a trading tradition, and the Quran stresses honesty in business dealings and forbids excessive profits earned through loans. Both Buddhism and Christianity were sometimes corrupted by the wealth their leaders acquired. Criticism of the caliphates often focused on the extravagance of their courts and the inequalities their rule fostered. Both Buddhists and Christians supported nuns and monks who chose to live simple lives apart from society, and Sufis were often mystics who honored simplicity.

All three faiths found an important place for good works. Theravada Buddhism left believers essentially to their own efforts to seek nirvana, but Mahayana Buddhism stressed compassion and service to others. Bodhisattvas delayed their own experience of nirvana in order to help all other beings attain the final goal. As Buddhism spread, many Buddhists focused on earning merit through service to others. Jesus stressed helping one's neighbor, and early Christian communities offered service to the poor. After the Catholic Church adopted Thomas Aquinas's theology, good works became an important Christian value and the church tried to infuse civic life with this ideal. Islam's focus on the community taught Muslims to care for one another, and Muslim governmental policies were expected to institutionalize Islamic principles.

The most obvious similarity between Christianity and Islam is that they worship the same God and share a common lineage from Abraham. For Muslims, Muhammad is the last of a long line of distinguished prophets, including Abraham, Moses, and Jesus, and the Quran makes numerous mention of Jesus, although it denies his divinity.

Both Islam and Christianity are infused with the concept of a final judgment and the coming of a heavenly kingdom. Jesus spoke frequently about the Day of Judgment and the Kingdom of God, and Paul expected Jesus to return to earth during his lifetime. The most familiar Christian prayer includes, "thy Kingdom come," although Christians do not agree on what that actually means. The Quran also speaks about the final judgment and describes heaven in some detail. Given the Indian concept of time, reincarnation, and repeated Big Bangs, Buddhists do not speak of one specific End of Days; they believe that the dissolution and re-creation of the world is an endless cycle. Instead of thinking of salvation as a form of self-realization, nirvana implies self-extinction when a person realizes he or she is one with the Infinite.[113] However, perhaps as a result of contact with Christianity, many Buddhists came to believe that Maitreya, the Buddha to come, will return at some future date, and believers who are alive at that time will gain instant salvation.

DIFFERENCES

The Judeo-Christian tradition initially stressed narrative and offered believers stories of how God acts in history. Only later did philosophy become an important aspect of these traditions. Muslims focused on revelations from God and the moral example of Muhammad, and later they infused their faith with Greek philosophy and reason. Buddhism, on the other hand, began with a system of philosophy, and stories about the Buddha and bodhisattvas were added later.

DIFFERENCES IN THE CONCEPT OF FOUNDER Differences exist about the nature of the founders of these faiths. Theravada Buddhists regard the Buddha as a great human teacher who showed his followers the way to salvation, while Mahayana Buddhists accepted the Buddha as a god, and also added many other transcendent Buddhas and bodhisattvas to their pantheon. Christians argued for centuries over whether Jesus was human, divine, or both, and the Christian Trinity was their attempt to combine humanity, divinity, and spirit in one person, although many feared such a representation acknowledged a creeping polytheism. Islam insists that Muhammad was a human being, stressing that "There is no God but God."

DUALISM AND NONDUALISM The Judeo-Christian-Islamic view of opposites also differs from the Buddhist conception of the "Oneness of all things." The dualism that animated Zoroastrianism had enormous influence on Judaism, Christianity, and Islam. All these religions accept divisions between good and evil, truth and falsehood, light and dark, and so on, and suggest that choosing correctly between opposites not only profoundly influences believers' actions but can also determine whether they are saved. A legacy of a dualistic worldview may help explain why contending armies have marched into battle each claiming God's blessing, as well as the frequent insistence on absolute certainty that many leaders who are heirs to this tradition seem to have. The long shadow of dualism may also help explain why many American politicians divide the world and its leaders into the categories of good and evil.

The Indian worldview recognized the distinction between opposites, but India never produced a Zarathustra or an Aristotle, who applied dualism in his famous axiom of the "excluded middle": A cannot be both "A" and "not A". Instead, at about the time of the first Upanishads (C.F. 700 B.C.E), Hindus developed monism, a belief in the oneness of all existence. Creation was seen as the process by which that oneness fragmented into an enormous pluralism of gods, goddesses, demigods, evil spirits and everything else. All the opposites we perceive in the cosmos are in reality aspects of that Universal One. Buddhism, coming out of that monistic/pluralistic worldview, attempted to embrace all pairs of opposites, suggesting they were humanly created categories that could be transcended. With the proper mental discipline, one could "go beyond the pairs of opposites" and experience pleasure and pain, happiness and sorrow, and all opposites as one reality. For some schools of Buddhism, to escape the pairs of opposites is tantamount to salvation.

Buddhism's enormous stress on tolerance may be one consequence of the absence of dualism. Unlike Christianity, as Buddhism developed, its leaders did not insist that all believers accept a single orthodoxy. Buddhism embraces a pluralism of schools and deities, none of which is exclusive. Christianity and Islam are replete with either/or images and ethical choices between good and evil, and Christian leaders were the most adamant about establishing one orthodox set of beliefs and a single system of theology that everyone had to accept. Even after the post-Reformation proliferation of new denominations of Protestants, many of them continued to insist that their way was the only way.

Although Islam grows out of a dualistic tradition, Muslims did not insist on only one expression of the faith. Muslims recognize four major schools of law, which do not always agree. Islam experienced no real church-state struggles such as those that punctuated Western Christendom for much of its history. There were a few martyrs in Islamic history, but nothing to parallel the large number of Christian "heretics" burned or otherwise put to death over the centuries.

FIGURE 5-2   WHICH SIDE IS GOD ON?

THE PLACE OF HISTORY   Another major difference between the Christian-Islamic and the Hindu-Buddhist traditions is the place of history. All three Abrahamic faiths emphasize the importance of history in explaining their worldviews. For both Christians and Muslims, God acts in history, and both traditions view history as the unfolding of God's plan. Buddhists are more likely to take the historic Buddha as a grand narrative and read the many tales about other Buddhas and bodhisattvas as metaphoric, mythic, and symbolic.

TIME AND SPACE   Conceptions of time and space differ widely as well. Buddhists accept the Hindu concept of reoccurring cosmic cycles of creation and destruction that last hundreds of millions of years. The universe periodically melts away, only to reemerge once more in a seemingly never-ending cycle of birth, death, and rebirth. Christians and Muslims believe there was only one creation, and when the End of Time occurs, life as we know it will end.

Members of the three religions not only lived and developed in very different conceptual worlds, but each had a different empirical understanding of the physical world in which they lived. Buddhists took their faith to Central and Southeast Asia, and for centuries maintained significant exchanges between south and east Asia. Chinese Buddhist pilgrims followed well-trodden paths along the Silk Roads to India, and Buddhists sailed with fleets that regularly visited ports along the Indian Ocean. Around 800, Buddhism included more than half of the world's people, and its geographical reach throughout Asia was enormous.

By contrast, the Christian world was quite small. Although Christians had contact with India, and Nestorians were active in central Asia, most Christians had little geographical knowledge of Asia. As Christianity spread into western Europe, Christians became more cut off from the trade routes that connected Europe and east Asia. In Europe, Christians lived for centuries in a "pre-Copernican straightjacket," which limited their imagination to planet Earth. As late as 1400, Christian maps placed Jerusalem in the center of the world.[114]

The Islamic world was larger than either the Christian or Buddhist world. Situated as they were between Christendom and the heart of Buddhist Asia, Muslims were familiar with Byzantine and Nestorian Christians, Buddhists, Manicheans, Zoroastrians, and Hindus. Muslim sailors and traders dominated commerce in the Indian Ocean. When Marco Polo, a Christian, traveled to China during the Yuan dynasty, he was a stranger wherever he went, but when the Muslim Ibn Batuta undertook his journey from Morocco to China in 1325, shortly after Polo's death, he was at home everywhere he went except in China, and even there he claimed to have found a Muslim community. He could communicate in a common language and share similar values with Muslims wherever he traveled, and he kept meeting people he knew.

ATTITUDES TOWARD SCIENCE   Prior to 1500, both Buddhist and Muslim scholarship and science were superior to scholarship in Christian Europe. Both Buddhism and Islam welcomed scientific inquiry, and heresy trials were rare in these two faiths. Both also supported large universities and groups of scholars. Early Buddhists were known for their medical knowledge, and Buddhists probably practiced the best medicine in the world until the twelfth century. Many people went to Buddhist monasteries for medical attention. Until the thirteenth century the Buddhist university at Nalanda in northern India attracted scholars from many parts of the world and housed a huge collection of books. Muslim physicians learned a great deal of medical knowledge from the Buddhists they met in central Asia, and Europeans relied chiefly on Muslim medical texts until the seventeenth century.

Moreover, Muslims made a conscious attempt, long before Christian scholars did, to learn from the scientists, mathematicians, and philosophers they met as their empire expanded. Muslims patronized scholars from many areas. During Islam's golden age, Muslims embraced Greek thinkers, particularly Aristotle, but Christian Europe only gained a deep knowledge about classic Greek thinkers in the thirteenth century, largely from Muslims in al-Andalus.

Scholarship in Muslim centers of learning was far superior to Christian levels of knowledge until the thirteenth century. Consequently Muslim intellectuals knew more about astronomy and the wider solar system than most Christians did. Muslim scholars brought the Indian decimal system and the concept of zero to Baghdad in the ninth century, and these concepts only reached northern Europe via Muslim Spain in the thirteenth century.

HUMAN SEXUALITY Proponents of the three universal religions had very different ideas about human sexuality. The Hindu context, out of which Buddhism developed, accepted sexuality as a given of nature. Although Hindus certainly believed that renunciation of sex and other earthly pleasures was necessary for ultimate salvation, their texts dealt openly with sexuality and gave counsel on its practice within defined social limits. *Kama*, which means pleasure, is one of the four goals of Hindu life, and the Kama Sutra, an important Hindu text, is a treatise on pleasure, including sexual desire. Hindus were expected to marry and raise a family.

Lay Buddhists were also free to marry and have children and regarded sex in much the same way as their fellow Hindus did. Monks and nuns took vows of celibacy and regarded sex as one of the major temptations that took believers away from the quest for nirvana. Early texts caution against being lured into the world of desire by attractive young women, and particularly harsh punishments were imposed if they violated proper sexual conduct. After the Buddha reluctantly accepted women as nuns, many joined. Becoming a nun offered women a socially accepted alternative to unhappy marriages and the demands that society placed on women, and nuns often became scholars.

Buddhists liken desire, the root of all suffering, to burning. The "burning, burning, burning" that the Buddha cautioned against often meant one's desire for women. Saint Paul also used burning as a metaphor for sexual desire. Because early Christians believed that the imminent second coming of Jesus would usher in the end of the world, there was no need to have children. Paul advised widows and those who were unmarried to stay single, adding: "But if they cannot exercise self-control, they should marry. For it is better to marry than to be aflame with passion." (1 Corinthians 67:8–9)

Desert Fathers and Mothers routinely remained celibate. After struggling with his passions, Augustine took the vow of celibacy and preached its virtues. Early priests sometimes remained celibate, but those appointed by the landed aristocracy usually did not. Only in the eleventh century were priests required to lead a celibate life. Christian monks and nuns were expected to follow strict rules of celibacy. Both Buddhists and Christians tempered their view on sexuality for the lay community, especially when some of its wealthy members began to make large donations.

By contrast, Muslims were never required to take vows of celibacy, and Muhammad, unlike the Buddha and Jesus, was very much a man of the world. He enjoyed the company of women and had several wives and concubines. Allah promised heaven to the righteous and used a variety of images to describe it: "Lo for the duteous is achievement— gardens and enclosed vineyards and maidens for companions and a full cup." (Sura 78:31–34) These very different attitudes toward sexuality may help explain why Christians often accused Muslims, and particularly Muhammad, of being licentious.

MONOTHEISM AND POLYTHEISM   The three universal religions also differed widely on their response to polytheism. Although the Buddha grew up in a polytheistic environment in India, the Buddha's message denied all gods and goddesses. However, as the faith spread among polytheistic populations in south and east Asia, it adapted local divinities and heroes and made them into bodhisattvas and even transcendent Buddhas. Buddhism has numerous female deities: Kwan Yin, originally the Indian male deity Avalokiteswara, gradually became the female Bodhisattva of Compassion. As the one who "hears the cries of the world," Kwan Yin is perhaps the most commonly worshiped figure in contemporary Buddhism.

Christianity, an avowedly monotheistic faith, vigorously fought to stamp out any remnants of polytheism and impose a uniform monotheism. In a sense, Christians served as the marines of monotheism, fighting polytheism first in lands around the Mediterranean and then in western Europe. Christianity transformed local deities and renowned historic figures into saints. However, nominal Christians, who probably composed the vast majority for centuries, just grafted Christian concepts onto earlier habits that they kept. As late as the sixteenth century, Bishop Martin, in Portugal, complained:

> . . . decorating tables, wearing laurels, taking omens from footsteps, putting fruit and wine on the log in the hearth, and bread in the well, what are these but worship of the Devil. For women to call upon Minerva when they spin, and to observe the day of Venus at weddings and to call upon her whenever they go out upon the public highway, what is that but worship of the devil.[115]

FIGURE 5-3   KWAN YIN

Islam has been the most fastidious in its commitment to monotheism. Muhammad quickly eliminated all the idols that surrounded the Ka'ba. From Arabia, Islam spread in Sasanid and Byzantine areas where most people were already familiar with monotheism and the Judaic, Zoroastrian, and Christian traditions. Overt evidence of polytheism was limited, and Muslim complaints about the survival of pagan rituals and beliefs were rare. The Muslim challenge was to win over elites already deeply infused with Greco-Roman-Persian values.

Feminine aspects of divinity, at least those aspects associated with wisdom and compassion, can be found in Christianity. Athena/Minerva symbolized wisdom in the pre-Christian Mediterranean world and Saraswati performs the same function in Hinduism. In the Hebrew Bible, wisdom is feminine. Many of the qualities attributed to Mary in both Christianity and Islam echo these older wisdom traditions, and the compassionate Mary can also be compared to the Kwan Yin. In its constant struggle against polytheism, early Christian leaders worked especially hard to eradicate any vestiges of mother-goddess worship. The emergence of Mary as a popular figure of veneration in Europe in the eleventh century suggests they were not entirely successful.

As strict monotheists, Islam was the most successful of the three universal religions in suppressing goddess worship, which was quite common in Arabia when Muhammad received his revelations. Interestingly, the Quran tells that when giving birth, Mary went out and held on to a palm tree. God told her to "shake towards thyself the trunk of the palm-tree. It will let fall fresh ripe dates upon thee." (Quran 19:24–26) This story reflects a common birth practice in west Asia as well as the story of the Buddha's birth that also occurred as his mother Maya held a branch of a tree as he was born.

ATTITUDES TOWARD WOMEN All three universal religions were ambivalent toward the feminine, although they all claimed they sought to uplift the status of women. Buddhist literature expresses two conceptions of women: one mysterious, sensual, destructive, elusive, close to nature, and potentially polluting and the other wise, maternal, creative, gentle, and compassionate caregivers. Kwan Yin reflects the second tradition. Christians were also ambivalent about women as evidenced in their concept of the "two faces of Eve" or the contrast between Mary and Mary Magdalene, one virginal and without sin and the other eventually transformed by the church into a prostitute.

Women were a vital force in building early Christianity. Many were active church leaders, and those who converted often brought their husbands and other male relatives to the faith. Christianity strengthened the institution of marriage by making it a sacrament and not allowing men to easily discard their wives. Men and women attended Christian services together and men were counseled to respect women.

Islam's effect on women's lives is much debated. Before Islam, many Arabian women had a great deal of freedom and authority in society. They were active in trade and had the right to divorce their husbands. However, infanticide was common and there was no limit on the number of wives a man could have. Islam put a stop to female infanticide, limited the number of wives to four if the husband could treat them all equally, and instituted some inheritance rights. However, Muslims adapted some of the social norms found in the urban areas into which Islam spread, such as keeping concubines and seclusion and veiling. Veiling, which had been a sign of status in Byzantium, became widespread in Islam.

INVOLVEMENT IN POLITICS The three religions had different attitudes toward involvement in politics and the use of violence. Siddhartha Gotama, who became the Buddha, was a prince in a small kingdom in northern India. His father tried unsuccessfully to keep him from seeing old age, sickness, or death, fearing they would lead him to religion and cause him to reject his responsibilities as king. Siddhartha turned his back on his family and caste obligations and focused instead on the individual's perception of reality. His message challenged the authority of the priestly caste but not the government.

A large number of stories originated in Asia about good kings who patronized Buddhism. Although many of them used religion to enhance their personal and political ambitions, the stories stress their moral qualities. The Legend of Ashoka, about the third emperor of the Mauryan dynasty, initially describes him as a wicked tyrant who delighted in violence and killed his brothers to get the throne. After he converts to Buddhism, he becomes a Cakravartan, one who maintains order in the cosmos and rules morally.

Ashoka's example had enormous influence in Southeast Asia, and he also served as a model for Chinese emperors. Kings who fought viciously to gain power and then reformed could point to Ashoka and claim that they, too, had moral authority. Even Kublai Khan was sometimes called a wise "Cakravartan King."[116] Later kings and leaders in China, Korea, and Japan called on the Buddha to support their use of violence, even though it is doubtful that the Buddha would have approved of such actions.

Jesus was not indifferent to political power. Palestine was part of the Roman Empire and scorning Roman authority would have been unacceptable. Jesus advised his followers to "Render unto Caesar that which is Caesar's and unto God that which is God's." (Mark 12:17) They were expected to be good citizens, but they were often persecuted and used as scapegoats. Jesus wanted to share a spiritual message about the Kingdom in Heaven, not lead a political revolt against the Romans. Because he believed that the world would soon end, he had little reason to stress political reforms or to advise his followers to engage in politics.

After the Edict of Milan in 313, which recognized Christianity, Christians' attitude toward power politics drastically changed. From that time forward, the church sought alliances with rulers who would advance Christendom, and church leaders blessed the use of military power to achieve that end. Within the Byzantine Empire, politics and faith were securely joined. The emperor was both nominal head of the church as well as head of state, and he selected the patriarchs. Like the Chinese and Japanese who used Buddhism to legitimize conquest and war, many European political leaders invoked the will of God as they invaded their neighbors and persecuted those who did not share their beliefs. With the rise of nation-states in Europe, it was common for princes and kings to combine devotion to God and the state, and many kings sponsored national religions.

Muhammad made no separation between his political and spiritual authority, and he gained many early followers by leading successful military campaigns. After the hijara, the flight from Mecca to Medina,

Muhammad served as military and political leader as well as religious reformer, and he successfully assumed leadership of Mecca. The early caliphs were also both military and religious leaders, although the ulama had the final religious authority. Periodically reform groups such as the Sufis criticized the opulent lives of the caliphs and sultans and the inequalities in society that their policies promoted, but few questioned the close association of the religious and secular realms.

CONVERSION POLICIES   Over the centuries there have been many misconceptions about whether the three religions used force to gain converts. The Buddha's message was a prescription to alleviate suffering and lead a person to new insights. It made little sense to try to force people to follow his Eightfold Path and become Buddhists. By the time Buddhism reached central Asia and China, rulers were using it to support their military exploits, but they seldom resorted to violence to force conversions.

Christians were more ambivalent about the use of force in conversion. For the first 300 years, Christians were a minority with no political power and there were no forced conversions. Instead, the Roman authorities often tried to force Christians to renounce their beliefs. After Christianity became the official religion of the Roman and Byzantine empires, measures were taken to encourage people to convert. Christians destroyed vestiges of the pre-Christian beliefs and appropriated their sacred groves and temples for Christian worship, and they worked tirelessly to destroy the remnants of European polytheism and often persecuted those groups. As a single Christian orthodoxy became the norm for Roman Catholics, leaders persecuted heretics such as the Waldensians, (followers of Waldo, who took the vow of poverty and opposed certain church doctrines). With the rise of empires and later national religions in Europe, religion was increasingly used to support the military and justify wars.

During the first century of its history, Muslims had no interest in converting non-Arabs. Arabs were expected to convert, but People of the Book were not and were free to follow their religion as long as they obeyed the caliph's rules and paid the protection tax. However, Muslims who renounced Islam risked death. From the beginning, Muslims claimed the right to defend their faith against other aggressors and did not have to deal with the contradictions over the use of violence that Buddhists and Christians faced. During the Abassid caliphate, many people became Muslims through the gradual process of Islamization.

The brutality that characterized European society from 500 to 1000 had been motivated mainly by threats to one's survival or by the desire for more land, goods, and power. Although Jesus had blessed the peacemakers and counseled that the meek would inherit the earth, Christians used their religion to justify their violence against Jews and Muslims during the crusades, and the crusades helped legitimize the use of violence to support Christianity.

The European conquest of the Americas, beginning in 1492, was accomplished by armed conflict and was often accompanied by forced conversions. Columbus testified many times that the purpose of his voyages was to bring Christianity to the "pagan isles." The Spanish missionary, Bartolome de las Casas, a champion of Native Americans rights who believed they had souls and were human, recorded many eyewitness accounts of Spanish atrocities. Once such onslaught he describes in detail:

> Such inhumanities and barbarisms were committed in my sight. . . .
> The soldiers . . . "made bets as to who would slit a man in two, or cut
> off his head at one blow: or they opened up his bowels. They tore the
> babes from their mothers' breast by the feet, and dashed their heads
> against the rocks. Others they seized by the shoulders and threw into
> the rivers, laughing and joking, and when they fell into the water they
> exclaimed: "boil the body of so and so!" They spitted the bodies of
> other babes, together with their mothers and all who were before them,
> on their swords."[117]

Spanish cruelty and atrocities in the Americas, which included many forced conversions, were so extreme they became known as the "Black Legend." About the same time in Spain, Christians gave Jews and Muslims the harsh choice of conversion, expulsion, or death.

COMMERCE AND TRADE   Involvement in commerce was another issue on which members of these faiths differed. The Buddha did not oppose members of the lay community becoming merchants. His discussion of "right livelihood" in the Eightfold Path cautions against occupations that might cause harm, but it does not forbid legitimate commerce. Wealthy merchants who contributed funds to the faith greatly stimulated Buddhism's continuing success. Merchants supported monasteries and were a vital factor in both attracting new followers and maintaining the Sangha. Lovely frescoes in the cave sanctuaries at Ajanta in India depict rich merchants and their wives who donated money for the excavations and in turn were given immortality in art.

Buddhism flourished in the hemispheric trade along the Silk Roads. Buddhism discouraged warfare and contributed to greater stability, and travel and the exchange of goods generally increase during periods of peace. Traders brought Buddhism to Southeast Asia and Buddhist missionaries traveled with traders to east Asia. Buddhists carried on a lively trade in relics and other materials useful in worship. Buddhists also established rest houses, hospitals, and centers of learning along the Silk Roads, providing vital services for the many traders who traveled these routes. Buddhist travelers who brought their faith to China stimulated exchanges between India and China that expanded far beyond the sale of religious objects.

Christians struggled over their attitude toward commerce and were often ambivalent. Christian scriptures repeatedly admonish the rich to give what they have to the poor, warning: "It is easier for a camel to go through the eye of a needle than for a rich man to enter the kingdom of God." (Matthew 19: 24) Although the Roman Church officially banned usury, both religious and political leaders knew that commerce was essential to their survival and prosperity, so they often invited small groups of non-Christians to carry on trade and other commercial functions. Large numbers of Jews served as middlemen and merchants throughout Christendom. At any time the church could turn Christians against Jews, and in this way it attempted to control the merchant class while keeping the majority of Europeans from participating in what the church officially labeled a "vile practice."

The church's belligerent attitude toward commerce led to many anomalies. The church was a huge market for silk, precious metals, and other paraphernalia that were essential for their rituals. This demand meant that Church officials routinely transacted business with Christian, Jewish, and Muslim merchants to secure the items they desired, especially silk. By the fifteenth century, the church was fully participating in the rise of European commercialism.

Islam supported trade from the beginning. Muhammad and his first wife were merchants, and Muslim practices such as the hajj encourage long-distance travel and trade. Wealthy Muslim merchants supported the cultural and intellectual life of Muslim cities by patronizing the arts and sciences and investing in the impressive building projects, and Muslim sailors were dominant in the Indian Ocean trading network. Merchants had high status, and the highest status was reserved for textile merchants. Muslims were to seek trading opportunities "even to China," but the Quran insists that merchants weigh their goods accurately and not charge interest. A Muslim source states: "The honest, truthful Muslim merchant will stand with the martyrs on the Day of Judgment."[118]

The lure of excessive wealth threatened both Buddhism and Christianity. As a result of donations offered to build merit, Buddhist monasteries, especially in east Asia, became very prosperous and worldly. Monks involved in commercial activities often became rich. On a personal level, avarice fundamentally violated the spirit of The Buddha's message. Politically, wealthy monasteries threatened the state and invited persecutions that dramatically undermined Buddhism's power and influence, especially in China.

The attraction of wealth also weakened the Roman Catholic Church. Symbolic of its involvement in business was the Medici family in Florence, arguably the most important commercial family in Europe in the fifteenth century, that installed some of its family members as popes. As Christians took advantage of expanding commercial opportunities, persecutions of Jews increased dramatically. Mendicant friars preached about the plight of the poor, but their voices made little impression on the church leadership. The church hierarchy's aggressive sale of indulgences caused many lay people to turn against the church, laying the ground for the Protestant Reformation.

REFORMS   Finally, periods of reform punctuated the history of all three religions. The Buddha himself was a major reformer who spoke against the caste system and the elaborate sacrifices that characterized the Brahminic religion of his time. His strong ethical message infused Indian mysticism with a set of concrete moral principles that humans should follow. Throughout Buddhism's career in east and Southeast Asia, numerous reformers began new schools to carry on the long tradition of Buddhist reforms.

The long periods of reform that both Islam and Christianity attempted were similar but led to different results. Sufi codes of conduct, not unlike the tradition of Buddhist and Christian monks, insisted on poverty and withdrawal from the world. Sufi brotherhoods were very similar to the rise of mendicant orders such as the Franciscans and the Dominicans. As Sufi sects increased in the subsequent centuries, they resembled the large number of Protestant denominations that developed after the Reformation. However, while Sufism blossomed into a major reform movement within Islam, reforms in Christianity ultimately led to a breakup of the Roman Catholic Church.

COMMON RELIGIOUS RITUALS AND PRACTICES

Several ubiquitous items have played a significant role in all three faiths. Silk was one. Not only was it widely used by followers of all three faiths, but the demand for silk affected trade patterns across Eurasia and the Indian Ocean. The Chinese had used silk in their ceremonies long before Buddhism arrived. It was especially important in burial rituals associated with reverence for ancestors. Chinese Buddhists wrapped their ancestors' bones in silk and used silk to protect relics as well.

At first, Indian Buddhists wore simple cotton robes, but by 300 C.E. monks were wearing silk clothing and using silk for other vestments in their rituals, increasing the demand for this unique product. Hindu textile workers who practiced ahimsa, noninjury of any living thing, were not keen on making silk because they were reluctant to kill the silkworms in their cocoons. After Muslims who had no such taboos came to India in large numbers, India became an active silk producer. Theravada monks, however, insisted on cotton robes because they also objected to killing the silkworms.

Church officials routinely transacted business with Christian, Jewish, and Muslim merchants to secure the items they desired. Islamic traders were the major suppliers of silk to Christian Europe, and many grew rich as a result. After Byzantine craftsmen learned the art of making silk, the demand for silk expanded dramatically. Purple robes symbolized high political and religious status. As the cult of saints and relic worship expanded in Christian Europe, silk was used for wrapping relics and for burials. Silk was also used as altar hangings, decorations, altar covers, wrappings for utensils, shrouds, tomb covers for bishops and kings, and vestments for church officials. A large portion of the church's income was used to purchase silk.

Under the Abbasid caliphs, silk was the most treasured cloth. One caliph's death inventory included 4,000 robes, 4,000 silk cloaks, 1,000 silk cushions and pillows, and 1,500 silk carpets.[119] Wealthy Muslim women routinely wore silk dresses and other silk items. Manicheans, Zoroastrians, and Nestorians in central Asia were also heavily involved in the silk trade and gave silk a privileged place among textiles.

Chinese Buddhists also wanted the precious stones known as the "Seven Treasures" for their rituals. The Chinese exported large quantities of silk to India in exchange for several of these stones which were only available in India, helping to stimulate a lively Sino-Indian trade that also included relics and jewels.

If silk was an ubiquitous presence in all three faiths, the use of prayer beads was even more prevalent. Using beads in prayer probably originated with Hindu worship of Shiva in India, perhaps as early as the eighth century B.C.E. Passing one's fingers over a string of beads enabled the devotee to keep track of the many names of the god being addressed or the sequence of specific prayers. Sandstone sculptures dated about 185 B.C.E. show Hindu sages and the god Brahma holding prayer beads.

Dried berries that symbolize particular events in the Buddha's life were used for prayer in early Buddhism. Devotees were supposed to recall events special to Buddhism as they fingered the beads. Some

Buddhists claim using prayer beads originated when the Buddha told a king to thread 108 seeds from the Bodhi tree, and, while passing the beads between his fingers, to repeat, "Hail to the Buddha, the law, and the Sangha" 2,000 times a day.[120] Many Buddhist monks carry a strand of 108 beads that can represent such things as names of the Buddha or the number of sinful desires the devotee must overcome. Laypersons usually carry strands of only 30 to 40 beads. Many Buddhists use prayer beads to help them still their thoughts and attain a state of serenity and oneness with their surroundings.

Buddhist prayer beads, called "court chains," were never very popular in China, where they were used as a status symbol rather than as an aid for prayer. By comparison, Korean Buddhists made extensive use of prayer beads until the end of the fourteenth century when the Yi dynasty banned Buddhism. The Japanese use prayer beads at funerals and other ceremonial occasions. Japanese teahouses commonly have strands of prayer beads hanging on the wall.

Tibetan prayer beads, which symbolize the Tripitaka (Buddhist scriptures), have three large beads dividing the 108 beads. Two smaller strings of beads attached to the main strand serve as an abacus, allowing devotees to count up to 10,800 prayers. More elaborate strands are available for counting even more devotional cycles.

Christians probably learned about prayer beads from the Muslims and began using them for good fortune in the seventh century. By the eleventh century, they were used for counting devotions rather than for protection. Because most European Christians were nonliterate, they were given a set of 150 prayers to say and the beads served as memory aids.[121] Roman Catholics call the prayer beads "rosaries," a term that comes from the Latin word "rosarium," suggesting the rose garden where people often went to pray. It also reminds devotees of the white rose that symbolizes Mary. Christian women sometimes wore elaborate prayer beads as jewelry. In the mid-sixteenth century, the pope decreed that St. Dominic (1170–1231) had invented the rosary, and Dominicans still make the official Catholic rosaries. The 150-bead rosary corresponds to the number of Psalms. Roman Catholics often reflect on past sins and seek forgiveness as they finger the beads.

Muslims also use prayer beads. Explorers and traders most likely spread the custom. Their 99 bead strand represents 99 names of Allah. Muslims hope their sins will be forgiven if they repeat Allah's names 100 times morning and night.[122] To ward off the "evil eye," a cord or tassel hangs from the one hundredth bead. The ubiquitous so-called worry beads found in Greece, Turkey, and Armenia were probably originally Islamic prayer beads.

FIGURE 5-4   PRAYER BEADS IN THREE FAITHS.

CHRISTIAN-MUSLIM RELATIONS: SIBLING RIVALRY, OR CLASH OF CIVILIZATIONS

In summarizing the similarities and differences among the three universal faiths, it is apparent that Christianity and Islam share a great deal, but Christians, especially, have not always realized or acknowledged the possibility of a common "Islamic-Christian Civilization."

Although Muslims knew that their faith was grounded in the Judeo-Christian tradition and that Christians and Muslims were worshiping the same God, most Christians either did not know these facts or chose to ignore them. European Christians were shockingly ignorant about Islam for centuries. Orthodox Christians in Byzantium initially confused Islam and Arianism because Muslims did not accept the divinity of Jesus. Some thought Muslims worshiped the morning star or Aphrodite[123] and others accused Muhammad of adultery and lechery. Venerable Bede, a leading eighth-century Christian writer, quoted Abraham's view of Ishmael as "a wild ass of a man," as proof that Islam had started with a troubled ancestor. He went on to argue that Muslims were "enemies of the church" and "hateful to God."[124]

After Frankish forces defeated the Muslims at the Battle of Tours in 732, most Western Europeans no longer worried much about a Muslim threat. Even though Christians continued to loath the faith and to characterize Muhammad as a false prophet and imposter, most did not think Muslims were intent on conquering more European land. By the ninth century some Christians even began to wonder if God preferred Islam, whereas others speculated that perhaps Muslim expansion was a sign that the "End of Days" was imminent.

In much European literature and folklore, Muslims were pictured as barbarians and called "Saracens," a derisive term that came to be associated with Muslims who opposed the crusades. In the Arthurian legends, Palomides, one of King Arthur's trusted knights, is told, "They have no honor, they are allied with the devil, and they are liable to emit a most unpleasant smell when their heads are cut off."[125] The French classic, *The Song of Roland,* a mythic account of Charlemagne's invasion of Spain, portrays Saracens praying to three golden idols: Muhammad, Apollo, and Tervagant (a devil). "Charlemagne's army smashed Muslim idols and they [Muslims] destroyed their own idols when they proved powerless against the army of God."[126] Ironically, most of the chroniclers of the first crusade used Muslim idolatry as the key reason for wanting to rescue the Holy Land.

Dominicans and Franciscans friars, who energized the twelfth and thirteenth century Christian revival in Europe, were especially hostile to Islam. Even the peace-loving Francis of Assisi (1182–1226) issued an impassioned call for missions to vanquish the infidels as proof of a revitalized Christianity. Hoping to become a Christian martyr, in 1212 he traveled to the Holy Land to preach against Islam. Illness forced his return to Spain, but seven years later he joined the fifth crusade and was surprised that during his meeting with Sultan al-Kamil, the sultan agreed to his plan to send Christian missionaries to west Asia.

Few Europeans saw any reason to study Islam, even though Muslims were building a sophisticated culture in al-Andalus. Even when Latin translation of the Quran became available, Christian apologists continued to invent accusations that completely distorted the faith. Peter the Venerable, Abbot of Cluny, who had commissioned the first Latin translations of the Quran in 1143, accused Muhammad of getting Jews and Nestorians to help him start a new religion by forging a document.

Although most Europeans up to the eleventh century had almost no accurate knowledge about the Muslim faith, a few scholars recognized and appreciated the scholarship taking place in the House of Wisdom in Baghdad and in various universities in al-Andalus. A thirteenth century assessment of Baghdad stated:

> There the Saracens have the greatest universities and great teachers.
> They receive me as if I were an angel of God—in the schools,
> classrooms, monasteries, churches, or synagogues. I was astounded at
> how, in such a perfidious law, one could find works of such great
> perfection.[127]

However, this same scholar, witnessing Christians in Baghdad being sold into slavery, asked God, "How can you allow this cruel beast [Islam] to dishonor your name, deflower your sanctified virgins, violate your churches?"[128]

When Christian forces conquered the Arab citadel of Toledo in 1085, the victorious Christian troops discovered a vast storehouse of literary and scientific information. Christian scholars then began reading classical texts and Muslim scientific treatises that Jewish and Muslim scholars had translated. James Burke, a contemporary historian who has focused on innovations and their impact, implies that this discovery was the day "the universe changed."[129]

Some leading Christian thinkers were fearful that young Christians might be Islamized. Paul Alvaras, a Christian intellectual, wrote:

> The Christians love to read the poems and romances of the Arabs; they
> study Arab theologians and philosophers, not to refute them but to

form a correct and elegant Arabic. . . . Alas! all talented young Christians read and study with enthusiasm the Arab books; they gather
immense libraries at great expense; they despise Christian literature as
unworthy of attention. They have forgotten their language.[130]

Christians living in al-Andalus under the Muslims could not help
but be impressed by Muslim society. Even while remaining Christians,
they became Islamisized. Many learned Arabic, read Arabic poetry, and
copied aspects of Muslim culture because that gave them greater status
and opened up opportunities for education and better jobs for them.
In Toledo, Cordoba, and Seville, Jews, Christians and Muslims freely
mingled and shared in research, translations, and discussions. Scholars
from all three groups worked together to translate Arabic and Syric
manuscripts into Latin.

Even after European scholars realized that Muslim scholarship was
far superior to anything known in Europe at the time, Christian leaders
still continued to vilify Muslims, depicting Islam as a heretical form of
Christianity and Muhammad as a false prophet and great imposter
(accusations that regularly appeared in nineteenth-century U.S. history
textbooks). Some argued that because the Quran did not report
Muhammad performing miracles, he was not as powerful as Jesus, dis-
missing the fact that Muhammad had received extended revelation from
Allah. One account even described Muhammad as having been a cardinal in the Roman Church, who, disappointed in his lack of success, fled
to Arabia and started a false religion.[131]

Muslim attitudes about Christianity were radically different from
Christian views of Islam. Muhammad fully intended his new faith to
build on both Jewish and Christian traditions. Muslims see themselves
as heirs of Abraham through his son Ishmael. Islam accepts Jewish
prophets including Noah and Moses and gives special homage to Jesus
and Mary. Of the Quran's 114 Sura (chapters), only eight individuals are
accorded chapters of their own. One of them is devoted to Mary and a
second to her father, Imran. Jesus is mentioned numerous times throughout the Quran.

Muhammad did not encourage his followers to try to convert People
of the Book. After all, they were already monotheists, praying to the
same God. Muslims have no theological basis for disdaining Christianity
or Judaism, groups that they regard as part of their larger family, and in
that context, "Islam and the West are historical twins whose resemblance
did not cease when their paths parted."[132] Muslims did oppose and even
kill Christians and criticized how many Christian acted, but Muslim
writers hardly ever condemned Christianity as a religion. In general,
Muslims were also far more tolerant of Jews than Christians were and

FIGURE 5-5   CATHEDRAL IN MOSQUE AT CORDOBA, SPAIN.

FIGURE 5-6   CHURCH CONVERTED TO MOSQUE, ISTANBUL.

did not produce anti-Jewish tracts. Areas under Muslim control also did not persecute Jews.

The experience of the crusaders, when thousands of European Christians actually encountered Muslims firsthand, might have caused average Christians to change their attitude about Islam. However, the fog of war makes it almost impossible to make a balanced assessment of one's enemy. Even so, many crusaders could not help but be impressed by what they saw of Muslim society. Saladin, the most distinguished of the Muslim leaders, impressed some of the crusaders who begrudgingly noted his skillful leadership and the compassion he showed to Christians after his forces regained Jerusalem.

Muslims, on the other hand, had little good to say about the crusaders. Muslims tended to characterize them as "barbarians" and frequently noted their "bestiality." When Christians reduced the Syrian city of Ma'arra to ruins and famine increased, word spread among Muslims that the crusaders "boiled the pagan adults in cooking pots; they impaled children on spits and devoured them grilled." A contemporary Arab chronicler wrote, "All those who are well informed about the Franj [crusaders] saw them as beasts superior in courage and fighting ardor but in nothing else, just as animals are superior in strength and aggression."[133]

The social and religious impact that the European crusaders had on west Asia was minimal, and the crusader states that were established proved short lived. Some Muslims served in crusader armies and there were a few conversions. Some soldiers exchanged sides depending on the success of the respective armies. Christians who stayed in west Asia after the crusades tended to adopt cultural practices of their Muslim neighbors. As small minority communities, ex-crusaders learned local languages, married Muslim women, and ate in the Muslim style. Even though most remained nominal Christians, they assimilated to the indigenous culture they had come to defeat.

None of these factors should obscure the long-lasting influence of the crusades as a source of deep animosity. Muslim hostility toward Christianity can be dated from these conflicts, and Christian misinformation about and prejudice toward Muslims intensified as a result. Although Jews, Muslims, and Christians had lived peacefully in al-Andalus for 600 years, the *reconquista* and the expulsion of Jews and Muslims from Spain contributed to the growing hostilities Muslims had toward Christians. Etched into the memories of both groups was a vision of the world divided between two warring faiths, a memory that has resurfaced periodically, especially in the aftermath of September 11, 2001, in the United States.

CONCLUSION

What conclusions might impartial observers in the middle of the sixteenth century have made about the future of Buddhism, Christianity, and Islam? They might initially have trouble locating Buddhism, which had attracted half the world's population in 800. In India, it had been gradually absorbed into Hinduism. Looking at east Asia, they would see Buddhism was an important, though not dominant, faith in China, where its teachings had become a part of Neo-Confucianism, which became the state religion in Korea in the fourteenth century. In Japan, Buddhism existed along with Shintoism. Looking more closely, observers might detect a great many Buddhist values and symbols in these areas and conclude that Buddhism had survived in new forms. Noting a significant number of people participating in Buddhist rituals, they might realize that Buddhism had infused the lives of hundreds of millions of east Asians, even many who did not recognize their enormous debt to its teachings.

When they turned their attention to Southeast Asia, they would see that the coastal regions of both mainland and Island Southeast Asia had come under the influence of Muslim merchants, and kings and princes had converted to Islam. Even so, Buddhism was still a vital ingredient in several regions. The newly emerging Thai kingdom was supported by Buddhist principles, and they might note that in the rest of mainland Southeast Asia, Buddhism was vibrant. In the Indonesian archipelago, Buddhism remained robust, but Islam was gaining strength.

Observers would see much evidence of Islam in west Asia, where millions of Christians had recently come under Muslim political control. Muslim kingdoms across central Asia had supplanted Nestorianism, which could be found only in small communities in the southern part of the Indian subcontinent. They would also note that the Ottoman Turks, who ruled Constantinople and most of the former Byzantine Empire, were threatening to spread Islam into the heart of Europe.

Ethiopia was still a Christian society, but Europe was the only area where Christianity was flourishing. Roman Catholicism had spread into Scandinavia and had recently been reestablished in Iberia. Observers might just barely make out the voices of Martin Luther and John Calvin calling Christians to look to the Bible rather than the Church to recover Jesus' original message.

Turning to the Western Hemisphere, the observers would realize that Roman Catholicism had jumped across the Atlantic Ocean and was establishing roots in the Caribbean and Mexico, but there was no hint that the whole hemisphere would one day become Christianity's most vibrant center.

The enormous reach of Islam could not help but stand out in bold relief. Islamisized newcomers such as the Ottoman Turks were controlling the former Byzantine Empire and other Christian strongholds from Hungary to west Asia, where Muslims constitute 90 percent of the population. Islam was strong among central Asian peoples and new converts were rapidly expanding its reach in Southeast Asia. In the subcontinent, they might note that Turkish/Mongol Muslims have taken Islam from Afghanistan into north India where Sufi saints were helping attract millions of converts. Islam also stretched along the east coast of Africa and into West African kingdoms where they can detect Islam and local beliefs all mixed up together.

If the observers were to make a reasonably objective analysis of the situation in 1550, they would probably assume that Buddhist influences are declining. They might wonder whether Christianity could withstand the challenge of Islam or survive its internal struggles, and they might speculate how the Amerindians will respond to Christianity's virulent conversion policy. The observer might well conclude that Islam will continue to thrive and prosper and might one day even become the major world religion.

But in predicting the future, these sixteenth-century observers and historians did not have to rely only on what they could see. They also had lessons from the past to inform their judgments, and they had seen history take many unexpected turns. They had seen the world changed by insights from a disillusioned prince, a humble carpenter's son, and by the revelations that an illiterate caravan merchant had received. They had seen Eternal Rome come and go, Christian Byzantium fall to Muslims, "Barbarian" Europe become urbanized and powerful, and China peacefully absorb many faiths. They knew that unanticipated factors such the spread of disease, new inventions, the support of powerful governments, charismatic leaders, or new ideas can dramatically change the course of events. And they understood the role that luck and chance play in human history. But even so, they could not have imagined that the three universal religions would one day attract two out of every three people in the twenty-first century.

Contemporary students of history are faced with at least two major options about the future relationships among the world's universal religions, especially between Islam and Christianity. One option pictures an emerging "clash of civilizations." This dualistic vision suggests that a "civilization" can be identified mainly by its dominant religious orientation. Samuel Huntington, a Harvard political scientist who has popularized this view, identifies eight major civilizations: the Western (Christian), Confucian, Japanese, Islamic, Hindu, Slavic-Orthodox, Latin American, and, possibly, African civilizations. He believes that the most vitriolic clash will occur between the "Western" and "Islamic" civilizations. Those who

FIGURE 5-7   COLLECTING, LETTERS TO GOD.

adhere to this view often cite recent terrorist attacks as a prelude to that great conflict.

A counter option rejects the idea that the "West" and "Islamic" areas constitute two competing civilizations. Richard Bulliet, a distinguished Islamic scholar, suggests there is actually one "Islamo-Christian Civilization." Far from imagining a clash between Christendom and Islam, Bulliet argues that "Islamo-Christian civilization denotes a prolonged and fateful intertwining of sibling societies enjoying sovereignty in neighboring geographical regions and following parallel historical trajectories."[134] The so-called West and Islam have not always fought one another. As Bulliet writes: "Looked at as a whole and in historical perspective, the Islamo Christian world has much more binding it together than forcing it apart."[135] He also states, "Neither the Muslim nor the Christian historical path can be fully understood without relation to the other."[136] If that is true, then the concept of an "Islamo-Christian" civilization makes the proposed clash of civilizations "nonsensical."

As history students we know that our worldviews impose "long lasting moods and motivations" that help shape some of our most fundamental responses. One strong "mood" in the West has been dualism, the tendency to see the world divided between moral opposites. At the same time, most of us would probably agree that the future is not predetermined.

We have options, and our choices can have major implications for the future. For example, if we believe in an impending clash of civilizations, we are in a sense casting our vote for violent conflict and will do little to prevent it from occurring. If, however, we take seriously the more inclusive concept of a single Islamo-Christian civilization, we are voting to work for inclusiveness and mutual respect so that such a clash never occurs.

Stating these options in this dualist fashion offers either/or choices and assumes that the future will lead to one of these results. In considering these issues, however, we might benefit from insights from Buddhism, the third universal religion. Buddhism remerged out of the Indian worldview that emphasized both/and more than either/or. As that pluralistic orientation spread to east Asia, it not only emphasized tolerance and compassion, it encouraged people to see all sides of an issue, including how their subjective values influence their perceptions. It also taught people to seek to create harmony among seeming opposites.

Instead of assuming that a stark choice exists between either conflict or coexistence, or that civilizations with differing views must clash, we can draw on historic insights, remembering that religions change over time and that both clashes and coexistence, accommodation and synthesis have taken place throughout history.

◀ ENDNOTES ▶

1. Herbert Gutman, lecture, New York University, March 12, 1982.

2. Clifford Geertz, *The Interpretation of Cultures* (New York: Basic Books, 1973), 94.

3. Geertz, 98.

4. Geertz, 99–108.

5. Edward L. Farmer, Gavin R. G. Hambly, David Kopf, Byron K. Marshall, and Romeyn Taylor, *Comparative History of Civilizations in Asia* (Reading, MA: Addison-Wesley Publishing Company, 1977), 220*ff*.

6. Ibn Khaldum, *Al-Muqaddima*, vol. 3, 375. http://www.ummah.com/islam/ taqwapalace/linguistics/arabic13.html.

7. John Sabini, *Islam: A Primer* (Washington, D.C.: AMIDEAST, 2001), 7.

8. Quoted in John L. Esposito, *Islam: The Straight Path* (New York: Oxford University Press, 1998), 11.

9. "Isidasi: The Story of a Buddhist Nun," in Kevin Rielly *Readings in World Civilizations, Volume One: The Great Traditions* (New York: St. Martins Press, 1995), 144–46.

10. John S. Strong, *The Legend of King Ashoka: A Study and Translation of the Asokavadana,* in *Emperor Ashoka of India: What Makes a Leader Legitimate?* Donald and Jean Johnson, (Los Angeles: National Center for History in the Schools, 1994), 109–18.

11. Donald Swearer, *The Buddhist World of Southeast Asia* (Albany, NY: State University of New York Press, 1995), 72–4.

12. Swearer, 72.

13. Jerry H. Bentley, *Old World Encounters: Cross-Cultural Contacts and Exchanges in Pre-Modern Times* (New York: Oxford University Press, 1993), 72.

14. James Scott. Presidental Address, Association of Asian Studies, March 27, 1998.

15. Geertz, Chapter III.

16. Frank E. Reynolds, and Mani B. Reynolds, trans., *Three Worlds According to King Ruang: A Thai Buddhist Cosmology* (Berkeley, CA: University of California, Berkeley Buddhist Studies Series 4, 1982), 89.

17. Arthur Wright, *Buddhism in Chinese History* (Stanford, CA: Stanford University Press, 1971), 34.

18. Wright, 1971, 36.

19. Wright, 1971, 37.

20. Arthur Wright, *Studies in Chinese Buddhism* (New Haven, CT: Yale University Press, 1990), 16.

21. Wright, 1990, 47–8.

22. Wright, 1971, 41.

23. John Kieschnick, *The Impact of Buddhism on Chinese Material Culture* (Princeton, NJ: Princeton University Press, 2003), 191.

24. Keischnick, 192.

25. Michael S. Diener, Franz-Karl Erhard, and Ingrid Fischer-Schreiber, translated by Michael H. Kohn, *The Shambhala Dictionary of Buddhism and Zen, A Glossary of Buddhist Terminology* (New York: Paperback Original Shambhala Dragon Editions, 1992), 159.

26. Wright, 1971, 67.

27. Amryrta Sen, "Passage to China," *New York Review of Books,* December 3, 2004, 61.

28. Swearer, 67.

29. Faxian Zhuan, No. 2085, vol. 51, p. 858c. *The Travels of Fa-hsien,* in H. A. Giles, *Record of the Buddhistic Kingdoms* (London: Routledge and Paul, 1956), 16.

30. Edward Conze, tran., quoted in Kiersenz, 164–5.

31. T. Samyuuktagama, no. 99, vol 2., 439b, quoted in Kiershnick, 3.

32. Eric Zurcher, *The Buddhist Conquest of China* (Leiden, The Netherlands: E. J. Brill, 1959), 262.

33. Jiu Tang Shu, quoted in Kieschnick, 12.

34. Sen, 102.

35. Liu Shao-ch'i, "Lun Kung-ch'an-tang-yuan ti hsiu-yang," *How To Be a Good Communist* (Beijing: Foreign Languages Press, Peking, First Edition, 1951), 50.

36. Ahn Kye-hyon "A Short History of Ancient Korean Buddhism," in *Introduction of Buddhism to Korea: New Cultural Patterns,* Lewis R. Lancaster and, Chai-Shin Yuin, eds. (Studies in Korean Religions and Culture; v. 3), (Berkeley, CA: Asian Humanities Press, 1989), 19.

37. Wonhyo, "The Way of Bringing Troubled Minds to Rest," quoted in *A New History of Korea,* Ki-bait, Lee (Cambridge, MA: Harvard University Press, 1992), 83.

38. Carter J. Eckert, Ki-baik Lee, Young Ick Lew, Michael Robinson, Edward W. Wagner, *Korea: Old and New, A History* (Cambridge, MA: Korea Institute, Harvard University, 1990), 81.

39. Eckert et. al, 130.

40. *Bushido: The Soul of Japan,* by Inazo Nitabe 1, p. 31 Tokyo: Charles E. Tuttle Inc., 1969.

41. Quoted in Dale T. Irvin, Scott W. Sunguist, *History of World Christian Movement, Volume I: Earliest Christianity to 1453* (New York: Orbis Books, 2003), 70.

42. See First Corinthians 16:20, Greet one another with a holy kiss.

43. Robert Royal, "Seeing Things," in *Crisis Magazine,* December, 2001.

44. Quoted in Monk Themistocles Adamop, "The Triumph of the Gospel of Love," hhtp://home.it.net.an/~jgrapsas/pages/Gospel.htm.

45. Bart D. Ehrman, *The New Testament: A Historical Introduction to the Early Christian Writers,* 3rd Edition. New York: Oxford University Press, 2004 pp. 3–7.

46. Quoted in Elaine Paegels, *Beyond Belief: The Secret Gospel of Thomas* (New York: Random House, 1998, 2003), 7.

47. Paul Brians, Mary Gallwey, Douglas Hughes, Azfar Hussain, Richard Law, Michael Myers, Michael Neville, Roger Schlesinger, Alice Spitzer, and Susan Swan, eds., "Tacitus," in *Reading About the World, Volume 1* (New York: Harcourt Brace Custom Books, 1993).

48. Eusebius, *Historia Ecclesiae, 10:7,* quoted in Pagels, 168.

49. Averil Cameron, *The Mediterranean World in Late Antiquity; A.D. 395–600* (London: Routlege, 1993), 146.

50. St. Ignatius of Antioch, who died in 117, was the first to use that term.

51. James Bentley, *Restless Bones: The Story of Relics* (London: Constable, 1985), 41.

52. Strabo, Geographica 2: 5:12 as quoted in Singhal, D. P. *India and World Civilization, Volume I,* (Bombay: Rupa & Co., 1972), 75.

53. Irvin et. al., 319.

54. Monk Filofei quoted in New Rome, Wikipedia http://www.answers.com/topic/new-rome.

55. Quoted in *The Jesus Sutras,* http://home.att.net/~fcclostr/jsutras.htm.

56. Irvin et. al., 321.

57. Richard M. Eaton, *Islamic History as Global History* (Washington, DC: American Historical Association, 1990), 14.

58. Eaton, 14.

59. Leila Ahmed, *Women and Gender in Islam Historical Roots of a Modern Debate* (New Haven, CT: Yale University Press, 1992), 62.

60. Ahmed, 62.

61. Esposito, 100–13.

62. Source of Rumi poem: Jelaluddin Rumi http://www.indranet.com/potpourri/poetry/rumi/rumi4.html, poems 5.

63. Esposito, 102.

64. Richard Bulliet, "Conversion to Islam and the Emergence of a Muslim Society in Iran," in *Conversion to Islam,* Nehemia Levtzion (New York: Holmes & Meier, 1979), 33.

65. Richard Bulliet, *Islam, A View From the Edge* (New York: Columbia University Press, 1994), 77.

66. Ira M. Lapidus, *A History of Islamic Societies,* 2nd ed. (Cambridge, MA: Cambridge University Press, 2002), 56–8.

67. Tertius Chandler, Gerald Fox, *3000 Years of Urban Growth* (New York: Academic Press, 1974).

68. Linda Norene Schaffer, *Maritime Southeast Asia to 1500* (Armonk, NY: M. E. Sharpe, 1996), 40.

69. Alfred Andrea and James H. Overfield, *The Human Record: Sources of Global History, to 1500,* 2nd ed. (Boston: Houghton Mifflin Company, 1994), 301.

70. Richard Bulliet, 1994, 99.

71. Eaton, 23.

72. Abu'l-Faraj al-Isfahani, Kitab al-Aghani, iii, pp. 45–46, quoted in *Islam from the Prophet Muhammad to the Capture of Constantinople,* Bernard Lewis, vol. II (New York: Oxford University Press, 1987), 47–8.

73. See Jessica A. Coope. "Religious and Cultural Conversion to Islam in Ninth-Century Umayyad Cordoba," *Journal of World History,* vol. 4, no 1, 50–1.

74. Karen Armstrong, *Islam: A Short History* (New York: Modern Library, 2000), 60.

75. Ahmed, 73.

76. Esposito, 82.

77. Lapidus, 103.

78. Bernard Lewis. *Race and Slavery in the Middle East An Historical Enquiry* (New York: Oxford University Press, 1990), 63–4.

79. Quoted in Lewis, 1990, 65.

80. Web http://www.wsu.edu:8080/~dee/ISLAM/ABASSID.HTM.

81. Richard Hillenbrand, "Medieval Cordoba as a Cultural Center," *The Legacy of Muslim Spain*, Salma Khadra Jayyusi, ed. (Leiden; New York: E. J. Brill, 1992), 118.

82. Quoted in Richard Hillenbrand, *Islamic Architecture Form, Function and Meaning* (New York: Columbia University Press, 1994), 455. Most of the poems are by Ibn Zamrak.

83. Quoted in Dominique Clevenot, *Splendors of Islam, Architecture, Decoration and Design* (New York: Vendome Press, 2000), 183. No author given.

84. Jan Knappert in Levtzion, 1979, 12.

85. Janet Abu-Lughod. *Before European Hegemony The World System A.D. 1250–1350* (New York: Oxford University Press, 1989), 291.

86. Raphael Israeli, "Islamization and Sinicization in Chinese Islam," in Levtizion, 164.

87. Israeli, 162.

88. Israeli, 162–3.

89. Menage, "The Islamization of Anatolia," in Levitzion, 52–3.

90. Menage, 66.

91. Menage, 67.

92. Robert Bulliet, Lecture given at Scarsdale High School, 2001.

93. Stanley Wolpert, *A New History of India*, 5th ed. (New York: Oxford University Press, 1997), 105.

94. See John Voll, "Islamic History as Global History," *Journal of World History* (Honolulu, HI: University of Hawaii Press) vol. 5, no. 2. (Fall, 1994).

95. Quoted in Bentley, 154.

96. Rock Edict XII *The Edicts of Asoka*, Footnote 2, p. 27, translated by N. A. Nikam & Richard McKeon (Asia Publishing House, 1959).

97. Barbara Stoller Miller The Bhagavad Gita: Krishna's Council in a Time New York, Penguin Books, 1986 Chapter II.

98. Quoted in Hans Wolfgang Schumann, *Buddhism: An Outline of Its Teachings and Schools* (Madras, India: Theosophical Publishing House, 1974), 54.

99. Epictetus, "My Life Is Worthwhile," quoted in *Notes for Class Twenty-Three: Stoicism, Buddhism, and the Meaning of Life,* http://www-phil.tamu.edu/~sdaniel/Notes/96class23.html.

100. Jainism grew up about the same time as Buddhism, but demanded a more self-punishing life and strict adherence to ahimsa, non-injury to any living thing.

101. Saints Barlaam and Josaphat.

102. L. N. Tolstoi, Polnoe Sobranie Sachineni (Moskva: Gosudarstvennoe, Isdatel'stvo. Khundhozhestvennoi, Literatury, 1957), 21–23.

103. Adrian Hastings, ed., *A World History of Christianity* (Grand Rapids, MI: William B. Eerdmans, 1999), 456.

104. Christopher Dawson, ed., *The Mongol Mission: Narratives and Letters of the Franciscan Missionaries in Mongolia and China in the Thirteenth and Fourteenth Centuries*, trans. by a nun of Stanbrook Abbey (London: Sheet and Ward, 1955), 81.

105. Morris Rossabi, *Khulibai Khan: His Life and Times* (Berkeley, CA: University of California Press, 1988), 20.

106. Rossabi, 20.

107. Quoted in Richard C. Foltz, *Religions of the Silk Road: Overland Trade and Cultural Exchange from Antiquity to the Fifteenth Century* (New York: St. Martin's Press, 1999), 122.

108. Foltz, 122.

109. Foltz, 122.

110. Rossabi, 127.

111. Quoted in Rossabi, 145.

112. Xijuan Zhou, "Buddhist or Manichaeans? Some Characteristics of the Manichaean Missionaries along the Silk Road." Paper delivered at the American Historical Association annual conference, 1998, 14. Quoted in Foltz, 87.

113. P. Lal in "Indian Influences on English, American and European Literature," in Donald Johnson and Jean Johnson, *The India Guide* (New York: The Asia Society, 2004), 11.7.

114. Ninian Smart, *Worldviews: Crosscultural Explorations of Human Beliefs*, 3rd ed., 1999 (New York: Prentice-Hall, 1999), 113.

115. Quoted in Richard Bulliet, *The Case for an Islamo-Christian Civilization*, (New York: Columbia University Press, 2004), 21–2.

116. Foltz, 122.

117. Marvin Lunenfeld, 1492: *Discovery, Invasion, Encounter* (Lexington, Massachusetts: D.C. Heath and Company, 1991), 207.

118. Bernard Lewis, 1987, 126.

119. Xinru Liu, *Silk and Religion: An Exploration of Material Life and the Thought of People, AD 600–1200* (New Delhi: Oxford University Press, 1998), 139.

120. Lois Sherr Dubin, *The History of Beads: From 30,000 B.C. to the Present* (Washington, DC: Harry N. Abrams Publishing Co., 1987), 80.

121. Dubin, 80.

122. Dubin, 88.

123. Xinru Liu, 139.

124. Benjamin Z. Kedar, *Crusade and Mission: European Approaches toward the Muslims* (Princeton, NJ: Princeton University Press, 1984), 6.

125. Dubin, 88.

126. Song of Roland, CLXXVIII, in Barnes and Noble, Spark Notes. http://www.sparknotes.com/lit/songofroland/section7.rhtml.

127. Riccoldo, quoted in John V. Tolan, *Saracens: Islam in the Medieval European Imagination* (New York: Columbia University Press, 2002), 248.

128. Tolan, 246.

129. See James Burke, *The Day the Universe Changed* (Boston: Little, Brown & Co., 1985).

130. Riccoldo, quoted in Tolan, p. 86.

131. Rollin Amour, Sr., *Islam, Christianity and the West* (Maryknoll, NY: Orbis Books, 2000), 52.

132. Bulleit, 2004, 43.

133. Amin Maalouf, *The Crusades through Arab Eyes* (NY: Schocken Books, 1984), 39.

134. Bulliet, 2004, 10.

135. Bulliet, 2004, 45.

136. Bulliet, 2004, 10.

◀ CREDITS ▶

⬛ INDEX ⬛